Balancing Acts

Balancing Acts

Youth Culture in the Global City

Natasha K. Warikoo

UNIVERSITY OF CALIFORNIA PRESS
Berkeley · Los Angeles · London

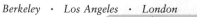

University of California Press, one of the most distinguished university presses in the United States, enriches lives around the world by advancing scholarship in the humanities, social sciences, and natural sciences. Its activities are supported by the UC Press Foundation and by philanthropic contributions from individuals and institutions. For more information, visit www.ucpress.edu.

University of California Press
Berkeley and Los Angeles, California

University of California Press, Ltd.
London, England

Portions of chapter 3 appeared in "Racial Authenticity among Second Generation Youth in Multiethnic New York and London," *Poetics: Journal of Empirical Research on Culture, the Media, and the Arts* 35, no. 6 (2007): 388–408. Portions of chapter 7 appeared in "Symbolic Boundaries and School Structure in Multiethnic Schools," *American Journal of Education* 116, no. 3 (2010): 423–51. Portions of the book appeared in "Youth Culture and Peer Status among Children of Immigrants in New York and London: Assessing the Cultural Explanation for Downward Assimilation," in *Beyond Stereotype: Minority Children of Immigrants in Urban Schools*, ed. R. Saran and R. Diaz (Rotterdam: Sense, 2010).

Library of Congress Cataloging-in-Publication Data

Warikoo, Natasha Kumar.
  Balancing acts : youth culture in the global city / Natasha Kumar Warikoo.
    p. cm.
  Includes bibliographical references and index.
  ISBN 978-0-520-26210-2 (cloth : alk. paper)
  ISBN 978-0-520-26211-9 (pbk. : alk. paper)
    1. Youth—Social life and customs—Cross-cultural studies. 2. Children of immigrants—Cross-cultural studies. 3. High school students—Social life and customs—Cross-cultural studies. 4. Assimilation (Sociology). 5. Academic achievement—Cross-cultural studies. 6. Group identity—Cross-cultural studies. I. Title.
  HQ796.W267 2011
  305.235086'91209421—dc22   2010013984

Manufactured in the United States of America

20 19 18 17 16 15 14 13 12 11
10 9 8 7 6 5 4 3 2 1

This book is printed on Cascades Enviro 100, a 100% post consumer waste, recycled, de-inked fiber. FSC recycled certified and processed chlorine free. It is acid free, Ecologo certified, and manufactured by BioGas energy.

For my parents, for pushing me to aim high
And for Ramesh, because you've made me a
better person

Contents

Preface

Growing up with immigrant parents in a small steel town in Pennsylvania, I knew I was different from my peers. For starters, I looked different, and at that time the contemporary "Indo-chic" had not made it big, so it wasn't cool to be Indian, or even "ethnically ambiguous," as it is today. Also, my brother and I were ace students. We attributed this to our parents' Indian background and culture, rather than to their professional status in comparison to our peers' fathers, most of whom worked in the steel mills of my town—and, sadly, eventually became unemployed as we grew and the mills closed during the 1980s. Ours was an easy enough assumption: the most obvious difference between us and our peers was our Indian culture, so culture seemed a likely explanation for our high academic achievement. Of course, it helped that our parents drilled it into our heads that excellence in education was expected in our culture. They saw American culture as something that we should stay away from, lest it steer us in the wrong direction. Even school-organized parties were prohibited by my strict parents, my mother frequently reminding me that "we are different." Friends (female only, boys not being allowed to call me until I got my own phone in college) often remarked on how intimidating it was to call me at home and deal with my father's stern "Who is calling?"

In contrast to my parents' fears of American culture, today Indians are, by many measures, one of the most assimilated ethnic groups in the United States. Indians have a high rate of intermarriage with whites;

we are more likely to live among whites than are blacks and Latinos; and we have high incomes and levels of education (Frey and Myers, 2005; C. N. Lee, 2007; U.S. Census Bureau, 2000c). These measures of assimilation are seen by many to signal success in American society—we have successfully assimilated into the mainstream, just as the Italians, Jews, Irish, Germans, and others did before us.

So did I excel in school by staying away from American culture? Or did academic excellence lead me to become more American? My experiences as a second-generation Indian American first sparked my interest in understanding how ethnic groups assimilate and experience academic and socioeconomic success and failure, and eventually led me to study the children of immigrants as a Ph.D. student. Cultural explanations for ethnic incorporation abound in popular discourse as well as among journalists and scholars. Asian Americans are commonly seen as "model minorities," their Asian cultures supposedly explaining success in school and work. African Americans and many Latino groups, on the other hand, are often stereotyped as lazy, culturally insular, and prone to undervaluing education, explaining lower-than-average outcomes.

As I began my Ph.D., I intuitively bristled at cultural explanations for ethnic and racial stratification, believing that scholars should instead focus on social structures that reproduce inequality and prevent social mobility. In my mind, the shift from my early understandings of my successes in school was due to a more complex perception of how disadvantage in American society negatively affects those at the bottom. I was not alone; sociologists after the 1970s grew leery of cultural explanations for inequality, scarred by the politics of earlier "culture of poverty" arguments that blamed African American culture for black disadvantage in American society, rather than historical discrimination and disadvantage, social policies that disproportionately disadvantage blacks, residential segregation, racism, and other structural constraints.

I later realized, however, that it is impossible to study the process of ethnic mobility in American society *without* talking about culture and how it matters, if only to discredit folk theories about why certain groups do better than others. I saw that ethnic identities evolve quite differently for different ethnic groups, depending on their race, structural constraints, modes of adaptation, and other factors. I had to take more seriously the diverse ways in which individuals and groups respond to structural constraints, and the fact that these variations matter for future outcomes. Just before I started the Ph.D. program, my adviser, Mary Waters, published a book that analyzed, among other things, the multiple ways in which black New Yorkers responded to racial discrimination (1999). African Americans emphasized experiences with interpersonal racism, while Afro-Caribbeans emphasized structural racism. These different cultural orientations, rooted in upbringings in different racial orders, in turn had implications for these black New Yorkers' success in the workforce. I also read studies by social psychologists that analyzed which types of group identities correlate with high self-esteem and school success (Phinney, 1991). I began to realize that I had to think about culture when trying to understand how ethnic groups adapt.

Culture, in fact, plays a key role in the predominant theory of ethnic incorporation in the United States today: segmented assimilation. This theory suggests that ethnic groups differ in their patterns of assimilation into U.S. society, in part because they assimilate into different segments of a highly stratified American society (Portes, Fernández-Kelly, and Haller, 2005; Portes and Rumbaut, 2001; Portes and Zhou, 1993). On the one hand, higher-skilled immigrants living in middle- to upper-class areas are reported to upwardly assimilate over generations, just as Italians and Jews did in previous generations. On the other hand, low-skilled minority groups in the inner city are reported to assimilate into the urban underclass; the second generation of these groups may experience "second-generation decline" (Gans, 1992), due in part to an "oppositional" culture that youth pick up from their African American peers. This oppositional culture includes anti-school attitudes and behaviors, as well as tastes for music and styles highly critical of mainstream society. Lastly, segmented assimilation theory suggests that living in an ethnic enclave can shield minority children of low-skilled immigrants from the problems and culture of the inner city, in part through an emphasis on ethnic culture and networks. Each of these assimilation trajectories results in part from a cultural orientation that immigrants and their children pick up from their surroundings: immigrants and their children in middle- to upper-class, predominantly white areas adopt "mainstream" American culture and values; those in the inner city adopt the counterculture of the urban underclass; and those in ethnic enclaves retain ethnic ties and ethnic culture, which promote high academic achievement.

The cultural explanations that this theory suggests never quite resonated with my own experiences as a second-generation young adult, nor with my experiences teaching children of immigrants in New York City public schools. As a teacher, I found that even the most poorly behaved students, when sat down and confronted, confessed sincere desires to straighten up, to earn better grades, and to finish school on time; these conversations were often heartfelt, and I truly believed most were not simply telling me what I wanted to hear, even when their behaviors in school compromised those aspirations. In terms of my personal experiences growing up, assimilation into the popular culture of my town meant watching the Pittsburgh Steelers play football and listening to Bruce Springsteen. Growing up in the late 1970s and early 1980s in small-town Pennsylvania, we had nothing like today's Bollywood–hip-hop remix music that blends popular urban music with Indian film songs. Instead, we enjoyed Springsteen's music about blue-collar America, especially appreciating the songs that mentioned our hometown and the industries that were closing in places like ours, even while our parents enjoyed job security as doctors. However, we pulled away from the crowd when it came to post–high school plans, choosing to apply to and attend Ivy League institutions far away from home. Most of our peers looked for work locally after high school, ending their formal education.

When I looked more carefully at what scholars had previously written about the second generation, I found that although many employed theories of culture to explain patterns of success and decline, none had taken an in-depth look at culture among the second generation. Instead, many drew a stereotype about a putative inner-city culture, whose adoption leads second-generation teens to oppose all that their parents and teachers hold near and dear with respect to academic achievement. Others idealized ethnic cultures and used them to explain why some Asian groups did better than black Americans and sometimes even white Americans. Both of these explanations resonated with my parents' explanations for our success and others' failures, but I found them lacking in evidence. In-depth studies of second-generation cultures—especially beyond the influence of their parents' ethnic cultures—were scant, and I had a hunch that such a project would improve our understanding of immigrant incorporation into American society. So I embarked on this study of youth culture among second-generation teens in New York City and London. I wondered: What meanings do teens see in their tastes in music and style? To what extent are second-generation youth influenced by popular culture and peer culture, and how? How does peer culture influence attitudes toward academic achievement? How do ethnicity and popular culture influence peer status groups? How do all of these cultural adaptations differ between ethnic and racial groups? What aspects of these cultural adaptations are uniquely American? In addition to my U.S.-based research, I decided to step out of the American context to understand what aspects of urban America affect these cultural adaptations uniquely.

I spent a year in two high schools with diverse student bodies and low achievement among students, one in New York and one in London. In the schools, I observed, talked to, and gathered data on children of immigrants, both formally—through in-depth interviews, a survey, and classroom observations—and informally—in the schoolyard, after school, and when I bumped into students on the subway or at corner shops. I found that children of immigrants attending these poor-performing schools nevertheless believe in the "immigrant dream": they think that if they work hard, they'll get ahead; they don't think that racism is holding them back; and they don't think that peers will shun them if they do well in school. Becoming American and becoming British for children of immigrants, even in disadvantaged areas, did not lead to rebellion against and rejection of conventional success such as academic achievement. Still, the children of immigrants I encountered sometimes dressed and behaved in ways that could impede their academic achievement. In New York, seemingly oppositional styles, music, and behaviors, however, stemmed not from an anti-school orientation picked up from African American peers, but rather from all teens' desires for *peer status*. London youth also prioritized peer status. That is, while they cared about academic success, they also cared about success among their peers—being cool, maintaining self-respect and pride, and being popular. I found remarkably similar tastes in music and style among children of immigrants in New York and London, which led me to conclude that today a taste for hip-hop and rap—assumed by many adults to signify rebellion—is actually a global, media-driven phenomenon rather than one adopted by local peers and rooted in critiques of mainstream society.

At times, engaging with peer culture came into conflict with the dominant culture's expectations, so that youth who focused exclusively on peer status sometimes found themselves slipping in school despite their best intentions. For example, defending one's pride by responding to bullying with shouts or even physical violence may maintain status among peers, but it can also lead to school suspension. This conflict between maintaining peer status and achieving school success explains cultural influences on underachievement among some minority youth. Still, the youth culture is not *opposed* to school norms.

The most successful children were those able to engage in "balancing acts": maintaining status in their youth subcultures while also maintaining focus on behaviors conducive to academic achievement. This skill in code-switching is what most youth strive for. I am not suggesting that downward assimilation does not happen. Both schools I studied have low rates of academic success. Rather, I show in this book that the *mechanism* for underachievement among some ethnic groups cannot be explained through oppositional youth cultures. The conflict between peer culture and dominant school norms can lead to downward assimilation, especially among youth who emphasize peer culture to the detriment of school success and among those who have not developed the skills to balance their two social worlds. Furthermore, structural factors such as underresourced schools, tracking, low parental education, and discrimination may further lead poor and working-class immigrant communities to poor academic outcomes.

Acknowledgments

The publication of this book marks the end of a long journey, and I was fortunate to have much support—intellectual and emotional—along the way. Central to this project was the guidance of my excellent Ph.D. committee. Mary Waters was an incredibly supportive adviser whose calm way often convinced me that everything was fine and would get done, even when I couldn't see the forest for the trees. Michele Lamont assiduously reads everything I send her, always providing detailed, insightful comments that improve my work immensely. The intellectual influence of Prudence Carter will be apparent to readers of this book. Her questions always push my thinking on matters of youth culture, race, and education, and for this I am grateful. All three continue to be outstanding mentors and colleagues, and I feel lucky to have had such brilliant and supportive women to work with. While I was at Harvard, Kathy Newman encouraged me to develop my then-fleeting interest in culture and helped me to shape my research questions during the early stages of this project. Harvard colleagues on the other side of Cambridge Common at the Graduate School of Education have also been very helpful, including Meira Levinson, Michal Kurlaender, Kay Merseth, and Marcelo Suarez-Orozco. Others at Harvard who pushed my thinking include Chris Bail, Patricia Banks, Irene Bloemraad, Michael Fortner, Renee Richardson Gosline, Corina Graif, Luisa Heredia, Richard Mora, Orlando Patterson, Wendy Roth, Bill Wilson, and Scott Winship. I am especially indebted to Cybelle Fox, who read numerous drafts of this manuscript in its many stages as a project proposal, dissertation, and finally as a completed book manuscript. Tomás Jiménez, Helen Marrow, and Laurel Cadwallader Stolte also generously read the manuscript in its entirety, helping me to clarify my ideas and tighten my writing. In Cambridge my friends Para Ambardar and Amit Rajparia often made me laugh and think outside the box as I planned this project and the rest of my life.

My two institutional homes in London provided intellectual support as well. John Hills, Jason Strelitz, Robert Cassen, and Ruth Lupton helped me think through my nascent ideas while I did my research and writing at the Centre for the Analysis of Social Exclusion (CASE) at the London School of Economics. At the University of London's Institute for the Study of the Americas (ISA), James Dunkerley and Iwan Morgan generously provided me with time to complete the dissertation and begin its evolution into this book. Outside CASE and ISA in Britain, Fiona Adamson, Claire Dwyer, Rahsaan Maxwell, Ephraim Nimni, Bhikhu Parekh, Eiko Thielemann, and Susanne Wessendorf all helped me develop my ideas.

Colleagues at Barnard College, UC Berkeley, Harvard, Hunter College, ISA, NYU, Queens College, University of Manchester, and University of Sussex all provided helpful feedback at talks I gave, as did participants in numerous conferences and seminars, including those of the American Sociological Association; the Canadian Institute for Advanced Research; the Council for European Studies; the Harvard-Manchester Summer Workshop on Immigration and Social Change; the London Migration Research Group; and Oxford University's Centre on Migration Policy and Society. Gilberto Conchas and Margaret Chin provided helpful comments as reviewers of this book, as did an anonymous reviewer. Naomi Schneider at the University of California Press provided continued support, and Steven Baker's copyediting made this manuscript more readable.

Generous funding allowed me to complete this project without delay. The NSF-IGERT Multidisciplinary Program in Inequality and Social Policy at Harvard University (Grant No. 9870661) provided funding during the year I did this research; Harvard's Center for European Studies provided funding for me to write the dissertation that became this book; and the National Science Foundation Dissertation Improvement Award (SES-0402248) saved time that would otherwise have been spent transcribing the interviews I conducted.

Qualitative research relies on supportive hosts, and in this project I had three generous ones. In London, Gerard McKenna made my research possible from the start: he welcomed a stranger from across the pond into his school; he responded almost immediately to my many requests for information; and he generously shared his personal office with me during my time at his school. In New York, Bernadette O'Reiley was a wonderful and warm host. She went out of her way to make me comfortable and to accommodate my research needs. Also in New York, when I needed another school at which to conduct research, Jonathan Barnett welcomed me back to his institution, and Kaiquon King introduced me to many thoughtful young men and women there.

Most important of all, the students and teachers at the schools where I conducted my research generously opened their classrooms and lives to me. I sincerely thank the dozens of teachers who allowed me into their classrooms. I was inspired by wonderful teaching, modeling, and mentorship by teachers I encountered on both sides of the pond. The candor with which the teens I met spoke and wrote was a gift for which I am immensely grateful. Their words, as you will read, are inspiring, heartbreaking, sincere, funny, insecure, and sweet. Many went out of their way to make my research easy and to make me comfortable, inviting me to sit with them during lunchtime, to join their conversations, to attend their school and community events, and even to join their classes.

Finally, my family. My in-laws, the Kumar family, have taught me to relax and laugh about most things in life. My parents, Shiban and Nanna Warikoo, provided my first encounter with immigrants, and I owe most of my life's accomplishments to their thoughtful parenting. My father's broad perspective on the world and talk of injustice developed my interest in fighting inequality at a young age. My mother has spent much of her vacation time with my children since they were born, taking care of them as I stole away to write and rewrite this book. My mother-in-law has done the same. Many years ago my brother Niraj taught me to be independent, to defend my ideas, and to pay attention to the world around me. I owe much of my intellectual development to him. My maternal grandmother, Jaikishori Mirakhur, or Nani as we affectionately called her, left this world as I put the finishing touches on this book. She gave me, my brother and cousins, and all our children unconditional love, and her sweet smile will remain in my heart forever.

The writing of this book spanned the births of my two wonderful children, Zoya and Kavi. They simultaneously bring deep meaning to my life and teach me to put less stake in worldly accomplishments. Coming home to their smiling faces puts everything in perspective. Their father, Ramesh Kumar, continues to be a wonderful partner with whom to share life's journey. Ramesh has pushed me to focus, to believe in myself and in my work, and to always remember the larger picture—of what I am doing, of why I'm doing it, and of why it matters. His infectious energy brings great joy to my life. Every morning when the four of us gather for a morning cuddle, I believe I am the luckiest woman in the world.

CHAPTER I

Understanding Cultural Incorporation

A simple explanation—offered by scholars, policy makers, and educators alike—for seemingly self-defeating youth behaviors such as fighting in school and talking back to teachers is that they stem from a rejection of the dominant ideology of equal opportunity and education as keys to success. This oppositional stance is thought to embody itself in hip-hop and rap music and style among minority youth. Using this logic, a bill passed in 2005 by the Virginia State House of Delegates would have fined the display of undergarments, a style popular with both boys and girls, especially in urban areas (the bill died in the senate). Similarly, a few months after Virginia's "Droopy Drawers Bill," a shopping mall in Kent, England, seeking to curb "anti-social behaviors" at the mall, banned the wearing of "hoodies"—hooded sweatshirts often worn by young men. These acts show that adults think that youth styles matter and that they believe styles can symbolize antisocial behaviors and outlooks. Theorists of immigration have applied these kinds of theories about oppositional culture to their analyses of ethnic assimilation, suggesting that the adoption of American youth cultures among the children of immigrants can lead to poor school outcomes. But, what do the cultural practices and outlooks of children of immigrants really look like? This is the central question of this book.

In the following pages I unpack the cultural lives of children of immigrants in multiethnic schools in two global cities, New York and London. I describe and analyze the aspects of youth cultures that adults most worry about: attitudes, music tastes and clothing styles, behaviors related to conflict, and influences on peer status. These are dimensions of children's cultural worlds that immigrants are most concerned about and that academics emphasize when trying to understand the second generation's incorporation into U.S. society. Parents, policymakers, and academics alike hope that children of immigrants will not develop negative attitudes toward schooling, that they won't learn to listen to music and don styles that signal a counterculture or rebellion, and that they won't get into fights and become as outspoken and defiant as many of their American peers. These behaviors, according to both conventional wisdom and some academic writing, are the determinants of whether children of immigrants will succeed in their lives. So I took some time to focus on the cultural lives of second-generation teenagers to find out what their attitudes are, what music and styles they prefer, what their tastes mean to them, how they deal with conflict, and what determines peer status. By delving deeply into not only *what* students are doing, listening to, and wearing but also *why* they make the choices they make and what *meanings* those cultural symbols have to them, I paint a picture of urban youth cultures very different from the one perceived by advocates of the "Droopy Drawers" bills.

I found little evidence for oppositional peer cultures, and no evidence that perceptions of discrimination lead to low aspirations. Academic achievement is quite low in both high schools of my research: less than half of students graduate in the New York school, and less than half in the London site leave school eligible to apply to university. Although a minority of students did have some negative perceptions of opportunities, those cannot account for the predominant patterns of academic failure in both schools. Students engaged in behaviors thought to signify disinterest in education—they got into fights, talked back to teachers, and came late to class. These behaviors, however, coincided with positive orientations toward school. What explained the behaviors was the high importance teens placed on *peer status,* for which they needed to socialize, defend self-pride, show toughness among peers, wear the "right" clothing, and listen to the "right" music. This was especially true for boys. The similarity between taste cultures in New York and London suggests that the local influence of African American peers cannot explain the cultural adaptation process for children of immigrants in these low-performing schools; rather, there appears to be a *global* urban youth culture in which American hip-hop and rap are popular and that leads to black racial identity having high peer status in both urban settings.

UNDERSTANDING ASSIMILATION

The predominant theory of assimilation in the United States today concerning the immigrant second generation (U.S.-born children of immigrants) is segmented assimilation theory (Portes et al., 2005; Portes and Rumbaut, 2001; Portes and Zhou, 1993). Segmented assimilation theory provides an explanation for divergent outcomes. Using an integrated structural-cultural explanation, it argues that the trajectory of ethnic communities depends on which segment of U.S. society—the upper-middle class, the ethnic enclave, or disadvantaged minority communities—families are incorporated into (Portes et al., 2005; Portes and Zhou, 1993). The theory suggests that three factors differentiate the post-1965 wave of immigrants from prior waves, leading to the possibility of downward assimilation: (1) a predominance of immigrants who are racial minorities in the United States; (2) a bifurcated labor market in which most jobs for the low-skilled are low-paying service-sector jobs rather than the unionized manufacturing jobs that many earlier immigrants were able to take; and (3) proximity (of some) to the problems of the urban inner city. The first two factors are structural explanations; the third includes a cultural explanation, suggesting that cultural influences, not just the structural hazards of proximity to poverty, lead children of immigrants to either a positive or a negative orientation toward U.S. society. The racial and class makeup of a child's neighborhood leads to either a positive or negative cultural orientation, and cultural identities, in turn, determine educational and delinquency outcomes. It is the cultural dimension of the third explanation—proximity to inner-city culture—that this book addresses.

These three influences lead to three possible trajectories, according to segmented assimilation theory: First, highly skilled immigrant families living in predominantly white, middle- and upper-class neighborhoods are most likely to experience upward assimilation, in part because the second generation adopts the American dream and becomes like their native white peers. Second, low-skilled minority immigrants and their children can be sheltered from the problems of the inner city by living among coethnics in ethnic enclaves; these families will experience "selective acculturation," assimilating well into the economy while retaining the positive influence of ethnic culture and ethnic social networks. Third, low-skilled minority immigrant families living among other disadvantaged minorities may assimilate into the urban underclass, and hence their children may demonstrate "reactive ethnicity" in response to perceived discrimination and experience downward assimilation. Youth in the last group adopt the "adversarial subculture" of the "values and norms" of the inner city's "outlooks and cultural ways," including "deviant lifestyles" (Portes et al., 2005; Portes and Zhou, 1993).

British sociologist Tariq Modood (2004) has suggested that segmented assimilation theory is applicable in the British context, as well, and can explain the high levels of university enrollment among Indians and Pakistanis and the relatively low levels for Afro-Caribbeans. Modood explains the different levels of university enrollment by pointing to differing modes of cultural assimilation, arguing that successful immigrant groups in Britain have managed to avoid British working-class culture, which he describes as "popular culture, often American-derived, . . . of Hollywood, . . . music, clothes, fashion." In contrast, Afro-Caribbeans "have come to be a leading-edge presence [in this working-class culture]," leading them to lower achievement (Modood, 2004, 102).

The segmented assimilation hypothesis of cultural incorporation into local settings begs for an empirical investigation into the cultural lives of children of immigrants from high-achieving and low-achieving groups, and into the meanings attached to participation in popular hip-hop culture. No major research in the United States has taken a holistic look at youth culture in all its dimensions among the second generation, across ethnic groups (Skrentny, 2008; Stevens, 2008). Researchers have assumed, however, that culture matters and influences processes of incorporation into American society, including academic achievement. This lacuna is in part due to the complexity of culture, and of academic achievement. We care about cultural assimilation because we think it plays a role in academic achievement. However, studies analyzing the myriad structural influences on academic achievement, in addition to cultural ones, cannot do justice to the complexity of the ways in which children of immigrants adopt and adapt the peer cultures in school.[1] In setting up my research, I recognized this tension in previous studies whose worthy goal was to explain differential academic achievement between ethnic groups. Attempts to do both, however, haven't allowed for the complexity of culture and its meanings and motivations and thus have lead to simplistic cultural explanations. That is why in this study I decided to hone in on culture.

The cultural explanation for downward assimilation theory is tied to *American*-style ghetto poverty and, in particular, the influence of urban African American culture. However, the theory has not been put to the test of international comparison. To understand the degree to which uniquely American residential patterns and racial formations shape cultural orientations among children of immigrants, I had to step outside the American context. London and New York City have much in common, but the history and contemporary significance of race in the United States and in Britain are significantly different. Among other things, the United States' legacy of slavery has led to a highly segregated African American population, in contrast to Britain, where the minority populations have come largely from former colonies and where blacks have high rates of residential and marital integration with whites (Massey and Denton, 1993; Peach, 1996; Model and Fisher, 2002). Still, I encountered surprisingly similar peer cultures among teens in New York and London, suggesting that the "contaminating effect" of African American peer culture cannot explain low achievement at the New York school. Scholars, it seems, have been too quick to accept and adopt explanations based on stereotypical accoutrements of African American poverty when explaining downward mobility in education among children of immigrants. Furthermore, I found that second-generation *Indian* students were the most likely group to report experiencing racial discrimination as part of their schooling experiences. This discrimination, however, came not from teachers and administrators but from peers. Second-generation Afro-Caribbeans, in contrast, reported experiences with discrimination *outside* school, in public places, from adults. Given these findings, one cannot explain attitudes and behaviors of low-achieving Afro-Caribbean students, as some have done, as stemming from a reaction to perceived discrimination from school authorities.

WHAT IS CULTURE, AND HOW SHOULD WE STUDY IT?

To embark on a study of second-generation youth cultures, I first had to figure out what culture really is. Culture is notoriously difficult to define. Some scholars focus on the *production* side, attempting to identify *who* and *what* defines the cultural products that individuals in society consume. Most often, these scholars are concerned about the hegemony of cultural production—that is to say, the subtle influences that corporations, the media, and other cultural producers have on consumers of culture. This perspective traces back to a Marxist orientation, in that it suggests that those who control the means of production dominate and control the production of culture in society. Horkheimer and Adorno (1972) of the Frankfurt School were the best-known early proponents of this perspective.

The problem with research focusing solely on cultural artifacts is that it does not address the *meanings* that individuals attribute to those objects and to cultural practices. Individuals are not passive sponges that absorb messages presented to them without critique. For example, the Black Youth Project at University of Chicago has found that although the majority of black youth listen to rap music daily, most black youth also agree that "rap music videos have too many references to violence" (C. J. Cohen, 2007). That is to say, individuals are able to consume a product without agreeing with the messages the cultural producers have expressed or intended. In my own previous research, I have shown how second-generation Indo-Caribbean young women consume popular Indian culture, including Bollywood films, yet also critique the traditional gender roles the films portray as foreign and not for them (Warikoo, 2005a).

In this book I unpack the meanings that hip-hop and rap music and style have for second-generation teens in New York and in London, as well as the meanings of seemingly anti-school behaviors such as fighting and talking back to teachers, to gain a more nuanced understanding of their peer cultures. Without a careful look at the meanings that styles, music, and behaviors have for teens, it is easy to read rebellious tendencies and anti-school attitudes into the process of Americanization. In fact, I found that although hip-hop and rap music and style are very popular in both New York and London, these tastes do not coincide with anti-school attitudes or with a greater propensity to believe that discrimination prevents school success. Students told me further that they attempt to mitigate misreadings of delinquency and anti-school orientations in their styles by dressing with moderation—for example, boys choosing jeans baggy enough to be cool among peers, yet not so baggy as to elicit perceptions of delinquency. I also found that seemingly anti-school behaviors like fighting and talking back to teachers had more to do with a peer culture that emphasizes maintaining pride and self-respect than with dissatisfaction with or disinterest in school.

Another way to understand culture is to analyze its influence on behaviors. To address the ways in which individuals and groups employ "culture in action," Ann Swidler (1986) developed a theory of culture as a set of "scripts" or "tool-kits," consisting of "symbols, stories, rituals, and world-views," from which individuals draw when deciding what actions to take. Swidler detaches culture from values, insisting that cultural practices and understandings should not be assumed to entail particular values. This perspective helps us understand, for example, how poor single mothers, although not engaging in marriage in *practice*, still *value* the institution of marriage (Edin and Kefalas, 2005). Their actions borrow from scripts for behavior that they have in their cultural tool-kits for decision-making and behavior, which may differ from those of young women living in different environments and drawing from different cultural tool-kits. This perspective became most useful to me as I tried to understand the "attitude-achievement paradox" (Mickelson, 1990)—the paradox of positive attitudes, aspirations, and beliefs coupled with poor academic achievement—among many students in the schools I studied. I found that analyzing peer scripts for behavior and tastes explained behaviors that others attribute to anti-school values, which contradict students' expressed values. I also use the tool-kit framework to understand gender differences. I found that the cultural scripts for masculine identity led boys to place even greater emphasis on maintaining self-pride among peers, in the process sometimes compromising their chances for school success.

Some theorists of culture have focused on *status* systems. French sociologist Pierre Bourdieu (1984; 1986; Bourdieu and Passeron, 1977) developed a theory of social status reproduction through cultural practices. Bourdieu argued that elites reproduce their high status by laying claim to an elite culture—cultural capital—that is inaccessible to those with lower status and that, though learned, is seen as natural and innate. This cultural capital helps high-status individuals maintain their elevated status through an unwritten set of rules for behavior and taste recognized and rewarded by other elites. For Bourdieu, cultural capital includes listening to classical music, knowing about art, preferring abstract art, and behaving in certain ways in school. Prudence Carter (2003) has extended Bourdieu's theory of cultural capital to a theory of a "black" or "nondominant" cultural capital that leads to status within a marginalized group such as African American youth. The children of immigrants I encountered also engaged in the quest for status among their peers, a goal that sometimes, despite their best intentions, con-flicted with their desires for school success.

Extending and refining Bourdieu's theory of social reproduction through cultural capital, Michèle Lamont (1992, 2000; Lamont and Molnár, 2002) has analyzed social groups' construction of *symbolic boundaries*. Rather than assuming that particular dimensions of culture matter for status, instead, to understand *which aspects* of culture matter, Lamont asks individuals to define the boundaries that separate them from those in other social groups.[2] In *Money, Morals, and Manners* (1992), Lamont shows how elite men value cultural characteristics common to other high-status individuals. At the same time, she shows how some of the characteristics that matter to elites differ between the United States and France. For example, financial status matters more among the American elite than among the French elite.

The symbolic boundaries approach proved useful in helping me to understand why students sometimes accused peers of "acting black." Although hip-hop defines urban popular culture among youth in both New York and London, it was racialized as black in both school con-texts. Peer expectations of racial authenticity often prevented teens from boundary crossing in their tastes. Accusations of "acting black" in comportment and style was one way of maintaining the racial order and maintaining black students' high status in the peer status hierarchy—a hierarchy that looked quite different from that of adults in the United States and Britain. By asking students about the symbolic boundaries between social groups in their schools, I also learned how the different high school structures lead New Yorkers to divide themselves much more along racial and ethnic lines compared to students in London. Urban American high schools are traditionally highly anonymous, with peers changing for every subject and again every year or even every semester. In contrast, British secondary schools keep students in home-room or "Form" classes that travel together for most subjects. This structural difference had a powerful impact on symbolic boundaries and race relations in the two sites.

THE STUDY OF YOUTH CULTURE

Researchers in the tradition of James Coleman (1961) have emphasized the importance of peer status in the high school youth culture experience (Brown, 1990; Milner, 2004; Rigsby and McDill, 1975). Coleman, in his classic *Adolescent Society*, written in 1961, suggested that American adolescents had begun to form a distinct culture oriented away from adult culture and having its own status system, norms, and goals. Coleman suggested that adolescent culture's scripts for high status were not the same as those that lead to high academic achievement (see also Rigsby and McDill, 1975).

Later, scholars in the tradition of subcultural studies both in the United States and Britain suggested further that adolescent subcultures explicitly *oppose* school norms (P. Cohen, 1997 [1972]; S. Hall and Jefferson, 1976; Willis, 1977; for an early critique of this argument, see Rigsby and McDill, 1975). Arguments in the subcultural theory tradition suggested that academic achievement has a negative effect on peer status, rather than having, as Coleman implied, a very weak, positive effect on peer status. In Britain these scholars were associated with the Birmingham School. Responding to analyses portraying disadvantaged youth as victims of class stratification in school (for example, Bowles and Gintis, 1976), these scholars sought to inject agency into analyses of youth behaviors and tastes by suggesting that subcultural teens and young adults make conscious choices to critique inequality in the larger society through their cultural practices and preferences, even while those peer cultures ultimately hinder their social mobility (S. Hall and Jefferson, 1976; Willis, 1977). Dick Hebdige (1979), in a classic study of working-class youth culture in Britain from the 1950s to the 1970s, suggested that youth used style to resist aspects of the dominant culture they disliked—for example, the British "mods" of the 1960s wearing suits askew.

The Birmingham School's early scholarship focused on the white working class; later, it influenced a new generation of scholars writing on minority youth cultures and styles in Britain. Paul Willis suggested that black British youth's adoption of African American and Jamaican dance and music styles demonstrates the use of "symbolic resources for the oppositional understanding" of "powerlessness and racial domination" (Willis, 1990; see also Sewell, 1997). More recently, Andy Bennett (2000, 2001) has suggested that white youth in northeastern England use the consumption of hip-hop music to reject the conservatism of those around them.

The late anthropologist John Ogbu (1990, 1991, 1995) made similar arguments about oppositional cultures among African Americans in an attempt to explain their relatively low academic achievement in school. Ogbu explained the differences in achievement between "immigrant" or "voluntary" minorities and "involuntary" or "caste-like" minorities by suggesting that groups like African Americans, because of their forced incorporation into American society, were likely to react against the racism and stunted opportunities they perceived around them by developing oppositional cultures, which ultimately led to their lack of achievement in school. As with explanations of the white working class in Britain, Ogbu saw African Americans as agents of their own school failure, though he also recognized structural constraints on them. Although Ogbu contrasted African American youth cultures with positive orientations among children of immigrants, segmented assimilation theory employs the oppositional culture frame to explain school failure among minority children of immigrants who live near African Americans in urban areas. This "contamination effect" is said to lead certain groups, such as Haitian Americans and other black immigrant groups, to downward assimilation (Portes and Zhou, 1993; Stepick, 1998; Waters, 1999).

Some new research calls Ogbu's framework into question. Sociologist Prudence Carter (2005) has investigated African American youth cultures in relation to academic achievement. She found no evidence that high academic achievement leads to social stigma among young African Americans living in a public housing complex in Yonkers, New York. Instead, Carter found that the youth in her study engaged in a black culture and demonstrated "black cultural capital" through their choices in style, music, and language. Carter's findings call into question the purported negative influence of African American oppositional culture on children of immigrants (see also Ainsworth-Darnell and Downey, 1998; Cook and Ludwig, 1998; Tyson, Darity, and Castellino, 2005). If the oppositional culture that is thought to motivate children of immigrants to adopt behaviors and outlooks detrimental to academic success does not exist, then it cannot explain low achievement among the second generation.

In the chapters that follow, I attempt to bridge the above perspectives on culture. I explain the meanings that teens attribute to the cultural objects they consume; hence, I focus on the reception side of culture. I am interested in what teens listen to and how they dress, and I am equally interested in the meanings they attach to their cultural tastes both consciously, through their descriptions of what their tastes mean, as well as unconsciously, through the relationship between individual tastes and attitudes. In addition to tastes and attitudes, I analyze teen *behaviors,* emphasizing how teens respond to peer conflict, in order to better understand the "tool-kits" guiding second-generation youth's behavior among peers. Lastly, I analyze the relationship between cultural practices and status among peers, identifying the symbolic boundaries students draw in the New York and London schools. I extend the previous theories of culture and status by applying them to *second-generation youth cultures,* by which I mean the systems of meaning-making and cultural practices among second-generation youth; these sometimes overlap with, but also differ from, adult cultures. Furthermore, I bring together the literature on peer cultures, peer status, and the immigrant second generation to provide a framework for understanding the cultural lives of the second generation in school. I extend the previous research on youth cultures and peer status by showing how children of immigrants adopt and engage peer status hierarchies in high school.

In this book I address second-generation youth cultures from the viewpoint of U.S.-born and British-born children of immigrants living in neighborhoods characterized by what some scholars call superdiversity (Vertovec, 2007). These neighborhoods are quite different from the largely white one in which I grew up, so it's less obvious what *American* or *British* really means in those contexts. Previous studies have either studied children of immigrants across multiple school settings or studied one particular ethnic group. Conducting my research in schools hosting multiple ethnic and racial groups meant that I could instead look across ethnic and racial groups within the same school settings to understand how groups adapt differently to the same school context. It also allowed me to document the types of youth cultures that arise when no racial or ethnic group dominates the social landscape, at least in terms of numbers.

DEFINITIONS

A word about terminology. I use *Indian* to refer to students whose parents were born in India; *Indo-Caribbean* to mean those whose parents are from the Caribbean and who have ancestors from India;[3] and *Afro-Caribbean* to mean those black respondents whose families are from the West Indies. I use *South Asian* as a more general term that includes both Indians and Indo-Caribbeans (as well as Pakistanis, Bangladeshis, and Sri Lankans, though I did not interview those groups). As will be seen, these labels do not always coincide with the myriad ethnic and racial identities that students reported to me in interviews. However, I use them to identify interview subjects and to evaluate patterns of behavior and culture suggested by previous scholars. At the same time, to avoid reifying ethnic and racial categories, I have focused on ethnic and racial labels only when there are marked differences to identify and clear theoretical hypotheses and explanations for them (Wimmer, 2007). In terms of generation, I define the second generation as those born in the United States or Britain to foreign-born parents, as well as the foreign-born who arrived before age five. I call individuals born abroad but arriving between the ages of five and ten the "1.5 generation." Throughout this book, because I am discussing primarily the second generation, someone described as "an Afro-Caribbean New Yorker," for example, can be assumed to have been born in the United States or to have arrived before age five. When a minority student is *not* second generation, I say so explicitly.

THE RESEARCH

For this research I wanted to contrast, in the same school context, the youth culture among a group thought to be high-achieving and positively oriented toward education with that among a group thought to be low-achieving and oppositional. Hence, I decided to compare Indian and Afro-Caribbean children of immigrants.[4] Why New York City and London, and why the two simultaneously? Both are cities where minorities are particularly diverse—not dominated by one or two national-origin groups as they are, for example, in Miami or Paris. I chose London as a comparison to New York because London's racial diversity is similar to New York's except in one crucial respect: there is no group in Britain equivalent to African Americans. That is to say, there is no native minority group in London thought to embody an oppositional culture among teens. Furthermore, Britain has nothing equivalent to black residential segregation in the United States, for any minority group (Peach, 1996). By comparing New York to London, I could disentangle the influence of African American cultures and life in New York—that is, I could understand the degree to which uniquely American neighborhood contexts determined cultural outcomes. The contrast would show me what was unique about the urban U.S. context, and what was not. I wanted to understand whether the presence of an oppositional culture among disadvantaged African American peers truly makes a difference in the cultural lives of children of immigrants, as some have suggested. If downward assimilation is related to the influence of an African American–influenced peer culture and U.S.-style urban poverty, then second-generation youth cultures should look different in London, where the native poor are whites and there is not as much racial segregation.

I decided on a mixed-method project in order to best triangulate complex questions of attitudes, behaviors, and self-presentation. I collected three types of data: 120 in-depth interviews (with 100 1.5- and second-generation youth in both cities and 20 white youth in London); a survey of 191 students in two schools—one survey in New York and the other in London; and an ethnography of the same two schools. The schools I chose in the two cities were similar in terms of their superdiversity, ethnic groups, and class. Both schools serve student populations in which no ethnic or racial group is in the majority, eliminating the possibility that youth were following the cultural orientations of their peers in the majority. Also, both mainly serve working-class ethnic minorities and are located in neighborhoods that are disadvantaged but not the most disadvantaged in their respective cities. Finally, both have significant numbers of Afro-Caribbean and Indian students, facilitating interview comparisons between the two cities.

Indians in both the United States and Britain have attained social mobility in terms of household income, have educational outcomes equal to or better than native whites, and are stereotyped as model minorities (Modood, 2004; Office for National Statistics, 2001d; Prashad, 2000; U.S. Census Bureau, 2000c).[5] Indians in my New York research were predominantly Punjabi Sikhs, while London Indians were predominantly Gujarati Hindus.[6] In contrast, second-generation Afro-Caribbeans in the United States—especially those living in working-class and poor areas—are frequently identified as African American and tend to live in similar areas as African Americans (Foner, 2005; Waters, 1999).[7] British Afro-Caribbeans have not attained socioeconomic parity with whites, have lower-than-average educational outcomes, and are stereotyped as dangerous and lazy (Majors, Gillborn, and Sewell, 2001; Modood, 1997; Sewell, 1997). Among all the students I interviewed in London, Afro-Caribbeans most commonly lived in low-income areas. The contrast between Indians and Afro-Caribbeans in terms of economic advancement, academic achievement, and stereotypes made for an informative comparison of youth culture across ethnic groups. Indo-Caribbeans in New York—a community from the West Indies whose ancestors were from India—provided an interesting comparison to Afro-Caribbeans and Indians there. Indo-Caribbeans allowed me to explore the differential influences of ethnicity (Caribbean) and race (South Asian) for Afro-Caribbeans and Indians, because Indo-Caribbeans are ethnically Caribbean yet racially Indian. Finally, whites in London served as a native group comparison, allowing me to tease out which social processes are unique to second-generation groups versus which are common to urban youth in general (Skrentny, 2008).[8]

York High School, New York City

I decided to base my New York research in Queens because of its diversity.[9] Blacks, Hispanics, and Asians each make up between 18 and 25 percent of the Queens population, making for a multiethnic borough known for its cultural diversity. According to school statistics, 34 percent of York High School's population is "Asian or Other" (including Indians, Indo-Caribbeans, and others); 47 percent is Hispanic; 13 percent, black (including Afro-Caribbeans, African Americans, and Africans); and 6 percent, white. One-third of the 3,100 students who attend York High are eligible for free student lunches (New York City Department of Education, 2004–5).[10] York High School's region, or catchment area, borders both Brooklyn and Long Island and ranges from some of the poorest neighborhoods of New York to lower-middle-class areas. Of the more than seven hundred students who entered the school in 2001, just 38 percent graduated four years later (New York State Education Department, 2005–6). The average combined math-and-verbal score for students who take the Scholastic Aptitude Test at York High is 785; New York City's combined average is 915 (out of 1600) (New York City Department of Education, 2004–5).

Relative to other New York City public high schools, performance at York is well below average, although not the worst in the city. The New York City Department of Education labeled York as a "School Requiring Academic Progress" in math and English language arts during the year of my research. I focused on grades 9–11, ages fourteen to seventeen, because these ages overlap in British and U.S. high schools. I found that outgoing students are often hard to track; hence, I excluded twelfth-grade (New York) and Upper Sixth (London) students from this research.

Survey results indicated that 81 percent of York High students' mothers are foreign-born and that just more than half the student body is second generation. Another 27 percent of survey respondents in New York were first or 1.5 generation. Eighteen percent of students at York High were "English Language Learners" at the time of my research

(New York City Department of Education, 2004–5). Of survey respondents who knew their parents' educational backgrounds, 43 percent at York High had mothers with less than a high school education, and 16 percent of mothers had a college education or higher.[11] At York High, Asian students performed better on standardized tests and had higher graduation rates than black students (New York City Department of Education, 2004). These overall school patterns were reflected in the performance of the students I interviewed: the second-generation Indians reported higher grade-point averages overall compared to their Afro-Caribbean peers.

I attended York High School in New York every day for four months during 2004, during which time I observed classes, chatted with students in the cafeteria, hung out in the ever-busy hallways, and generally got to know the culture of the school. In addition, I conducted a survey of four classes of students (mixed by race/ethnicity and gender), and I interviewed sixty students. The students I interviewed came from three groups of twenty, half boys and half girls: second-generation Indians, second-generation Afro-Caribbeans, and second-generation Indo-Caribbeans. Because of the low number of Afro-Caribbeans attending York High (the vast majority of black students were African American), I conducted some of the interviews with second-generation Afro-Caribbeans at a similar neighboring school.[12]

Long Meadow Community School, London

My research in London paralleled my research in New York. The school, Long Meadow Community School, lies in the poorer part of the London borough of Brent, which is in the 23rd percentile in England in terms of socioeconomic deprivation (with the most deprived boroughs falling into the 1st percentile) (Department for Communities and Local Government, 2004). Fifty-five percent of Brent's population consists of ethnic minorities (Office for National Statistics, 2001b). Much like Queens, New York, Brent is known for its ethnic diversity.

Long Meadow's 1,100 students reflect the ethnic and racial diversity of the borough. No ethnic group predominates, and there is also a significant "mixed race" population.[13] The largest ethnoracial groups are white British students (17 percent), Indians (16 percent), and Afro-Caribbeans (15 percent); still, these groups together constitute less than half the student population. Based on the survey data I collected, two-thirds of the student body is second generation. In terms of educational outcomes, in 2003, 43 percent of Long Meadow eleventh-grade students attained five grades of C or above on the General Certificate of Secondary Education (GCSE) exams (the national average is 52 percent) (Ofsted, 2004).[14] Although Long Meadow hosts students between ages eleven and eighteen (including a Sixth Form for ages sixteen to eighteen),[15] I focused my research on Years 10–11 (ages fourteen to sixteen) and the Lower Sixth Form (ages sixteen to seventeen) to coincide with the ages of my New York respondents.

Long Meadow's student body is largely working class, with about one-third of all students eligible for free lunches (24 percent of all secondary public school students in London are eligible for free lunches). In terms of parental education, according to my survey, 18 percent of Long Meadow mothers had less than a Year 11 education (equivalent of U.S. grade 10, but marking the end of high school in Britain), and another 11 percent had ended their education after Year 11. On the other end of the spectrum, 25 percent of students reported that their mothers had a university degree or higher.[16] As at York High School, the Indian students I interviewed outperformed Afro-Caribbean students academically. In the school as a whole, Afro-Caribbean students had higher rates of school suspension compared to their Indian peers (Ofsted, 2004) The measures seen in table 1 suggest that both schools are somewhat below average for their respective cities in terms of social class and academic achievement, although neither is the worst off in its respective city.

I spent six months at Long Meadow Community School in London during the 2003–2004 academic year, attending school three days a week. I roamed the halls, sat with students during breaks between classes and during lunch, and joined class field trips. As in New York, I conducted a survey of four classes (mixed by race/ethnicity, skill, and gender) and sixty in-depth interviews, with twenty second-generation Indians, twenty second-generation Afro-Caribbeans, and twenty native whites for comparison. As in the New York research, half of the students I interviewed in each group were girls, half boys.

The research sites are quite comparable, but, of course, differences do exist. First, Brent's immigrant population is somewhat more established, highlighted by the fact that many students' parents came to Britain at young ages and that I met very few immigrants at Long Meadow Community School. In contrast, York High had a very active English as a Second Language program, and I encountered many

TABLE I   THE RESEARCH SITES: A COMPARISON *(Percentages unless otherwise noted)*

	York High School		Long Meadow Community School
Neighborhood SES			
Families below poverty line	14	Ranking of overall deprivation	23rd percentile in England (from bottom)
Parents			
Mother did not finish high school	43	Mother ended education at Year 11 or less	29
Mother completed 4-year college degree	16	Mother completed 4-year university degree	25
Mother foreign-born	81	Mother foreign-born	72
Student Populations			
Second generation	54	Second generation	66
First or 1.5 generation	27	First or 1.5 generation	6
Eligible for free lunch	34	Eligible for free lunch	31
Graduation rate	38	Five A*–C GCSEs*	43
Race			
Asian or other	34	Afro-Caribbean	15
Black	13	Black (non-Caribbean)	13
Hispanic	47	Indian	16
White	6	Other Asian	11
		White British	17
		Other White	9
		Mixed, other, unspecified	19

5 GCSE A–C grades are required for university admission.

SOURCES: Department for Communities and Local Government, 2004; New York City Department of Education, 2004–5; Ofsted, 2004; survey data (*n* = 191); U.S. Census Bureau, 2000b.

more immigrant students. Second, urban Britain, including London, has significantly lower residential segregation than urban America has (Peach, 1996). In a classic study, social geographer Ceri Peach famously answered the question "Does Britain have ghettos?" with a resounding no (Peach, 1996). Even London's historically "minority" areas, such as Brixton, have a majority white population.[17] These two factors, in addition to the "one-drop rule" in the United States, which defines anyone with African heritage as black, led to a much greater "mixed race" population at Long Meadow, where students who identify as "mixed race" make up 12 percent of the student population (Ofsted, 2004). It also meant that there were many more white students attending Long Meadow than attending York High School. Hence, Long Meadow's student population was 17 percent white, in contrast to just 6 percent of York High's population. According to segmented assimilation theory, segregation is one of three causes of some minorities experiencing downward assimilation. The difference in levels of segregation between London and New York allowed me to evaluate the influence of life in a highly segregated city and in a school whose African American students mostly live in ghetto neighborhoods. Many of York High's black students were African American, and most African American students lived in a traditionally African American, poor community included in the school's catchment area. Third, high schools are traditionally structured quite differently in Britain and urban America, with British schools emphasizing continuity of peers through the Form Class and American schools emphasizing diversity of class choices and levels. For more details on the how and why of my research, see the appendix to this book.

PLAN OF THE BOOK

Each chapter of this book unpacks an aspect of culture as it relates to the second-generation students I met during the course of my research. In chapter 2, I focus on taste preferences in music and style. Readers who follow popular music will not be surprised that by far the most popular music and style was hip-hop. Hip-hop's predominance in both schools led some rebellious teens to reject it in favor of rock and punk music along with the associated "Goth" or "grunge" styles. However, neither a taste for hip-hop nor for rock or punk led to anti-achievement attitudes or oppositional orientations. I found tastes in New York and London to be remarkably similar. Globalization appears to have made hip-hop a currency for status among urban youth worldwide, suggesting that proximity to African American peers cannot explain the taste preferences of New York youth, as some have suggested. Indeed, students in both cities and of all ethnic and racial groups were more likely to cite the media than peers as influences on their styles and tastes in music. I did find significant gender differences. Boys expressed a greater taste for rap music and hip-hop style, associated with delinquency by some authorities, though I found no evidence that a taste for rap music leads to oppositional attitudes. This may explain the perception that minority boys are more likely to engage in oppositional cultures.

In chapter 3, I turn to ethnic differences in teen styles and tastes in music. I discuss how the drawing of symbolic boundaries between ethnic and racial groups and peer expectations of racial authenticity affected teens' taste preferences; I focus on the subtle differences in taste preferences between the Indian, Afro-Caribbean, Indo-Caribbean, and white students I interviewed. Hip-hop's association with African Americans elevated black racial identity to high status among peers. Nonblack students were sometimes chastised for "acting black," or inauthentic consumption of black popular culture. Hence, ethnic groups found ways of engaging with hip-hop that connected with ethnicity. Afro-Caribbean youth in my research found themselves with the most authentic claim to hip-hop because of hip-hop's black roots. South Asian youth engaged in hybrid bhangra–hip-hop and Hindi-hip-hop styles;[18] because they couldn't easily boundary-cross in their consumption without being seen as racially inauthentic, they blurred the boundary between Indian and hip-hop music. White youth in London chose from myriad cultural styles. Hence, although popular youth culture and status considerations exist in all social contexts, regardless of race and class, their manifestations differ by race and ethnicity.

In chapter 4, I turn to the ramifications of popular urban youth culture's racialization as black for student perceptions of racial discrimination. Some scholars have suggested that certain children of immigrants, like their African American peers, react to the racial discrimination they perceive in their school environments by rejecting formal education for an oppositional peer culture. However, I found that not Afro-Caribbean but Indian students—high-achieving in both national contexts—most likely to report experiences with racial discrimination in school. This discrimination did not come from school authorities, but rather from peers with higher status in their youth cultures. Students of all backgrounds explained Indians' low peer status through their weaker engagement with peer cultures. Furthermore, the Asian male stereotype is one of hypomasculinity, which may lead to low status among peers but also coincides with a model minority stereotype among adults. Afro-Caribbean students, on the other hand, reported racial discrimination exclusively from unknown adults *outside* school, in public places. In contrast to the Asian stereotypes, in mainstream culture, black boys face a hypermasculine, dangerous stereotype, which stigmatizes them among adults but may bring status among peers. These findings suggest that, regardless of *actual* racism and discrimination, reactions to *perceived* discrimination from teachers and school administrators cannot explain low achievement among Afro-Caribbean students in the two schools. The very different types of racial stigma for second-generation Indians and Afro-Caribbeans lead to different consequences for status in the peer social world, and also for future opportunities for success in the adult social world. In the latter, perceptions of hypermasculinity can lead to discrimination against young black men in employment, housing, and encounters with the police.

In chapter 5, I turn to other aspects of peer culture that have been thought to conflict with academic achievement: attitudes and beliefs (including beliefs about racism and discrimination, peer culture attitudes, and perceptions of opportunities) and behavioral scripts with respect to conflict. In terms of attitudes and beliefs, I found little evidence for oppositional peer cultures and no evidence that perceptions of discrimination lead to low aspirations. Furthermore, the few students who *did* express oppositional attitudes cannot account for the overall low achievement rates in both schools, where only a minority of students leave qualified to start a university education. In terms of behavior, I found that teens placed much importance on defending self-pride and showing toughness when it came to conflict with peers. Conflicts sometimes, as a last resort, ended in physical fighting. Engaging in peer conflicts served two purposes: it prevented real, physical violence, because in both schools, appearing weak led to being bullied; and it brought peer status, by demonstrating self-pride and toughness. These conflicts, however, did not signal defiance of school authorities or opposition to school norms. Nor did they stem from a lack of interest in academic excellence. Rather, they were described by teens as inevitable and sometimes necessary responses to situations at school. As with consumption, gender mattered. For young men, masculinity was tied to toughness, defending self-pride, and being seen as hip. Pressures of masculinity led boys to place more importance on maintaining self-pride among peers. This connection made boys even more invested in peer status than their girl counterparts, for whom femininity was less likely to come into conflict with adult school culture.

In chapter 6, I synthesize the findings of the previous chapters to develop a theory of peer culture in schools that is relevant for children of immigrants in both cities, emphasizing the role of peer status. I found that peer culture involves maintaining and defending one's status in front of peers, which sometimes comes into conflict with adult expectations for school achievement—this was especially true for boys. Furthermore, the quest for peer status, rather than oppositional culture, best explains second-generation teen attitudes, behaviors, and tastes. As I looked carefully at youth cultures in these two schools, I found a distinct youth subculture in school, but not an oppositional culture. Instead, the subculture involves a distinct set of cultural accoutrements related to a status hierarchy in which racial authenticity, pride, toughness, having the right tastes in music, style, and language, and having the right comportment are all important. I found that an emphasis on peer status drives youth cultures and that this, rather than rebellion or rejection of the dominant society, explains the taste preferences and behaviors of the teens I encountered, which some might interpret as oppositional. According to the youth in my study, success was the balancing act of maintaining high status in the peer social world and in the "dominant" or academic world.

Although I designed this study as a comparison to understand how American-style urban poverty and the influence of African American peers on some second-generation teens' cultural orientations lead to different outcomes in New York and London, I encountered remarkably similar youth cultures in both cities with respect to taste preferences, attitudes, behaviors, and influences on peer status. Where students did differ between New York and London was in the drawing of symbolic boundaries; that is, although they were similar in terms of *what* led to peer status, New York and London teens diverged in terms of *who* had peer status. In chapter 7, I take a symbolic boundaries approach to youth cultures to understand the boundaries of "us" and "them" that students drew. New Yorkers divided much more along racial and ethnic lines than did their London counterparts. New York youth were more than three times more likely to mention race and ethnic groups when asked to describe their school's social groups than were teens in London. Also, New Yorkers most frequently cited race or ethnic groups when asked who is popular and unpopular in their school, while only two Londoners did so. Lastly, New Yorkers were less likely to have close friendships with peers of different backgrounds; they were less likely to feel comfortable talking with other races; and they were more likely to have an in-group preference for dating. The contrasting organizational structures of the two schools, typical of their respective cities, had a strong influence on the relatively greater salience of race and ethnicity for symbolic boundaries in New York compared to London.

Finally, I conclude the book in chapter 8 with some reflections on how the peer cultures of students in my study may change as they grow older; on the lives of teens in other school contexts; and on the cultural and structural influences on second-generation academic achievement. I then draw from the book's findings to make some key policy recommendations for improving academic achievement among children of immigrants.

CHAPTER 2

Music and Style

Americanization or Globalization?

Sixteen-year-old Shivon describes his London neighborhood as "kinda, just, ghetto." He lives in a public housing complex known to be one of London's more notorious for drugs and gang activity. Shivon's parents came to Britain from Jamaica as teenagers and met in London. One day during a school break, I observed Shivon rapping among his friends—he later told me he was "freestyling" (making up the rap as he went along) and that he's known among friends for his rapping. Shivon mostly listens to rap music: "I just like rap music, everything—the beats, the videos, the clothes, the lyrics." American rappers are his favorite artists: Lil' Flip, Ludacris, G-Unit. Shivon's style is "just like them [rappers], that's what my mom says. . . . Hip-hop style, American." On the day I interviewed him, Shivon wore diamondlike earrings, a gold-link chain with a cross pendant, a long-sleeved oversized T-shirt, and oversized jeans. Already in post-secondary education as a Sixth Form student, Shivon told me that school is very important to him: "Because everyone—you have to have education. Everyone in my family is telling me, yeah. It's best I get my education and then I can go get proper jobs." He plans to attend university after he finishes his A-levels. He strongly agrees that working hard will lead him to success, and he doesn't believe that discrimination affects his performance in school.

It is common knowledge that young people place great importance on music tastes and style. Indeed, this is what comes to mind when most people think of youth cultures. Although music and styles may seem frivolous and unimportant, many think that tastes and styles embody great meaning. State legislatures and city councils across the country have tried to ban baggy pants for fear of their negative influence

(Koppel, 2007; Warikoo, 2005b). Among American scholars of immigration, some have suggested that certain second-generation youth's taste preferences for styles associated with urban African Americans are symbolic of an oppositional culture that can lead to downward assimilation (Portes et al., 2005; Portes and Zhou, 1993; Zhou and Bankston, 1998). British scholars of race and immigration have suggested that some disadvantaged youth adopt an adversarial style of dress, expressing a rejection of the dominant society through their clothing and tastes in music—what some have termed "resistance through rituals" (A. Bennett, 2000, 2001; S. Hall and Jefferson, 1976; Hebdige, 1979; Sewell, 1997; Willis, 1990). At a time when scholars were emphasizing structural forces that led to class reproduction, these scholars of Britain's Birmingham School attempted to bring youth agency into analyses of youth cultures by showing how some anti-achievement styles and behaviors were actually political acts. These previous discussions of youth taste cultures, however, lack empirical evidence of the resistance that researchers tie to styles. Some suggest that the resistance is unconscious, and the acts alone signify resistance; however, this provides no means for empirical verification (Davies, 1995; Giroux, 1983). In this chapter I analyze what second-generation teens in both cities are listening to and how they dress. In addition to *what* tastes teens prefer, I analyze the *meanings* they assign to those tastes and the influences on their tastes. Through the voices of teens themselves, I analyze what motivates particular styles and consumption patterns for teens, rather than assuming that tastes have unitary meanings.

I found that hip-hop music and style are most popular in both of the school contexts I studied.[1] Although hip-hop was favored among teens in both cities, a taste for hip-hop music and style generally did not signal oppositional attitudes or orientations. This was even true of lovers of rap music: their attitudes toward success and education were remarkably similar to those of their peers who had different or more diverse musical tastes. Students were more influenced in their styles by the media than by peers; tastes in New York and especially in London drew more from *global* than from *local* influences. These findings suggest that for these second-generation teens, hip-hop is not embedded with an oppositional meaning through the influence of local peers, as scholars of downward assimilation have assumed. As a result, the findings suggest a need to rethink common understandings of second generation teen styles and choices in music.

Gender plays an important role in youth cultures, as I will describe. Previous research on youth cultures has largely focused on young *men,* either explicitly or implicitly (Mirza, 1999). Young men and women express different taste preferences, however, and the ways in which adults understand their styles are quite different. Schools are institutions with gender regimes—sets of arrangements about gender (Connell, 2002)—that instill norms of masculinity and femininity in children through gendered behavioral and stylistic expectations; different modes of punishment and rewards for males and females; and other means (López, 2002; Martin, 1998; Thorne, 1993). These expectations come not only from school authorities but also from peer cultures. I observed both boys and girls struggling to maintain norms of masculinity and femininity, respectively, through their styles. However, boys' tastes were more likely to be misread by adults who assumed baggy jeans and rap music lead to delinquency among young minority men.

MUSIC: GLOBAL HIP-HOP

Dressed in all your fancy clothes
Sneakers looking fresh to death I'm loving those Shell Toes.[2]
Walking that walk, talking that slick talk
I'm liking this American boy.

—Estelle, "American Boy" (Top Ten song in the U.S. and Britain, summer 2008)

British singer Estelle's hit song featuring American rapper Kanye West, "American Boy," highlights the popularity of hip-hop and American-based urban popular culture in Britain. In the song, Estelle mentions major U.S. urban centers that she would like to visit: Brooklyn, Los Angeles, New York. Hip-hop music and its concomitant style have become mainstream popular culture among youth, especially urban youth, in the United States and Britain. Hip-hop artists dominate the Top Ten songs of popular radio, and hip-hop music is played at fraternity parties at elite U.S. universities and at parties at elite institutions in Britain (Pattillo-McCoy, 1999; Sewell, 1997).[3] In both sites of my research, hip-hop was understood to be the music that most students listened to and the source of their styles. This meant listening to music including rap usually performed by men, R&B music sung by men and women, and music that involved some amount of singing, rapping, and remixed samples of old songs. Those who never listened to hip-hop or its related forms (R&B, rap, U.K. garage) did so most often as a rejection of the popular culture among their peers.

TABLE 2   FAVORITE ARTISTS

New York	London
1. Usher	1. Sean Paul
2. Sean Paul/50 Cent	2. 50 Cent
3. Mario Winans	3. Beyoncé/Eminem/Kevin Lyttle
4. Puff Daddy	4. Black Eyed Peas
5. Nas/Ludacris	5. Tupac Shakur

SOURCE: Survey data, $n = 191$.

When I asked students in interviews what kinds of music they regularly listen to, 80 percent told me some form of hip-hop. This included 94 percent of boys in both cities, and all but one of the Afro-Caribbean respondents. Of the top twelve artists named in both cities when students were asked about their favorite music artists or songs, seven are African American male rappers or R&B singers; one is an African American female R&B singer (Beyoncé); two are Caribbean singers of reggae (Sean Paul) and soca (Kevin Lyttle); one is the controversial white rapper Eminem; and one is the multiracial hip-hop group from L.A. the Black Eyed Peas. These data were quite similar in London and New York, and by ethnic group. Over half of students listed all hip-hop songs and artists as their favorites.

Although teens were similar in their music tastes across the two cities, boys had a stronger preference for rap, while girls were more likely to prefer pop. Twenty-eight percent of boys listed all rappers as their favorite artists when surveyed, while just one girl did so; on the other hand, 12 percent of girls listed all pop artists, while no boys did so. Pop was associated with femininity. Some boys told me that they had listened to pop when they were younger, but not as they grew older. One Indian boy in London, Ajay, told me that he listens to "lots of different types like hip-hop, R&B, bhangra music. And rap, garage." When I asked him if he always listened to those, Ajay said no: "Before, when I was small, I used to, like, listen to pop and stuff, but now I don't like that very much." This shift may be the result of marketing strategies that sell rap to urban boys, and pop to girls. Rap music, especially popular rap, expresses highly masculine behaviors, and most top artists are male. Only one student identified a female rapper (Missy Elliott)[4] as a favorite music artist. The greater consumption of rap by boys, then, is not so surprising.

These differences, however, make boys more vulnerable to stereotyping and perceptions of opposition and delinquency by adults they encounter. Adults more strongly associate rap with oppositional cultures and a rejection of the dominant society in both Britain and the United States than they do pop or hip-hop, and they associate it with contemporary urban youth. Rap music is one of the few genres rejected by Americans with diverse music tastes, and taste for rap decreases with higher education levels (Bryson, 1996). Media depictions of rap music suggest it is a danger to society, in contrast to media depictions of white-identified heavy metal music as causing moral panic and as dangerous only to individual consumers of the genre (Binder, 1993). In Britain, just 9 percent of adults report hip-hop or rap as their favorite kind of music, in contrast to pop, chosen by 27 percent of British adults (Smith, 2005). Although more than one-third of British adults say they have participated in a youth subculture, hip-hop and rap's relative recency means that just 4 percent of adults report having participated in a hip-hop subculture (Smith, 2005).

Although adults seem to perceive hip-hop and especially rap as low-status, countercultural, and dangerous to society, this is not how teens in my research related to the music. Rap did not lead these fans to a greater propensity for negative attitudes and beliefs. To understand the link between a taste for rap and attitudes, I compared the attitudes of "rap aficionados" with those of students with other music tastes. Of the 191 students surveyed, 27 listed all rappers and rap songs as their favorites. I labeled these students rap aficionados for their inclusion of only rap among their music tastes (rather than, for example, those with more general tastes in hip-hop, including for example, R&B singers). If any taste for African American–based music coincides with opposition, it should be strongest among those who listen only to rap.

I did not find that rap aficionados had a greater propensity to oppositional attitudes than did others. The differences in attitudes were statistically insignificant for all but one measure. For example, although 45 percent of rap aficionados agreed with the statement "Discrimination affects my achievement in school negatively," a *greater* percentage of other students agreed (53 percent). Similarly, just 8 percent of rap aficionados disagreed with the statement "I would like to attend and complete university," as compared to 5 percent of other students; this is a statistically insignificant difference. In terms of peer culture, a taste for rap had no effect on responses to the statement "Among my friends, it is not cool to do well in school." However, the degree to which academic achievement actually leads to *higher* peer status was affected by a taste for rap: 33 percent of rap aficionados disagreed with the statement "Among my

TABLE 3   RAP'S INFLUENCE IN BOTH SCHOOLS

	Rap Aficionados	Other Tastes
Discrimination affects my achievement in school negatively.	45% agree	53% agree
I would like to attend and complete university.	8% disagree	5% disagree
Among my friends it is *not* cool to do well in school.	18% agree	15% agree
Among my friends, it is cool to do well in school.	33% disagree	14% disagree*

*Statistically significant difference at p = .05.
SOURCE: Survey data, n = 191.

friends, it is cool to do well in school," while 14 percent of others did. Although a minority in both groups disagreed, this indeed is a statistically significant difference. It means that doing well in school does not gain peer status for a minority—albeit a significant percentage—of rap aficionados. Again, note that the converse statement—"Among my friends it is *not* cool to do well in school"—showed an insignificant difference between rap aficionados and others. Thus, tastes for rap were not associated with greater anti-school attitudes or perceptions of discrimination, although rap fans were more likely to have friends who don't find it cool to do well in school. This finding runs counter to the notion that teens choose rap music as rebellion or to express or reflect countercultural attitudes. Regardless of what rappers are saying in their lyrics, teens in this research who listen to their music seem not to be using it as a tool for expressing discontent, anger, or opposition.

In terms of behaviors related to school success, rap aficionados reported spending less time on homework per night than peers with other tastes: nearly two-thirds of rap aficionados reported spending less than thirty minutes per night on homework on average, compared to just under one-third of students with other or more diverse music tastes. However, this difference may be more a result of gender differences, because all rap aficionados but one were boys, and boys were twice as likely to report doing less than thirty minutes of homework per night than girls. Rap aficionados and their peers were more similar in their reports of skipping school than were boys and girls. Fifty-nine percent of rap aficionados reported that they never skip school, compared to 54 percent of students with other music tastes. This suggests that although a strong preference for rap music does not seem to have a strong correlation with delinquency *within* school, it does have a relationship to gender and perhaps achievement-related behaviors *outside* school.

Next I turn to style, often closely related to tastes in music, especially among youth.

WEARING CULTURE: HIP-HOP STYLE AND EXPRESSIONS OF MASCULINITY AND FEMININITY

In terms of style, again, hip-hop was most popular. For boys this meant some or all of the following accoutrements: the latest Nike sneakers, Timberland boots, baggy jeans (often low enough that their boxers were visible), baggy T-shirts and basketball jerseys, hooded sweatshirts, big jackets, do-rags, new-looking baseball hats worn to the side often with tags still on, and bandanas. Girls' clothing included name-brand sneakers, tight jeans, tight shirts, matching zip-up hooded sweatshirts and bottoms, light makeup, nails styled long with designs on them, and belts bearing their names. Both boys and girls might wear big, gold-looking jewelry, including necklaces with pendants bearing the wearer's name or a religious symbol, bracelets, and rings. Girls' earrings tended to be hoops, whereas boys' earrings tended to be big "diamonds," often in just one ear.

Although students in New York had much more leeway in self-expression because of the lack of school uniforms in that city, London youth found many ways to express their identities through clothes and accessories. The uniform in the London school consisted of a casual, unisex outfit. The school encouraged students to wear their choice of sneakers to school. Although prominent accessories were officially not allowed, both boys and girls regularly wore visible earrings, necklaces, hats, and bracelets. Hair was another means of self-expression. London students had a few opportunities to come to school in nonuniform clothes. Every semester there was a designated day during which they could wear their own clothing. They also came in street clothes to parent-teacher meetings and to the winter evening performance. In what follows, I outline the style preferences for youth in each city and describe, in particular, how norms of masculinity and femininity influenced students' choices about clothing. I wanted to understand how teens saw their styles, how gender expectations influenced what they wore, and, as with music, what styles said about orientations toward the dominant society.

TABLE 4   SELF-SELECTED TERMS FOR STYLE, BY CITY
(Percentages)

	New York	London
Casual	45	59
Stylish	31	47
Hip-hop	50	28
Urban	10	24
Sophisticated	11	12
Alternative	13	5

NOTE: Students could choose more than one response, so percentages do not add up to 100.
SOURCE: Survey data, n = 191.

In a survey question, I asked students to choose one or more words from a list to describe their style of clothing (they could also write in any answer). The most common choices were *casual* and *stylish,* followed by *hip-hop* and *urban.* British youth were more likely to choose general terms like *casual, stylish,* and *urban,* in contrast to New York youth, 50 percent of whom chose *hip-hop.* Still, overall I found remarkable congruity between the word choices that youth in the two cities made to describe their clothing style.

The relationship between hip-hop style and attitudes and behaviors was similar to the relationship between a taste for rap music and attitudes and behaviors. Those who described their style as hip-hop expressed perceptions of discrimination, desires to attend university, and perceptions of peer attitudes toward achievement similar to those who described their style with other adjectives. Also, as with rap aficionados, students having hip-hop style were not more likely to skip school than peers with other styles, though they did report spending less time on their homework.

Boys had a stronger preference than girls for styles associated by authorities with delinquency—namely, hip-hop and urban. Girls most frequently described their clothing styles in more general terms such as *casual* and *stylish.*

During interviews, girls described how norms of femininity were upheld with their chosen fashion. When I asked Renee, an eleventh-grade Afro-Caribbean student in New York, if anyone ever misunderstands her based on what she wears, she told me that her friends chastised her for not looking feminine enough:

TABLE 5   SELF-SELECTED TERMS FOR STYLE, BY GENDER
(Percentages)

	Boys	Girls
Casual	43	62
Stylish	33	48
Hip-hop	46	27
Urban	26	11
Sophisticated	11	11
Alternative	8	9

NOTE: Students could choose more than one response, so percentages do not add up to 100.
SOURCE: Survey data, $n = 191$.

Like once I was wearing these boyish pants and a boy's shirt and they said, "Why do I dress like a boy?" I said, "I like it. It's comfortable. . . . My friend . . . said, "Why you dress like a boy?" because she dresses more like a girl, with tight shirts and the tight jeans. And I said, "I don't feel comfortable at all in your type of stuff because, you know, it's hot and I am not very comfortable."

On the day I interviewed her, Renee wore sweats over black pants. She explained to me that she had two gym classes that semester, with two academic classes in between them. She didn't like changing in the locker room, so she simply put the required sweats over her pants and kept them on between the gym sessions. She seemed not to be wearing any makeup.

Although many girls took care to maintain a feminine appearance (and stigmatized those who did not, like Renee), they had to avoid letting their appearance go too far lest they be seen as sexually loose. If a girl went too far in her sexiness, male and female peers alike would disapprove. For example, Sharon, a white English girl, told me that most of her friends in the neighborhood were boys because the neighborhood girls were too "tarty": "There is very few girls in my estate [public housing complex], actually. And the people that I stay out with don't know about the girls. They are not involved. . . . Like I think they are too sluttified. [laughs] Sorry! They are too tarty and everything. So I wouldn't wanna hang around with them. . . . They dress so their chest is sticking out, wearing short clothes." Sharon's explanation of "sluttified" suggests that the girls she dislikes and avoids hanging out with go too far with their sexiness.

In New York, students expressed similar sentiments about girls who are too sexy. Jamal, when describing his coethnic Guyanese girls, said this to me: "The Guyanese girls, they are so wild, you know. I mean, I don't mind if you [a girl] go out, but like in public, you know, you have to be conservative, mature. . . . These Guyanese girls are, you know . . . they like to party a lot, but unless [only if] she is a ho. So, I mean, I don't really, you know, mess around with them unless I know for sure that they are not that type of person." In other words, Jamal doesn't like girls he knows to party too much or to be too liberal. Young men and women inhabited a shared social space, but the norms and expectations for them were quite different, both in how they dressed, described above, and also in how they engage in conflict, as I show in chapter 5. Popular style considerations served to reinforce traditional gender norms through girls' sexiness (but with chastity) and boys' toughness.

For boys, norms of heterosexuality influenced style, masculine iden tity being tied to heterosexuality (Ferguson, 2000; Kimmel and Mahler, 2003). For example, when I asked twelfth-grader Rajbir about his style, he told me that he takes care not to wear brands that may signal gay identity to his peers:

> R: What influences my dress? Okay, like in, in school I tend to wear, like, not the clothes I wear outside. Because, like, when I go outside I hang out with my friends—they're all from suburban areas and stuff, so they dress, like, I don't know how to say. Like, more like white, proper. All right—at school I try not to wear clothes like that, because they will think I am gay or something, so.

> N: So what are those clothes? Can you describe them?

> R: Like, I will wear, I don't know. I wouldn't wear, like, an Armani shirt to school. . . . Like, I don't wear clothes from, like, stores like French Connection, Armani, and stuff like that in school. I wear more, like, just like whatever, Gap or something like that.

Rajbir was a high-achieving student who met his suburban friends through Sikh summer camps that he attended. His ability to engage in the peer culture of his school and then switch to the peer culture of his suburban Sikh friends involved changes in dress code; it appears that the urban, disadvantaged environment of his school places more stigma on possible gay signals than do the suburban, "white, proper" areas where his (Indian Sikh) suburban friends live. Although he carefully navigated the different norms of masculinity in the two environments, Rajbir felt free to express his ethno-religious identity. He wore his uncut hair in a turban as prescribed by his Sikh faith, and his bookbag had a large *khanda* embroidered on it, a symbol of Sikh identity (akin to Catholics' cross). Some researchers have suggested that the norms of masculinity are stronger among working-class men and boys than among middle-class males (Coleman, 1961; Davies, 1995; Martin, 1996). It may be that middle-class males have other forms of capital—social (dominant), cultural, and economic—from which to draw and hence place less emphasis on peer culture via masculinity.

SNEAKERS: "MY ADIDAS" TO "STOMPIN' IN MY AIR FORCE ONES"

Hip-hop music has long had a connection with branded sneakers, as far back as the first rap group to become popular with a wide audience, Run-DMC, and its 1986 song "My Adidas," which led to a wave of popularity for Adidas sneakers among urban youth. In a 2002 rap song, Nelly famously described all the versions of Nike Air Force Ones that he owns. At the same time that hip-hop music has popularized Nike sneakers among urban teens, the marketing industry has looked to gain insight on future trends by observing urban poor youth and marketing branded products to them (Klein, 2002; Pattillo-McCoy, 1999; Rose, 1994). This strategy works. Sixty-three percent of the New York students expressed a strong preference for brand-name sneakers. For many in New York, this meant a specific preference for Air Jordans, made popular for Nike by the African American basketball star Michael Jordan. In London, there was even more affinity for name-brand sneakers. Not only did the majority of students in all ethnic and gender groups say in interviews that they wore only brand-name sneakers (77 percent), but well over half overall specifically mentioned preferring Nikes. Note that although it obviously takes much money to constantly have "the sneakers that just came out," wealth was not a marker for status among peers in and of itself. In fact, teens took pride in experiences with hardship and poverty. One Afro-Caribbean girl in New York told me proudly, "I was raised on the hard streets of Crown Heights!," the poor, predominantly black neighborhood in Brooklyn. John Jackson, in his research with Harlem youth (2001), similarly finds status in material things yet also through experiences with poverty.

Respondents gave two main reasons for preferring Nikes and name-brands. First, they were seen as high quality. For example, Sanjay, who helped his Indian mother maintain the liquor store his deceased father opened, told me: "It's not like name brands, just like, what look goods on me, like boots, sneakers. I really like Nike, yeah, Nike Jordans. No other brand. . . . Because they make good sneakers. The others are too colored, and not good shapes. Nike and Timberlands are the best ones."

In addition to a belief in the higher quality and style of name brands, teens also expressed a desire to fit in and be seen as cool. Jamela, a ninth-grade 1.5-generation Afro-Caribbean girl in New York, told me that she prefers name brands for their look and for the recognition of others: "I like name brands. I like name brand sneakers. . . . Because you know everybody's wearing them and they look nice sometimes, you know. They look very nice." Jamela, like Sanjay, suggests that brand-name sneakers happen to look nice. However, she also expresses an instrumental desire to fit in with peers.

Nikki emphasized the coolness factor. A ninth-grade student whose African American mother is from the American South and whose father is Afro-Caribbean, she pointed out that to be cool, one must have up-to-date sneakers: "It's like, if you want to hang out with the cool group, you gotta have the sneakers that just came out." Nikki's observation illustrates the relationship between cultural symbols and peer status. The "latest" Nikes can be converted to symbolic status among peers. There was a tone of slight criticism in Nikki's observation of the need to have the latest sneakers to have high status among her peers, and in fact she told me that her social group is the "middle" group and that the popular students in her school often bullied other students.

Terry, an Afro-Caribbean boy in London, also told me he prefers branded sneakers so that he can keep up with peers and be seen as hip. Furthermore, the shoes would prevent social stigma. When I asked if his sneakers are really important to him, he replied: "Yeah, really clothes and trainers [sneakers]. Just that most people, you gotta mind what you wear because people might diss you [disrespect you, or put you down]. . . . For not wearing what they are wearing. Like, you can't wear something too cheap, you know. You will probably get dissed. That's how it is these days." Terry recognized the peer status that the right clothing and sneakers would buy him. He spoke earnestly and seemed to take very seriously the need to maintain his status among peers.

The data on style and sneakers, like that on music, indicate great similarity between New York and London youth in their tastes for hip-hop. This suggests that hip-hop has become a global currency for status among urban youth worldwide and is no longer confined to a local, neighborhood-based subculture in New York. Hip-hop now reaches far beyond the African American neighborhoods of Brooklyn, Queens, and the Bronx in which it developed more than thirty years ago. What meaning do teens make of this global music and style? What ideas, attitudes, or perspectives do teens express through their styles, as they see it? To better understand how teens themselves see the cultural choices they make, I turn next to the meanings of style as reported by the students I met. I focus on their own perceptions of meaning, rather than assuming meanings based on particular styles. Scholars of immigration have too often assumed singular meanings for the tastes of children of immigrants without probing further into teens' self-perceptions.

(MIS)UNDERSTANDING TEEN STYLES

What did these global, media-influenced styles mean to teens? Most teens when asked said that style and music are an important parts of their identities, and this was true among both high and low achievers in both cities. However, many students of all ethnicities reported that others misinterpret their styles of dressing. When I asked students in interviews about the meanings of their styles ("What does your style of dress say about who you are?"), the most common response was that *others attribute a meaning that is wrong*—most often delinquency. This response was given by one-fifth of respondents asked in interviews in both cities. Students cited many experiences of wrong signals read by adults. These misperceptions happened in myriad ways on both sides of the Atlantic, including perceptions of low skills, low motivation, and delinquency.

Many in both cities felt that authorities might see them as lacking skills or desire for success. When I asked Grace, an Afro-Caribbean and African student in London, about how her style relates to her identity, she told me that some adults might, based on her clothing and hairstyles, see a different person from who she is inside:

> What my style means? . . . I'll still be to one style, but it doesn't mean I am like that. You have to talk to me first to see what kind of person I am, but people always think that "she is one of them." Like if I was going to a job interview or something—obviously I know how to present myself—but even if you went to ask me on a job, they will just think, "You are not likely to work here." But . . . I know when to just take my hairstyle and put it normal.

I asked Grace to clarify what she meant by people thinking "she is one of them":

They will think, "street child." . . . Like, say, if I came and my hair was bright with colors, they will think I am not—it's happened a lot like in a lot of shops—they just think you are not good enough to work there and you ain't got the brains and you ain't been to school. And they think, just think you are one of them wasted children.

Grace often wore her hair very styled, and changed her style often. For a period she wore blue extensions, and on other days her hair was coiffed high above her head. Her nails often were done with long extensions as well. She was acutely aware of the stereotypes that those outside her peer circle hold of her style, as her words show; yet among her peers, she was seen as very stylish. She also suggests that she would change her style for instrumental reasons, such as for a job interview, to mitigate others' misperceptions. Grace's grades in school were in the middle range of students I interviewed, though she reported spending much more time on homework than most of her peers and never skipped school (41 percent of British students reported skipping school at least once a year). Mary Pattillo-McCoy (1999) describes the possibility of others' misperceptions—similar to those Grace described—as the danger that style will "send an unintended signal" (132). Grace's fears were confirmed by a conversation I had with an immigrant Afro-Caribbean teaching assistant I met at Long Meadow. She asked me about my research, and when I described the topic, she told me about what she called her "baggy pants theory": students who wear baggy pants lack focus and consequently don't do well in school.

Boys' understandings of others' misperceptions were based around the thug image. In a study of inner-city black youth in Philadelphia, sociologist Elijah Anderson (1999) found that authorities such as school faculty and police mistook "decent" youth for "street" youth because of their accoutrements. This led to a self-fulfilling prophecy of failure to stay out of trouble and achieve mainstream success. When I asked John, a fourteen-year-old working-class Afro-Caribbean boy in London, what his style of dress says about him, he told me that it means very little, though others misread delinquent meanings:

It don't honestly really say that much about me. Sometimes people get first impressions wrong, the impression about the way I am, by the way I dress. . . . Sometimes they might think I am a bit thugged out. Like, rude and all that. . . . Because sometimes, if my trousers might be baggy, a bit baggy or something like that.

John's response resonates with Nancy Lopez's findings among Dominican boys in New York who are stereotyped as dangerous (López, 2002).

A soft-spoken young man, John wore his hair in braids and his uniform sweatpants somewhat baggy. He was in the top academic track for science, though he reported spending less than thirty minutes average on homework each night.

Just as adults and youth had different understandings of individuals' styles, urban and suburban contexts also led to different meanings of the same styles. That is, the same styles could elicit different reactions and hold different meanings depending on the social context. Recall Rajbir's preference for clothes from The Gap in school versus French Connection and Armani among his suburban friends. Another student, Indo-Caribbean Roshan, told me that a key to success is the way one presents oneself and that the norms of proper dress are different in different areas:

> Like how I am, this is normal for like kids now. But if you wearing like do-rags—well, not do-rags, but something like bandanas, chains—something that represents gangs, all that kind of stuff [that signal delinquency]. . . . This [points to his own clothes] is normal for us, [but] if you go up into the suburbs, they probably wear polo shirts and khakis and loafers. You know, [that's] normal for them. This [points to self] is normal for us.

Roshan suggests that the norms of proper dressing vary between his home in Queens and his relatives' home in upstate New York, and that suburban adults would read his style as gangster, while Queens peers would not. He does make distinctions among his peers, however—between those who wear do-rags and those who wear bandanas. I often observed Roshan in class, and he usually wore baggy jeans, Timberland boots, and big hooded sweatshirts that he used to hide his face on days when he chose not to engage in class. His example illustrates the point that the further one moves away from the social group that shares a certain style culture, the more room there is for misunderstanding. In this case, both age and urbanicity matter. Hence, adults outside Roshan's Queens neighborhood are even more likely to interpret his clothing wrongly than are peers in Queens. What Roshan seems not to realize, however, is that adults will often read the same style on young men of different races differently, so that a young minority male may elicit fear or assumptions of delinquency in a suburban context in ways that a young white male with the same style may not (Pattillo-McCoy, 1999). In fact, hip-hop style is quite popular among suburban white youth as well (Perry, 2002).

Others reported that their styles signaled *moderation*. This was especially true in New York, where students were not limited in stylistic expressions by a school uniform. That is, these students took pains to distinguish themselves from peers whose styles were too extreme. This distinction took three forms: signaling moderation; signaling *not* being in a gang, for boys; and signaling "normal" identity and the right amount of sexuality for girls.

Some students wanted to show moderation in terms of self-pride and to prevent antagonism from peers. Marc, an eleventh-grade Indo-Guyanese student in New York, told me that his immigrant parents preferred that he dress moderately, and he agreed with them:

> My parents, they dress different than I do because they're not really that into the U.S. style and stuff. They came from Guyana, but they don't have a problem with me dressing like a regular kid. As long as I don't overdo it, and wear really, really big clothing, then they don't have a problem with it. My dad says he sees some kids with pants that are falling down and stuff when they walk, so he just tells me to dress proper. So I'm like, "Okay."

Assuming this parental management of style was a source of conflict, I asked Marc if he ever fought with his parents about their regulation of his style. But I was wrong:

> No, I agree with them too. . . . Like they're right, I shouldn't dress [with] really, really baggy clothes and. . . . You know, I mean when you wear big clothing, people look at you and they're like, "He think he's big" and stuff. And they're going to keep watching you, and they might want to beat you up.

In school, Marc wore glasses, stylishly big jeans (but not huge, as he described), and lots of gel in his curly hair. The pains he took to wear just the right level of bagginess to signal hipness yet not too much pride earned him the respect of his peers as well as his parents. The balance kept him out of trouble with both.

Certain styles could signal gang involvement among boys in New York, a perception that many wanted to avoid.[5] Shamsher, an Indian student in New York, also told me he likes to dress moderately and not to be seen as a "gangster": "I like the way I dress . . . you, sometimes you feel like fresh, you don't wanna look like bad people, be neat and good. . . . Like you don't wanna be a gangster. Like wear simple clothes! It's good." I asked Shamsher to clarify what he meant by dressing like a gangster: "Like you wear hats, do-rags. It shows like a sign of gangs, like that."

Shamsher wore his hair heavily gelled, and on the day I interviewed him, he wore a bright-red, new-looking T-shirt and a black leather necklace that had a gold pendant with his name on it inside a khanda.

The necklace's similarity to many rappers' necklaces symbolized the influence of hip-hop style combined with his ethnic identity. On most days, Shamsher also wore a big earring in one ear that looked like a fake diamond. To peers, Shamsher's dress probably signaled "normal" style. As he explained, his lack of hats and do-rags signaled that he did not identify with gangs, and this was the image he wanted to convey. This delicate balance between wanting to be seen as hip and cool and also wanting to avoid perceptions of deviance was common among both girls and boys.

For girls, moderation in style also meant fitting into style norms. Nikki, a fourteen-year-old Afro-Caribbean and African American girl, told me that her style had just the right amount of "ghetto" influence: "[My style is] not ghetto, but it's not, like, plain. Like I am always saying, 'It's too tight for me!' But I don't like wearing things loose. I'm in the middle." I asked Nikki to clarify what she meant by "ghetto":

> Ghetto is like—I have a name belt [belt with her name on the buckle in cursive lettering]; it is ghetto, but the reason I have one is because my family got it for me. So I had to wear it. I can't stop wearing it. I'm also not like ghetto like, let's see, like I didn't get my name chain because my mother thought it was ghetto. I didn't get my name earrings because she thought it was ghetto.[6]

Nikki does not want to appear "ghetto," which implies a lack of moderation. Rather, she modulates her participation in "ghetto" style. Some participation, however, is necessary for hipness and status with her social group. Recall Nikki's earlier discussion of the need to wear the latest sneakers to have high peer status. She seemed content with being in the "middle" group, as she described it, in terms of style and peer status, to mitigate extreme expectations from her peers.

When I asked Baljit, a sixteen-year-old girl in New York who came to the United States at age nine from India, to describe her style, she said she wanted to dress like "regular" people: "Very simple, like, I don't like, you know, like not really baggy clothes or really tight clothes, you know. I just dress like regular people dress, that's it." Baljit's words illustrate the difference for hip-hop style between boys and girls. For girls, it involved very tight jeans and, for boys, very loose jeans. Although the clothes I saw Baljit wear in school signaled her participation in youth styles (her jeans looked quite tight to me!), she identified her style as moderate.

For girls, moderation also signaled a balance between dressing with feminine style and avoiding *too* feminine a style. When I asked Sophie, an Afro-Caribbean girl in London, about what her style says about her, she told me that it says she's neither "girlie" nor "boyish": "Basically we [my friends] are the kind of people—we are not girly. We are not too boyish. So we're just in the middle." Earlier in this chapter I describe the norms of femininity that require girls to appear feminine, but not so feminine as to be seen as frivolous or, worse, sexually loose. Sophie's description of the meaning of her style indicates her awareness of those norms.

Teenagers were aware of the messages that others read from their clothing styles. In general, they seemed adept at deciphering their peers' subtle style differences. Most, similar to those whose words appear above, chose to signal in their styles a balance between hipness and an orientation toward mainstream success including academic achievement (disinterest in gangs and overly "ghetto" behaviors). This is one way in which style involved meanings for individuals. The problem urban minority teenagers face, however, is that outside their peer cultures, adults are not nearly as adept at reading their subtle differences. Hence, even a moderately baggy shirt can elicit assumptions of delinquency and oppositional culture, despite the best intentions of the individual wearing it. These (mis)understandings of style on the part of underinformed adults can lead to presumptions of delinquency. Although the styles are in fact quite benign, adults may interpret them as oppositional and treat students accordingly, with possible implications for their academic achievement.

IDENTIFYING THE SOURCE: INFLUENCES ON STYLE

The findings above show that styles were often misunderstood. But where exactly did these styles come from? Although the similarity between New York and London students' tastes in music and style suggest global influences such as MTV, some scholars have suggested that children of immigrants in disadvantaged neighborhoods adopt the oppositional hip-hop styles of their African American peers. Which matters more in shaping teen choices?

In interviews I asked students what influences their styles of dressing. The most common influence on style in both cities was the media, followed by peers. Forty percent of students in both cities told me that the media (music artists, actors and actresses) influenced their style. These students gave answers similar to Sandra's, an Afro-Caribbean Londoner: "A lot of things [influence my style], like if I am watching telly, if I see, like, a music channel and they have got this video showing and stuff and they have got this outfit and I am like, 'Oh, my God, that's so nice, I wish I could have it!' Like that." Media such as Music Television (MTV and MTV Base),[7] Black Entertainment Television (BET), and hip-hop music were the most frequently named influences on style among boys and girls and among all ethnic and racial groups except Indians, who were evenly divided between media and peer influences.

In addition to media influences, 22 percent got their sense of style from their peers. These youth tended to place more emphasis on fitting in among peers. They said things like what Angela, an Indian girl in London, said: "I like mostly the clothes that my sister wears, so I just go and shop, like, her kind of clothes. And then I have to ask my friends first like, 'Does this look nice?' If they say no, then that's it; I won't get it." During a break between lesson periods, Angela came to chat with me and talked about her upcoming trip with her best friend and the friend's parents to New York over Christmas to go shopping for clothes. She asked me about the best New York neighborhoods to shop in. A bubbly and friendly student, Angela was frequently chastised by teachers for talking in class. Nevertheless, her English teacher mentioned that she was among the top students in her class, which was confirmed by the grades she reported to me. When I asked Gurdaas, an Indian boy in London, about what influences his style, he said simply: "Like my surroundings, the kids. Like, what they wear, I wanna wear that too, so that's pretty much it, yeah."

London youth were three times as likely to mention media influences on style—singers, rappers, and movie stars—than to say their peers around them influenced their style, in contrast to New York youth, who were just 41 percent more likely to mention media influences than peer influences. The significantly greater media influence in London resonates with the roots of hip-hop: historically, Queens, New York has been a major center for hip-hop music production. Many rap songs mention the main streets of Queens—Linden Boulevard, Rockaway Boulevard, and others. In contrast, only recently are British-born rappers becoming well known (in Britain), and even so, the most popular hip-hop artists in Britain are American, as shown earlier in this chapter and as evidenced by music charts in Britain. Still, even in New York the media influence on styles was stronger than the peer influence.

This strong media influence suggests that peer cultures cannot adequately explain youth styles for the vast majority of teens. Furthermore, although peer cultures expressing resistance are generally identi-

TABLE 6   PEER AND MEDIA INFLUENCES ON STYLE *(Percentages)*

	Peers	Media
Afro-Caribbeans	20	55
Boys	16	63
Girls	25	50
Whites	6	47
Indians	25	25
Indo-Caribbeans	32	42

SOURCE: Interview data, *n* = 120.

fied with boys—especially black boys—either explicitly or implicitly (Mirza, 1992), boys and especially Afro-Caribbean boys in my study were *less* likely to cite peer influences than were their female counterparts.[8] Afro-Caribbeans were also the ethnic group most likely to mention media influences. This suggests that those groups thought to engage in oppositional peer cultures are in fact influenced more by the media than by their peers. The commercialization of hip-hop has made its popular forms less embedded with meaning today than they were, say, twenty-five years ago, when hip-hop was an underground genre of music among New York City African American youth (Gilroy, 1993; Rose, 1994). Hip-hop critiques of the dominant society and an underground hip-hop scene do exist in both New York and London. However, the vast majority of students in these two schools consumed popular hip-hop artists rather than artists whose messages are more critical of the dominant society. Furthermore, high achievers and low achievers were equally likely to name media and peer influences on their clothing style.

GLOBALIZATION AND STYLE

David Held (1999) defines globalization as "the speeding up of worldwide interconnectedness in all aspects of contemporary social life, from the cultural to the criminal, the financial to the spiritual" (2). The great similarity between youth in London and New York with respect to taste preferences in music and style, along with the strong media influence on style, speaks to globalization's powerful impact on youth. This is especially true for children of immigrants, whose families already tend to be globalized. The commercialization of hip-hop has led urban youth around the world—including Britain—to favor styles rooted in urban African American influences (Dolby, 2001; Gates, 1997; Gillespie, 1995; S. Hall, 1997; Klein, 2002; Maira, 2002; Perry, 2002; Sewell, 1997). Some suggest that this preference has caused hip-hop to lose its "roots" in political expression and voicings of disaffection. Nevertheless, this globalization of popular culture can best explain the similar findings in New York and London music tastes and styles. It suggests that rather than local, peer-based cultures, students in both cities engaged in global, media-driven popular cultures.

Students in London were keenly aware of the strong influence and popularity of American-born styles, brands, and artists in their social worlds, and they often identified their tastes as American. One Afro-Caribbean girl in London remarked while filling out her survey: "Isn't that interesting. Everyone I put down [for favorite artists and songs and for artists whose music you have obtained recently] is American!" Often after hearing me speak for the first time, students in London would ask me with excitement, "You American, miss?!" One time in the computer room, London students chatted with me about sneakers:

> Nathaniel went to the website niketown.com to look at the latest Nikes, asking Devon if he should buy them. The two of them and Ali, a second-generation Pakistani, chatted with me about how expensive things are in London compared to prices in the U.S. They mentioned the exchange rate, which had been increasing in favor of the pound. Ali said that what's old (and hence discounted) in the U.S. is new in the U.K., because new sneakers are released first in the U.S. One of the others said, "No, Foot Locker now releases them at the same time." Both Nathaniel and Devon appeared to be mixed race. (Fieldnotes, January 14, 2004)

This concern with the latest Nike sneakers and American dominance rang true in other conversations as well: one white working-class boy asked if he could give me money to bring back the latest Nikes from the United States for him when I was about to go for a short visit. Their knowledge of the exchange rate between pounds and dollars indicated a global perspective, at least with respect to fashion. Some girls (and boys) asked me to describe in detail American prom parties, graduation ceremonies, and cheerleading squads. When I asked how they had heard about these American traditions, most said they had seen movies featuring these American teenage traditions, and they were eager to institute the traditions in their own school.

Music Television also played a large role. Paradoxically, global media like MTV could lead to very local knowledge of the United States. Stan, a white English student with a visible hip-hop style (diamond-like earrings with his initials on them, baseball hat, very baggy school uniform, large gold necklace), asked if I knew of a particular park in Harlem:

> In science class Stan and Charles were playing and laughing while others worked on their experiment. Stan asked me what the boroughs of New York are. After I told him, he said, "What about Harlem?" I explained that Harlem is part of Manhattan, and then he asked if I knew a particular park. I said I didn't, and he explained that it is a park in Harlem where the best amateur basketball is played and where there is an amateur basketball tournament every year. I was surprised by his specific knowledge, and when I asked how he'd heard about the place, he told me he saw it on MTV. (Fieldnotes, November 19, 2003)

Globalization and mass consumption led to this teenager's detailed local knowledge of a place that I—someone who had lived in New York for five years, including two years close to Harlem—knew nothing about.

The American image that dominated popular music and style in London was generally identified with urban African Americans, as described earlier in this chapter. MTV in Britain, in fact, has a separate station, MTV Base, that exclusively plays hip-hop, R&B, and rap music, similar to BET in the United States. When I asked Grace, an Afro-Caribbean Londoner, whether the movies she watches influence her, she told me about the American movie *Bring It On*, which features two rival cheerleading squads. The squad from a middle-class white area of San Diego competes with the black, inner-city squad of East Compton. The San Diego squad had previously stolen its award-winning moves from the East Compton squad, heavily influenced by hip-hop dance. This conflict between the white middle class and "authentic" poor blacks speaks to popular notions of hipness embodied in blackness. When I asked Grace how the film influenced her, she told me it led her to attempt to set up a cheerleading squad at Long Meadow Comprehensive: "[*Bring It On*] is like an American film. It's a cheerleader film, really. . . . That's why we wanted to do cheerleading in our school. . . . That's a movie that's influenced me." Hence, American popular culture, via hip-hop and Hollywood, looms large in London.[9]

Globalization, then, makes youth in London and New York more similar than different in their taste preferences and consumption choices: hip hop music, big, gold jewelry, gelled-down hair for girls, baggy clothing for boys, tight clothing for girls, Hollywood movies. Moreover, in New York the media was 41 percent more likely to influence a teen's style than were peers, and in London the media was even more influential. These findings call into question the cultural trajectory described by downward assimilation theory, which suggests that *neighborhood* influences lead to cultural practices and, consequently, either upward or downward assimilation. Furthermore, the native poor group in London is white, but I found little evidence that style stemmed from that group, as might be predicted by the cultural explanations of downward assimilation theory as applied to the British context. Working-class white students in London usually engaged in hip-hop–inspired styles (see also Gates, 1997; Hewitt, 1986). Rather than adopting *local* cultural scripts for consumption, as segmented assimilation theory and theories of resistance through rituals presume, youth in both cities accessed *global* scripts in their taste preferences.

In this chapter I describe youth's taste preferences in music, style, and sneakers, finding many similarities between London and New York, due in part to global influences on peer taste cultures. In the following chapter I further detail teen tastes in music and style and explore the subtle differences between ethnic groups' taste preferences. I show how race influences the ways in which second-generation teens engage their youth cultures, and how and why consumption practices differ by ethnicity among the second generation.

CHAPTER 3

Racial Authenticity, "Acting Black," and Cultural Consumption

Fourteen-year-old Mary, a white English student, told me she listens to hip-hop, R&B, and U.K. garage music. Her style, as she described it, was "townie"—the style of hip-hop fans, the opposite of "grungy." She told me that some kids in her school are "wiggers": "A white person trying to act black, and it's not working. . . . They can't do it properly. Doing their hair like it. Talking like them and putting bandanas on and that. . . . But they can't act. They can't do it." Mary's voice grew annoyed as she described peers who "act black" because of their apparent inability to enact racially authentic behaviors and styles. Although Mary herself preferred black-identified music and style (hip-hop), she drew a line in the sand that whites implicitly should not cross, in order to maintain racial authenticity and avoid encroaching on black peers' territory. Mary's words suggest that although hip-hop has become popular among all youth, ethnic and racial groups are expected to maintain racial authenticity and not cross boundaries of ethnicity and race when it comes to taste preferences.

In what follows, I show how students navigated the complex terrain of popular culture, ethnic culture, and peer expectations of racially authentic cultural practices in their tastes in music and style. In chapter 2, I show how talking to second-generation teens about their music tastes and styles revealed meanings that adults may not have guessed. Here, I use the same lens of cultural consumption, this time to understand processes by which children of immigrants cross, blur, and shift ethnic and racial boundaries in the realm of culture. Ethnic and racial identities—constructed differently for different groups—led to peer status among both coethnic and noncoethnic peers. However, although adherence to the scripts for racial identity led to status, so too did the consumption of black-identified hip-hop music and style. And yet, the consumption of black-identified popular culture sometimes led non-black students to be seen as "acting black" (sociologically, lacking racial authenticity or attempting to boundary-cross), both by coethnic peers (for example, Mary's critique of "wiggers") and by black peers.

RACIAL AUTHENTICITY

Scholars have conceptualized authenticity as being true to oneself, achieving self-fulfillment, or maintaining "commitment to self-values" (Bendix, 1997; R. Erickson, 1995; Fine, 2003; Taylor, 1992; Trilling, 1972). The criteria by which authenticity is determined are socially constructed—that is, an amalgamation of elements from the past are chosen to meet present needs—by processes of "fabricating authenticity" (R. A. Peterson, 1997). Stephen Cornell and Douglas Hartmann (1998), in their classic account of racial and ethnic identities, describe authenticity with respect to identities as "social convention." They explain the process of defining authenticity in terms of ethnic and racial identities: "Some set of group members or outsiders selects a version of an identity and defines it as 'authentic,' granting it a privileged status. They then use it to distinguish among persons and identities, past and present. The grounds of supposed authenticity, however, are essentially arbitrary" (94).

Let me illustrate this point with an example. Sociologist Paul Gilroy, in his classic book *The Black Atlantic* (1993), explains that although hip-hop grew out of Caribbean speech styles via early hip-hop artists' Caribbean heritage, African Americans have claimed hip-hop as their own. Gilroy observes that today African Americans are seen as the authentic producers and consumers of hip-hop music, suggesting that they have used hip-hop "to legitimate African American particularity" (108). Some Afro-Caribbeans in my research reflected this identification of hip-hop as African American when they expressed feelings of inauthenticity in their consumption of hip-hop relative to African American peers. Constructed authentic identities take on a life of their own and develop real meanings for individuals and groups, in spite of their mutability and the limitations they place on individuals (for example, the expectation that African Americans do not listen to rock music) (Appiah, 1996; Cornell and Hartmann, 1998; Grazian, 2003; Jackson, 2005; Maira, 1999). Given popular understandings of ethnic and racial identities as essential and unchanging, the authenticity of those identities can be claimed by individuals or questioned by others, using fixed criteria, or scripts, for defining identities. "Authentic" cultural practices thus determine perceptions of group membership and of status, by both in-group members and outsiders. Perceptions of authenticity, as I show in this chapter, can also determine status within a social group—in the two schools of my research, peer status (see also Fine, 2003; Milner, 2004). Some students did critique peer expectations of racial authenticity, just as some scholars have critiqued the notion of racial authenticity (Appiah, 1996; Jackson, 2005; Mahon, 2004; Maira, 1999); still, it mattered a great deal in their peer social worlds.

The fabrication of racial authenticity serves to prevent boundary crossing in cultural tastes and practices. Sociologists of immigration have analyzed the crossing and blurring of boundaries by ethnic groups in the realms of citizenship, language, religion, and skin color, emphasizing how a country's social policies and history in these areas can influence the ways people divide themselves in society (Alba, 2005; Alba and Nee, 2003; Zolberg and Long, 1999). Sociologists of culture have looked at symbolic boundaries from a different perspective, focusing on cultural practices and products; for example, the defining of artistic genres (DiMaggio, 1987; Lamont and Fournier, 1992; Zerubavel, 1991). I integrate these two ways of thinking about symbolic boundaries by analyzing how processes of ethnic and racial boundary maintenance via racial authenticity among the second generation inhibit boundary crossing and consequently lead to blurred boundaries with respect to cultural tastes and practices.

COETHNIC EXPECTATIONS OF RACIAL AND ETHNIC AUTHENTICITY

Students expected peers to adhere to "authentic" scripts for their respective ethnic and racial identities. These expectations came from both coethnics and peers of different groups. I often heard accusations of someone "trying to be someone he is not"—in other words, adopting the cultural scripts—be it style, music, slang, or other markers—of another ethnic or racial group. For example, Rajbir, an Indian boy in

New York who strongly identified with his Sikh faith, told me that he hung out with Sikh friends from outside school more than he did with Sikhs in school.[1] When I asked him to explain why, he said:

> Because, I don't know, kids in this school, it's like I can't relate to them as much. . . . I just hang out with kids who . . . are baptized for the religion. They still hold their culture, and they follow the religion at the same time. . . . Like, I mean these kids [at Rajbir's school] don't probably—I don't believe that they hold, like, values as they say, because all I know is that every year I see two, three Sikhs cut their hair. And when they do it I ask them why they did it, and they just say because some kids make fun of them. I am like, "Yo, kids make fun of me all the time, but if it gets to me, like, I talk to them a bit and they will be angry at me. But I just ignore and then walk away."

Although many Sikhs in the United States and at his high school do not maintain uncut hair, Rajbir suggests that he more authentically practices the Sikh religion common to them by continuing to grow his hair and wear a turban in spite of teasing at school. He faults some peers at school for not continuing an authentic Sikh identity in the face of discrimination at school.[2]

Indo-Caribbeans also faulted each other for not adhering to traditional Indo-Caribbean cultural scripts. When I asked Roshan, an Indo-Caribbean New Yorker, about the different social groups in his school, one he mentioned was the "coolie" group,[3] consisting of "West Indian and gangster mixed up. They act like something they are not." When I asked Roshan to clarify this description, he told me that members of the "coolie" social group forget their Caribbean roots: "They forget where they come from. They try to pretend like they do [remember], but they have no sense of where they came from. They only know about now and these times." I asked Roshan what specifically they don't remember. He replied: "The way they come off. Some of them come off aggressive." Roshan's implicit critique of the coolie group is that they attempt to copy some other image rather than adhering to their cultural roots. "Gangster" was another of the school social groups Roshan identified; he told me this group was "black, West Indian [probably implying Afro-Caribbean], and Spanish." Roshan's critique of his fellow Indo-Caribbeans who fall into the "coolie" social group suggests that he thinks they inauthentically imitate their black and Latino "gangster" peers.

Afro-Caribbeans criticized coethnic tastes for "white" forms of music—punk, rock, grunge—and, in so doing, pushed conformity to the expected scripts for authentic black identity. Just as nonblack students might sometimes be censured for "acting black" if they engaged with hip-hop too much, black students were pressured to conform to the expected "black" taste preferences. For example, Nicole, the one Afro-Caribbean student in London who preferred rock over hip-hop, still listened to much hip-hop because her mother bought only hip-hop CDs: "I don't buy CDs; my mom buys R&B and hip-hop and stuff like that. But if I had money, I would go and buy Evanescence and Linkin Park [rock bands] and stuff like that." I asked Nicole why her mother wouldn't let her buy rock music.

> She would let me, but she just, she is not racist or anything, yeah, but she just sees that as white people music. She'll listen to it as a joke sometimes, but I just think it's kinda rude, though. And other, my peers, they are all like, "Why you listen to white music?" But just because white people sing it doesn't mean it's for white people. I can't say that I am like a grunger or anything like that, just because I am my own person, and I like music that has good beats. [If] it has good beats, I like it. So it could be anything.

Both Nicole's mother and her peers chastised her for her taste in "white" music. Later in her interview she told me that her best friend is Zohra, a second-generation Moroccan peer whom Nicole credited with teaching her to be herself; in the explanation quoted above, Nicole seems to refer to other peers. She defends her tastes as owing to the "good beats" of the bands she likes, and she is critical of the racial identification of music. Nicole's dilemma resonates with that faced by the Black Rock Coalition, an organization set up in 1985 to bring together black musicians performing rock music as a response to music executives and audiences (both black and white) that expected them to perform "black" music such as R&B and hip-hop, and consequently often rejected their music as "not black enough" (Mahon, 2004).

Adults, too, like Nicole's mother, sometimes questioned behaviors outside the expected scripts for ethnic identities. Renee in New York told me that she liked to "dress different ways. I will dress like how people would call a pop way, gothic, and yeah, I just mix it around." But adult coethnic Afro-Caribbeans questioned her tastes: "People ask why I have to wear certain things I wear. Like, I was on the street buying a soda, and this guy asked me why I'm wearing . . . a Puerto Rico shirt, if I am not from Puerto Rico." I asked Renee how she knew the man. "He used to see me around the way and he knows my mother. He used to go out with my cousin actually. And she said nobody from my family is from Puerto Rico, except one person my uncle is about to marry." This censuring demonstrates the salience of ethnicity in Renee's environment, where showing signs of an ethnicity other than one's own is seen as inauthentic, even if someone in the family has that heritage.

The examples of Renee, Nicole, Roshan, Rajbir, and Mary show that teens (and adults) in a setting with multiple ethnic groups still police the ethnoracial authenticity of coethnic peers. This finding resonates with previous research that analyzes the dynamics of racial authenticity via cultural practices within particular ethnic groups, in some cases between different generations (Carter, 2003; Jackson, 2001; Maira, 1999, 2002; Tuan, 1998, 1999). What about peers *outside* the ethnic group? The uniqueness of my study lies in part in the opportunity I had to examine the dynamics of authenticity *across* ethnic groups, thanks to the multiethnic school environments I observed. Do kids care about racial authenticity among other racial and ethnic groups? The answer is yes, especially when it comes to black (in)authenticity, or "acting black." Black-identified cultural scripts were the most common ones used by out-group members, because of popular culture's (hip-hop's) racialization as black. That is, because black-identified taste culture had high status within youth culture, it was the most common taste culture consumed by students, who in doing so sometimes crossed ethnic and racial boundaries and risked accusations of racial inauthenticity.

POPULAR CULTURE, BLACK IDENTITY, AND (IN)AUTHENTICITY

Although hip-hop's roots are in the African diaspora, its appeal today goes beyond black youth, as demonstrated in chapter 2. Still, hip-hop culture, though global, remains black-identified, and lay understandings of popular culture seem to buy into culturally essentialist notions of racial identities (Gilroy, 1993; S. Hall, 1997). This was true in the London school, even though it included no African American students. Thus hip-hop was seen as "belonging" to black youth because it stems from their community; this authentic identification with popular culture gave black students status among their peers. When I asked Michelle, a Haitian New Yorker, how she defines herself in terms of race, she told me, black. I asked her to explain what it means to be black: "It means to be cool. . . . It's hot to be black! . . . Like you go to the parties. You know all the dances! You could dance, you could dress, yeah!" Being black gave Michelle automatic status, because it meant knowing the popular music and its concomitant dance moves and clothing styles. That is, she is authentic in her consumption of popular culture because it is black-identified.

My observations at a celebration of India's independence day in London, attended by thousands, illustrate this point well. A South Asian comedian on stage described a young "desi" (a colloquialism for South Asian) man whom he heard in a shop speaking "with a Caribbean accent." As he went on to imitate the alleged imposter, the comedian used what sounded to me like an urban African American way of speaking, rather than a Caribbean or British accent. He then joked, "Why do we never hear Caribbeans talking like Asians [the opposite of what he described]?[4] It's like they're in the club and [switches to sing-song South Asian accent] 'Hello, girl, do you want to come home with me?' [switches back] Somehow I don't think that's gonna get them the girls!" The comedian's joke about South Asian young men adopting a Caribbean (or African American) manner of speech, rather than a South Asian way of speaking, to woo young women illustrates the higher peer status and hipness associated with black male identity and the lower status associated with South Asian masculinity, even among South Asians.

Although most youth engaged with hip-hop (aside from the small minority who explicitly rejected it), nonblacks perceived as engaging "too much" or inauthentically were sometimes criticized. "Trying too hard" or "posing" were dismissed as *inauthentic*, and sometimes as "acting black." Just as elites use subtle cultural markers to signal high status and to exclude low-status individuals from mainstream success, a culture exists among teens in which access to the "right" cultural accoutrements is restricted. Evaluations of racial authenticity with respect to hip-hop consumption could be made by anyone—coethnics, black peers, and other out-group members. Recall white English Mary's dislike of other whites who "act black": "It's not working!"

I asked Terry, who lives in London with his Jamaican mother but is in touch with his Ghanaian father, what the phrase *acting black* means. Terry explained:

Yeah, some people try to act black for some reason, because people think . . . I don't know why, but black these days means cool. Like . . . when people act black, yeah—like, you know . . . how black people will act—they will try and act [like that]. . . . They will be saying words, yeah, as if they were black . . . and dressing like a, like a black person. . . .

Mostly, because these days, yeah, people like wearing, like, good, good clothes. Like, like if you watch the movies, . . . like *Don't Be a Menace*,[5] and all them movies. All them black kind of comedy movies, you see the way they dress hip-hoppy. . . . Like dressing with all these chains, all these rings, and just copying mainly. You see a lot of that in this school. So people might be acting black.

. . . Like, yeah, have you seen *Barbershop?* . . . Yeah, because there is a white guy in there that acts like he is black. So it's like kinda like that.

In other words, the clothing, speech patterns, and music associated with "blackness" are marked as high status ("cool," in Terry's words), and hence even nonblack students engage in them. The character in the movie *Barbershop* to which Terry refers is a white man using taste signals and language in ways that seem not to "match" him: the humor lies in the character's lack of authenticity in exhibiting "black" cultural traits, which as a result seem forced and unnatural. Terry and many other black students in both cities critiqued the authenticity of outgroup members by suggesting that some nonblack peers adopted black cultural scripts. Note that the two references Terry gives are of black *American* characters. When I asked Terry *who* at school behaves in these inauthentic ways, he told me that Somalis try to "act black": "I'm not being racist, but . . . you know Somalians [*sic*], yeah, most of them try to act black." According to Terry, Somalis in contemporary Britain are not accepted into the category "black" by other black youth (Frosh, Phoenix, and Pattman, 2002, find similarly negative views of Somali students), and hence their authenticity in "black" cultural consumption is questioned by peers like Terry.

South Asian students also noticed the status associated with black racial identity among their peers. Indira, a fifteen-year-old Londoner whose Indian-origin parents were born in East Africa but nevertheless taught their daughter Gujarati, told me that she hears the phrase "acting black" at her school. When I asked her what "acting black" meant, she explained: "You know how different races have their own way, because of their background and how they're raised? [Some] say, 'Oh, look, she's popular. If I do that, I'll be [popular].' [Other] people go, 'Why you copying the black way?'" That is to say, teens expected peers to adhere to scripts for behavior associated with their races, yet the scripts that outsiders most copied were those associated with blacks, because they were associated with popularity.

I found a similar relationship between race and popular culture in New York. Christine, a sixteen-year-old Indo-Guyanese student, told me that when students "act black" in their clothing and conversational styles, they forget about their ethnic backgrounds, and they do so to be cool, or to gain peer status. When I asked her why someone would say someone else is "acting black," she told me: "Because, like, I guess because the way they dressing and the way they talk and they forget about their background, yeah." I asked why someone would do that, and she said: "It's partly to fit in, you know. Because they want friends who can, like, who are tough and can have their back and stuff, yeah. And they want to try to be like them." Christine suggests that some of her peers sacrifice their ethnic cultures to gain friends and to create a tough image.

One might have expected that in multiethnic settings in which no group dominates, kids would have fewer expectations of racial authenticity, and that hip-hop, given its universal appeal, would no longer be racialized as black. However, this was not the case in either city. Both coethnic and non-coethnic peers pressured students of all ethnic and racial backgrounds to adhere to racially authentic cultural practices and stigmatized those who attempted to boundary-cross in their choice of music and style. A means of maintaining a hierarchy in which black students had high peer status, this process is analogous to that in the larger society in which high-status groups use cultural practices and tastes (e.g., for golf and classical music) to maintain their position and prevent low-status groups from social mobility (Bourdieu, 1984).

Although most students bought into essentialized notions of ethnic and racial identities that led to expectations of racial authenticity in cultural practices, some resisted peer pressure to conform to narrow definitions of what it means to be "black," "white," or "Indian." Cultural anthropologist John Jackson (2001) has pointed out that the essentialization of racial identities as *cultural* rather than *biological* creates room for the categories to be challenged. Recall Afro-Caribbean Nicole's taste for rock music, despite her friends' and mother's disapproval. Despite annoyance at her friends' chastising her for listening to what they called "white people music," Nicole sometimes described others as "acting black": "I sometimes I say it ['acting black']. I notice that and I say it, but it's not right, because . . . what is it? I don't understand what is 'trying to act black.' . . . So I think it's not a good term to use. But I use it sometimes and it's not good." I asked Nicole when she would use the phrase "trying to act black." "Like, say if I see a white girl and she's got her hair slicked and she is listening to ragga,[6] doing like dances that Jamaican people do, I might say, 'Why is she trying to act black?' But that really isn't what she—well, it is not a good thing because . . . if you like the music, then, like . . . you should listen to it. And if you are trying to do the dance, why not do it?" Just as Nicole questioned the expectation that she listen to "black" music, she problematized her occasional critique of nonblacks' consumption of "black" popular culture.

In the reverse, Stan, a working-class white Londoner with friends of many different ethnic backgrounds, was a hip-hop fan and wore clothes to indicate his style. When I asked him if he ever heard the phrase "acting black," he said: "Yeah. . . . [P]eople might say I act black, but I don't really see it. I don't think that [I am] acting black—I am just acting in a certain way. Like, it's not that we wanna own that, but I guess because it's come from a black sort of music that people think [we act black]. . . ." I asked Stan to clarify what he meant by "own that." "Like . . . it's just style. They . . . can't say, 'It's our style; you can't do it.' It's like, it's for the different races, and if I like a music then I like it. So I am gonna do what I want. [It's] not for them to say, 'You can't do that.'" One day in class Stan sat next to me and asked about New York City. He asked me where he could stay for cheap in the city, mentioning that he had found a YMCA near Harlem for $20 a night. He asked me whether he would stick out in Harlem, presumably because he is white. Stan understood that race, regardless of style, influences others' perceptions of him; still, he loathed racially exclusive expectations of hip-hop style and music. Although students like Stan and Nicole found the phrase *acting black* problematic, it was a common phrase, used sometimes to describe style (very baggy pants, a style of walking, and so forth) and sometimes to refer to attitudes (acting tough, posturing, being loud).

Although the vast majority of students in both cities did not question the cultural essentialism of racial authenticity expectations, a handful in each city did, like Stan and Nicole. This questioning was more common in London, most likely because of the greater salience of race and ethnicity in the social lives of New York youth, which I describe further in chapter 7. Londoners tied their social lives less to race and ethnicity, and this may have led more of them to question expectations of racial authenticity in their cultural practices.

STUDENT RESPONSES TO RACIAL AUTHENTICITY AND POPULAR CULTURE

How did different ethnic groups respond to expectations of racial authenticity and a black-identified popular culture, given that con-

TABLE 7   PATTERNS OF TASTE IN MUSIC ACROSS ETHNIC GROUPS

Afro-Caribbeans	South Asians (Indians, Indo-Caribbeans)	British Whites
1. Hip-hop	1. Hip-hop–bhangra remix	1. Hip-hop
2. Caribbean (limited)	2. Hip-hop–Hindi remix	2. Rock and punk
		3. Diverse

sumption of popular culture led to peer status? In terms of navigating popular culture, a student asks himself or herself: What styles and music can I make legitimate claim to and thereby be seen as authentic? Because popular culture (hip-hop) is racialized as black, for Afro-Caribbean youth, hip-hop was the most obvious choice. For Indian youth, the increasingly established hip hop Indian remix styles meant that they could demonstrate racial authenticity while also signaling a taste for high-status popular culture in the hip-hop elements of the genre. Hip-hop–Indian styles blend Bollywood film songs, hip-hop, and bhangra—Punjabi folk music now popular with youth from all parts of the South Asian diaspora.[7] White youth navigated this world in diverse ways, as I will show.

Overall, although ethnicity strongly influenced youth's tastes in music and style, it did not determine it. An experience in a New York school cafeteria illustrates this point. On a June day I bumped into Joelle there, who was friendly as usual. A boy approached and chatted with her a bit, but she couldn't remember his name:

> "What's your name again?" she asked him. He reminded her by saying it sounds like a cartoon character—Tig. She asked him, "You Guyanese?" "No." "Trini?" "No." (Those would have been my guesses, too.) "Where are you from, then?" "I was born here." Joelle sucked her teeth in friendly irritation—"No! Where's your family from!" "Bangladesh." "Bangladesh? That's like Indian!"

Tig wore a baseball hat with the bill very flat, a very big T-shirt, and baggy jeans and spoke using urban slang and cadence. The three of us got to talking about music. Joelle said she listens to many kinds of music, including some rock, and she mentioned Limp Bizkit. Familiar only with the name, I asked Joelle to describe Limp Bizkit's music or tell me what the group's popular songs were.

> Joelle responded, "I thought you'd know about rock music?!" I asked why. She replied, "Oh, for a minute I forgot you was Indian!" "Why, does being

white mean you listen to rock music?" "Yeah, cuz most white people listen to rock music." Tig jumped in: "No, that's not true!" Joelle said, "Did you hear me? I said *most!*" I then asked, "What do Indians listen to, then?" Joelle said, "That Indian music. I listen to Indian music. I like that one song from the movie *B-A-G-H-B-A* . . ." "*Baghban*?" I said. Tig looked at me and smiled knowingly—I couldn't tell if he was laughing at how she said "*Baghban*" or at the fact that I was familiar with the Bollywood hit. Joelle then showed us the Bollywood music CD she had in her bookbag. (Fieldnotes, June 4, 2003.)

When Joelle was thinking I was white, she assumed I would know about Limp Bizkit. Yet, as an Afro-Caribbean she was familiar with Indian Bollywood music. The encounter with Tig and Joelle illustrates the assumed link between ethnicity and tastes, even while individuals such as Joelle prided themselves on having "omnivorous" tastes (R. Peterson and Kern, 1996).

AFRO-CARIBBEANS: IT'S HOT TO BE BLACK!

Afro-Caribbean youth expressed stronger preferences for hip-hop music and style (brand-named sneakers, hip-hop music, and so forth) than their South Asian and white British counterparts. Only one Afro-Caribbean student in both cities did not respond by naming some form of hip-hop music when asked in interviews about the type of music he or she listened to regularly (compared to twenty-eight of forty Indians, eleven of twenty Indo-Caribbeans, and thirteen of twenty whites). In addition to African American–inspired music types, well over half of Afro-Caribbeans in both cities said they listen regularly to some type of Caribbean music, including reggae, ragga (London), *bashment* (London), dancehall (London), soca, calypso, and reggaeton (New York).

Recall from the previous chapter that sneakers are an important element of hip-hop style among teens. Afro-Caribbeans were most likely to be brand-conscious when it came to sneakers. Of the Afro-Caribbean students interviewed in London, only one said he was not particular about having name-brand sneakers, compared to seven Indian students (35 percent) and seven whites (35 percent). Similarly, in New York more than three-fourths of Afro-Caribbean students expressed a preference for name-brand sneakers, compared to two-thirds of Indo-Caribbean students and half of Indian students.

Afro-Caribbeans also placed the most importance on style overall. In response to a question asking students how important, on a scale of 1 to 10, looking good is to them (10 being most important), in New York, Afro-Caribbeans averaged 8.4, while Indians averaged 6.9. Similarly, in London 70 percent of Afro-Caribbean youth said that the way they dressed was an important part of their identities, in contrast to a minority of Indians. These results resonate with Murray Milner's finding (2004) that African American youth in U.S. high schools tend to place more emphasis on style than their nonblack peers. Carl Nightingale (1993) also has suggested that inner-city African American youth focus on consumption as one means of symbolic status in a world in which they have little else. Although this is true, *non*black youth *also* employ consumption in the quest for peer status. I found, however, that racial authenticity makes hip-hop consumption more valuable in terms of peer status for black youth than it does for other groups. That is to say, consuming popular culture gains peer status, especially if youth perceive that consumption to be racially authentic, as they do for Afro-Caribbeans. Afro-Caribbean youth had more to gain among peers in terms of status by taking pains to engage popular styles and music. This emphasis on peer status, however, may make Afro-Caribbean students more likely to privilege the cultural expectations of their peers over those of adults in their balancing act between peer status and school achievement, to the detriment of their academic achievement. (I turn to this question in more detail in chapter 6.)

Ethnic and racial identities reinforced Afro-Caribbean students' ties to hip-hop. When asked about their ethnic and racial identities, well more than half of Afro-Caribbeans called themselves black or African American (sometimes in combination with other identities, such as "black British" or "black Caribbean"). Mary Waters, in a study of second-generation Afro-Caribbean high school students in Brooklyn (1999), similarly found that many of those students identified racially with African Americans. This identity allows Afro-Caribbean teens to claim authentic consumption of popular hip-hop culture. Given the Caribbean influence on early hip-hop (Gilroy, 1993; Rose, 1994), it is ironic that New York Afro-Caribbean students had to identify themselves as African American in order to assert authenticity in their consumption of hip-hop culture. In fact, some Afro-Caribbean students did not feel completely authentic. When I asked Joe, an Afro-Caribbean student who came to New York at age eight, about his racial identity, he told me: "I am American, but I wasn't born in this country. I was born in Guyana. I am black, yeah." I asked Joe what it means to be American. "I wouldn't even know, to tell you the truth. I mean, I just don't feel like I am a pure American. I guess you have to be born in America to feel like a pure American. . . . I feel like I am trying to be something I am really not, you know. I am trying to be American, but I am really not American." Given the preferences Joe expressed earlier in his interview for hip-hop music and style, I gathered that the American identity he alluded to is African American. Still, in terms of others' perceptions, Joe was likely to be perceived by peers— African Americans and others—as racially authentic in his cultural repertoire. In contrast, South Asians could not so easily pass for African American.

SOUTH ASIANS: BHANGRA–HIP-HOP AND HINDI–HIP-HOP HYBRIDITY

Because of the larger South Asian presence in Britain compared to the United States, both historically and demographically,[8] South Asian and South Asian–influenced popular culture are more commonly available in Britain. Two radio stations broadcasting nationally cater exclusively to South Asians in Britain; no parallel stations exist in New York or anywhere else in the United States. Youth in my London research preferred these stations: one-half of the twenty Indians surveyed in London listed a South Asian–oriented station as one of the radio stations they listen to regularly. Indians in London commonly reported Rishi Rich, a British music producer who formed a group of British remix artists called the Rishi Rich Project, as a favorite. With influences from Hindi film songs, bhangra, and hip-hop, Rishi Rich's music is sung sometimes in Punjabi and other times in English. The "British Asian" music and style have made their way to American second-generation Indians (Maira, 2002); hence, despite the greater accessibility in London, Indian students' tastes in Indian-derived forms of music and style between the two cities were quite similar. Two-thirds of South Asian interview respondents (Indians and Indo-Caribbeans) in both cities combined expressed a taste for Indian or bhangra music. Much of this music is remixed with hip-hop. Because expectations of racial authenticity prevented most South Asians from complete boundary crossing to consume high-status hip-hop music and style exclusively, they blurred the boundary between "South Asian" and "black" forms. In addition to hip-hop remixed with South Asian styles of music, two-thirds of South Asian students in both cities also had some taste for hip-hop, rap, R&B, or U.K. garage.

In 2003, the year this research began, the song "Mundian To Bach Ke," by British-born Panjabi MC, was a hit on popular American and British hip-hop stations. The song was remixed in collaboration with American rapper Jay-Z, who raps in English over the song sung in Punjabi. Indians in both cities appreciated this broader appeal and exposure. Reena, a fourteen-year-old Londoner, said to me: "I love the desi [South Asian] music. I am not sure if—I don't know if it's popular in New York, but over here, yeah, it's so good. . . . I think it's good in a way because it, it gives everybody a chance to express themselves, especially now that, um, . . . the *Asian* side of music has come, because it's also getting into the English charts [as the Panjabi MC song has]. Yeah, everyone has their own little bit in there." I asked Reena how it makes her feel when she hears desi music on the radio: "Just get up and dance, yeah. I just think it's a good thing . . . because everyone enjoys it now. All the different, all different people because they have all heard it and it's become popular, it's actually *in Britain.*" Hearing Indian remix music on popular radio stations exposed non-Indians to Indian music, which Reena appreciated. It also made Reena an authentic consumer of part of popular culture. Vikram, a fourteen-year-old Indian student in New York, told me that his taste in music switched from hip-hop to bhangra–hip-hop remixed music when the same Panjabi MC song became popular on the radio: "I used to listen to rap before, but I am not really into rap now because I really love bhangra. . . . You heard that song of Panjabi MC? So that's how. It came on the radio and I started to like bhangra music. So now I'm just kinda, you know, in love with bhangra." Bhangra music's presence on popular hip-hop radio was especially important in New York, which lacks a South Asian–focused radio station. For Indian teenagers, this was an aspect of hip-hop radio they could claim as authentically their own, just as ordinary hip-hop was claimed by African American and Afro-Caribbean students. The South Asian youth engaged with the popular culture of their general peer culture, but they also gained status by hybridizing it with something with which they had more authenticity in the eyes of peers, bhangra.

Although the Panjabi MC song made it to popular hip-hop radio, in general Punjabi remix music strongly appealed only to Indian students, including the predominantly Gujarati Indian population in London. Indo-Caribbeans preferred not bhangra remix but Hindi remix music, in addition to other distinctly Caribbean styles like soca, calypso, and chutney. In interviews half of Indo-Caribbean girls and 30 percent of

Indo-Caribbean boys said they listen to Hindi music regularly; none said they listen to bhangra. The distaste for bhangra may be a combination of the popularity of Hindi music and the lack of bhangra in the Caribbean, and a distancing from Punjabis (bhangra traditionally stems from Punjab)—the most stigmatized ethnoracial group in their school's peer culture, especially for boys (recall that most Indians at York High were Punjabi). Richie was one Indo-Caribbean student in New York who distanced himself from Punjabi Indians in his school. Identifying racially as black,[9] he told me about the interracial problems he saw in his school that target Punjabis: "Like, a lot of people don't like Punjabi people and they would just fight them because of their race." Richie points out the differential treatment some Indians get because of their race, while he himself identifies racially as black—although to me he looked more like his Punjabi peers than his Afro-Caribbean or African American peers. He reported that he listens exclusively to rap music and that his closest friend is Hispanic. Richie distanced himself from Indian identity perhaps because of its low status among his peers. He sought to resolve the dilemma of low status for South Asian identity by attempting to boundary-cross by consuming exclusively black-identified taste culture and maintaining non–South Asian social ties.

Students thus consumed music and style based not only on the racial and ethnic identities with which they wanted to engage but also on those from which they wanted to distance themselves. This active participation in the maintenance of their ethnic and racial boundaries was done strategically to maximize peer status. Still, the choice was generally limited to the cultural scripts that peers would accept as racially authentic to the individual.

SOUTH ASIANS, TASTE, AND GENDER: BOYS IN HIP-HOP STYLE, GIRLS IN *SALWAR KAMEEZ*

Indian boys in London had a distinct style of clothing, influenced by hip-hop but not determined by it. Many wore their hair heavily gelled and styled with short spikes, a style I also observed in London on South Asian British music stars like JuggyD and Rishi Rich and on adult British South Asians as well. In addition, the boys often wore their pants baggy and accessorized with large, gold jewelry, similar to the style of hip-hop artists. This jewelry, however, had a South Asian character: instead of having their names on necklaces in hip-hop style, for example, many South Asians in both cities wore gold necklaces with a religious symbol—Muslim, Hindu, or Sikh.

Compared to South Asian boys, South Asian girls in both cities had a style in school less distinct from that of their non–South Asian peers, perhaps preferring to express ethnic identity through ethnic clothing worn elsewhere. Almost all the South Asian girls (both Indian and Indo-Caribbean) I interviewed in both cities had some ethnic clothing, which they wore to weekly religious functions, family parties, or special occasions. In contrast, only half of the Indian boys I interviewed in both cities had ethnic clothing, and just one Indo-Caribbean boy did. Boys wore dressy Indian suits only to family weddings and a few special occasions. In my New York research site I occasionally saw South Asian girls in *salwar kameezes* at school,[10] but I never saw boys in ethnic Indian clothing (Londoners had no such option because of their school uniform). Similarly, the Fourth National Survey of Ethnic Minorities in Britain found that 91 percent of Indian young women in Britain always or sometimes wear ethnic Indian clothing, in contrast to 48 percent of their male counterparts (Modood, 1997).[11] This pattern resonates with dress patterns in South Asia, where professional women more commonly wear ethnic clothing in public, while professional men usually wear Western clothing.

Gender differences in music tastes paralleled those in style. Although among South Asians, both boys and girls expressed tastes for hip-hop and Indian music, girls favored Indian styles of music: just less than half of South Asian girls listened to hip-hop regularly, but two-thirds listened to Indian music styles. In contrast, more than 80 percent of South Asian boys listened to hip-hop regularly, while just more than half listened to Indian styles regularly (see table 8).

Why the gender difference? In both Britain and the United States today, black male identity has been stereotyped as highly masculine, bordering on violent and dangerous. This image can be appealing for boys developing their masculine selves (Haywood and Mac an Ghaill, 2003; López, 2002; Majors and Billson, 1992; Marriott, 1996). The association of hip-hop with a tough, black male identity may increase its appeal to South Asian boys (see also Maira, 2002; Warikoo, 2005a). On the other hand, girls can develop their feminine identities through highly feminine and traditional roles for women in Hindi movies and songs, which appeal to many girls. Also, South Asian girls can gain symbolic status among non–South Asian peers via ethnic identity, due to the popularization of South Asian female fashions such as *bindis*,

TABLE 8   SOUTH ASIAN TASTE PREFERENCES IN MUSIC

	Rap/Hip-Hop/R&B	Hindi/Bhangra
Indian boys, London	10 of 10	8 of 10 (mostly bhangra)
Indian boys, NYC	8 of 10	6 of 10 (mostly bhangra)
Indo-Caribbean boys, NYC	7 of 10	3 of 10 (all Hindi)
South Asian boys, total	25 of 30 (83%)	17 of 30 (57%)
Indian girls, London	7 of 10	6 of 10 (mostly bhangra)
Indian girls, NYC	3 of 10	10 of 10
Indo-Caribbean girls, NYC	4 of 10	5 of 10 (all Hindi)
South Asian girls, total	14 of 30 (47%)	21 of 30 (70%)

SOURCE: Interview data, n = 60.

henna, and sari fabrics (Durham, 1999; Maira, 2002; Sandhu, 2004; Warikoo, 2005a). Scenes from a recent American movie illustrate this point. In *Dude, Where's the Party?* a second-generation Indian college student goes on a date with another second-generation Indian student: he looks hip in his baggy pants and hip-hop style, while she looks beautiful in a *salwar kameez*. At the Indian party they later attend, we see boys break-dancing (a hip-hop style of dancing) and girls in ethnic clothing dancing with boys dressed in hip-hop style.[12]

Although in South Asia the Punjabi male image is one of heightened masculinity—similar to the black male stereotype in the United States and Britain—this is not an image recognized among non–South Asian peers in New York and London; hence, that cultural script is not drawn upon as much as hip-hop images of masculinity. Students based their consumption practices on the degree to which particular styles and music would not only lead to higher peer status based on popular culture and racial authenticity but would also maintain feminine and masculine gender identities. Popular understandings of South Asian masculinity and femininity in their social context, together with the desire to maintain racial authenticity in the eyes of peers, led second-generation Indian boys and girls to access different cultural scripts in the realms of clothing styles and music tastes. Just as Indo-Caribbeans made cultural choices that distanced themselves from a low-status Indian identity, Indian boys were less likely to emphasize Indian identity than were their female counterparts, because South Asian masculinity carried less peer status than South Asian femininity in their cultural milieu. Given a choice, students choose cultural scripts that maximized peer status, often in unexpected ways.

WHITE ENGLISH STUDENTS IN LONDON: "WIGGERS," "GRUNGIES," AND MIDDLE-CLASS "CULTURAL OMNIVORES"

Because so few white students attend York High School (whites compose 6 percent of the student population), I focus in this section only on white English students in the London school.[13] White students at Long Meadow Comprehensive were the school's most diverse group in terms of their cultural identities. One Indian boy noticed that "all the black kids will have their, like, Afros. The Indian kids will have their hair gelled up. . . . [White kids are] a bit more different, yeah. . . . They will be their own person, yeah."

Some white students engaged with the "black" hip-hop scene (they tended to be more working-class, often living in predominantly minority public housing); others rejected the kids they called "townies" (those who preferred hip-hop music and style) and instead engaged with an alternative rock/punk identity; and still other, middle-class kids did not have strong taste culture identities. I turn now to the "townies," "grungies," and "cultural omnivores."[14] One white student, Stan, explained the different styles as stemming from neighborhood differences:

> It depends on area. . . . Like, if you live in a mostly white estate [public housing complex], you're gonna wear like, like, you know, the waterproof kind of track suits. Those like don't wear their trousers low, but just like normal. And it's just like different sorts of caps they wear, like not these sort of straight caps [hip-hop style]. They wear like bent ones. . . . And then if you go into like H— [an area with more blacks], the people wear jeans like low and baggy, Air Force One trainers, and like bomber jackets, Avirex.

From a poor family, Stan always wore the accoutrements of hip-hop style—pants very low, Air Force One Nike sneakers barely tied, baseball hat tipped to the side, big gold jewelry. With a style similar to Stan's, Frank, a Year 10 (ninth-grade equivalent) working-class white student, told me that he prefers Nike when I asked him what influences his style of dress: "I don't know. If I like it, I will wear it. Maybe just a pair of Nike tracksuit bottoms and a jumper [sweater]." One of his Afro-Caribbean friends one day told me about Frank's impressive collection of Nike sneakers. Frank later said that when his mother gives him money to buy new clothes, she becomes furious when he comes home with another pair of sneakers rather than new pants or shirts. White teens with hip-hop style were subject to accusations of racial boundary crossing or "acting black," as Stan explained earlier in this chapter. They responded to these accusations in two ways. First, some made sure not to go too far in emulating hip-hop style and artists. For example, Jake, a white English student who told me he listens to rap and hip-hop music, preferred Adidas and Nike sneakers, but not Air Force Ones (a particular type of Nike very popular at the time of this research and the subject of a popular song by Nelly, a famous rapper). Jake expressed a desire not to consume products that were too common. Also, recall Mary's taste for hip-hop but distaste for peers she called "wiggers . . . a white person who acts black, and it's not working." Second, other white students questioned the concept of racial authenticity altogether; in the words of Stan, "They can't say, 'It's our style, you can't do it.' It's for the different races and if I like a music, then I like it."

In contrast, white students who rejected the dominant hip-hop style—"grungies"—usually attributed their preference for more underground tastes explicitly to a rejection of the dominant society, its consumerism, and conformity. These students escaped the accusation of racial inauthenticity by choosing music and styles identified as white (rock and punk), even though that music was unpopular and held low status among their peers overall (including among other white peers). In other words, they traded popular tastes for racial authenticity. Lisa was one example. A white Sixth Form student, Lisa told me that she did not wear name-brand sneakers. She used left political discourse as well as economics to explain her distaste: "I find a lot of them [brand-name sneakers], they are really expensive for what they are. I don't really like them. And they're made in sweatshops for like ten p[ence], and they charge like fifty to sixty quid [pounds] for them. It's a rip-off, really." I asked Lisa how she learned about sneakers being produced in sweatshops, and she cited the Internet: "Just the websites I go to, on like vegetarianism, things like that."

Lisa often wore large black combat boots to school, black nail polish, and a dog collar around her neck. She told me that she listened to punk music. Her style was perceived by peers to be racially authentic, yet marginal because of her distaste for hip-hop. In her interview, Lisa described conflicts in school between her social group—the "grungies"—and her school's dominant youth culture group—the "townies." One day when Lisa talked to me after a school field trip, she was upset because the "townies" had been making fun of her. On other days, she complained that her mother forced her to take GCSC mathematics, a required course if she wanted to go on to university. She was doing poorly and had little interest in the class, often skipping it. When she did attend, she did little work. On days that I shadowed Lisa's classes, I frequently found her in one class and not in others. Tellingly, grungies were the only social group that explicitly rejected something mainstream—but what was defined as mainstream was hip-hop and black-identified, not posh and white.

Although Lisa's rebellion happened to coincide with less-than-stellar school performance, rock and punk fans' academic performance varied. Stan, the working-class white student described earlier who openly displayed his preference for hip-hop in his dress style, suggested that "grungies" like Lisa rebel, yet they still do better than others academically. I asked him to explain why:

Most grungies that I have seen that are like trying to rebel . . . they probably, their parents are probably like, like quite high up in the BBC or a news reader or something like that, and their mom might not even work, just stay at home like a typical family. Their parents are together. And with me it's that my parents were never together, and we have benefits, and I am not so much of a rebel, I am just me. And I think they . . . kinda go against society wearing baggy and ripped jeans, stains on them, and T-shirts like that.

I asked Stan to clarify why he thought rebellious students are actually doing well in school:

Their background comes out. Like their mom and dad are pressuring them to do well because—I don't even know why working-class parents don't, but it's like there is more pressure on them to do well. And they probably been to better schools in a way, like their primary school is probably better or their mom, dad like are more pushing them to do well. So even though they are rebelling, they are not.

Stan's insight into the social dynamics at school is quite telling because it suggests that rebellion is seen as the domain of those not engaging with the hip-hop popular among peers. And, rebellion has to do with taste and style, not with performance in school. Indeed, I did encounter a few boys with "grungy" style in the Year 10 high-track math class I frequently observed. They wore their hair long in the front, often covering their eyes; carried around army-green canvas shoulder bags with Nine Inch Nails pins and the like; and wore Converse canvas sneakers, in contrast to the Nikes that their peers more commonly wore (Stan does overlook the other half of "grungy" students who are, indeed, working-class, such as Lisa). In 2004 the *New York Times* reported a similar phenomenon in the New York City punk scene: many upper-middle-class white youth wore Mohawks and went to punk concerts at CBGB's (a famous punk music club opened in 1973, recently closed) by night, but attended posh private schools and did not reject formal education by day (Stapinski, 2004). According to Stan, the "rebels" in his school are middle-class white students who do well in school; these are the only students who consciously define themselves and their taste practices as oppositional—in contrast to the attribution of opposition by many scholars to black-oriented and working-class styles (Bennett, 2000; S. Hall and Jefferson, 1976; Ogbu, 1990, 1991; Portes and Zhou, 1993; Sewell, 1997; Willis, 1990).

"Grungy" teenagers, as Stan and others described them (and as they described themselves), listened to music identified with "white" traditions—rock, punk, and grunge. For some, a preference for punk and rock music and a rejection of hip-hop paralleled a disdain for minorities and a feeling that minorities' accusations of racism and discrimination in society are unfair—a perception of reverse racism. For example, when I asked Sally, a working-class white student who enjoyed BMX biking and punk rock music, whether there is any racial tension in her school, she said:

> Yeah, there is. . . . And normally if—say, if you are doing racism in a class. When you see a black person, you feel quite bad. Well, I do anyway, because—I don't know why. It just makes you feel a bit bad. . . . They sort of don't forget the slavery past. You know, I can't change that. No one can change it. It happened in the past, and you don't have to carry it on. . . . And personally I have no problem with, uh, black people. It's only people with like chips on their shoulders, that talk with the Jamaican accent, which there is no need to do.

Earlier in her interview Sally complained about the rude behaviors of people in her neighborhood, which was predominantly black. She later told me that she had no racial or religious preference in someone she would date, but that her parents would not allow her to bring a nonwhite partner home: "Religion doesn't matter, yeah. But I think my parents would go a bit crazy if I brought someone of a different ethnicity home. And so, I don't stick to it, but I don't bring them home."

Sally later spoke of feeling as though people in her neighborhood did not have "manners," in contrast to the way her parents raised her to behave. Her words indicate alienation from black peers, especially those who exhibit ethnic markers such as foreign accents. Blacks aroused feelings of guilt from "the slavery past" for Sally. In spite of living in a largely minority neighborhood, she had taken up BMX biking, which she described as a "mainly English, white" sport, perhaps as a way to disengage from her minority surroundings. Also, her rejection of urban popular youth culture in favor of punk music and BMX biking meant that black peers could not accuse her of "acting black." On the day I first observed Sally's classes, she wore baggy sweatpants that did not conform to the school uniform (but were the same color, so it was not obvious), and her bookbag had an image of a marijuana leaf and the words "Grow it, roll it, smoke it." I sometimes saw Sally on my way in to school smoking cigarettes in the far corner of the schoolyard among a group of predominantly white peers.

Similarly, Anna, a working-class nonpracticing Jew, reported that she is becoming more and more interested in rock and punk music and feeling tired of the R&B and hip-hop that she used to listen to. She expressed the belief that some peers with hip-hop tastes were disrespectful of difference. Her brother had recently shaved his hair into a Mohawk, and was bullied in school as a result. He preferred punk music. Anna told me: "[Some people] are just rude. There are a few groups, like people who hang out in school, who are just rude. I mean, my brother got punched in the face yesterday by a group of idiots. . . . But I don't blame them. I like to blame it on the parents." I asked Anna of what race the rude students tend to be: "Sort of a mix. I don't really want to say, because it might sound racist, but it's not, because I am not racist. But it might sound [that way], so I am not gonna say." Anna's frustration with the targeting of her brother's different style led her to dislike certain peers—from her words, one may presume racial minorities. Like Anna and Sally, some white students seemed to construct identities outside mainstream peer culture in reaction to perceptions of reverse racism. If they chose unpopular styles and music, they, like minority peers, could claim that others target them for harassment, albeit on the basis of taste preferences and style rather than race or ethnicity.[15]

Finally, some middle-class white students in London had more diverse tastes than their Indian, Afro-Caribbean, and working-class peers. I call these teens middle-class "cultural omnivores." Derek, for example, listened to rock music and refused to wear name-brand sneakers because of many brands' production in Third World sweatshops. His best friend, Frank, however, had many different pairs of expensive Nike sneakers and spoke with a strong working-class accent. Derek told me he didn't have a strong group identity. After Derek brought up "grungies" as one of the social groups at school, I asked him if he would call himself a grungy: "No, I wouldn't. I wouldn't put myself in any category, really. I mean, I am not like someone who just goes around, like, you know, 'I want to be like this, I want to be like that.' I just do, like, whatever. I—I just dress like I want to dress, and, you know, it's nothing to do with trying to be grunge or trying not to, or trying to be a townie or something like that." He told me about his friendship with Frank: "I mean, I get a little shit from [Frank] and them when I listen to punk and stuff like that, because they don't really like that sort of thing." Derek and Frank connected mainly through their mutual love of soccer. On more than one occasion I noticed the two passing notes in class—the notes had possible positions on a team on which they played together. Derek lives in the school's vicinity, known for being a relatively expensive area, while Frank lives farther from school, in a rented apartment.

Peter, a Year 10 student whose parents both completed university, told me that he listens to diverse styles of music: "I listen to music at night or like from my bed. I normally listen to music on the radio. . . . Sometimes dance music, sometimes kind of the popular music that's not too kind of, not like the kind of teenager stuff, but maybe like if an Eminem song or something [comes on]." He told me that music is not a big part of his identity. Peter's description of his taste in music contrasts sharply with the majority of his peers, for whom the music they listen to is a big part of personal identity. His father works as a freelance writer, his mother as an events planner. Eclectic tastes are perhaps one tool for acceptance when attending such a culturally diverse school. Peter's and Derek's preferences resonate with studies describing an increase in "culturally omnivorous" tastes in the United States, especially among elites (R. Peterson and Kern, 1996; R. Peterson and Simkus, 1992). This "cultural omnivorousness" escapes the pressures of racial authenticity and popular culture altogether by not engaging *any* strong identity or preferences in terms of music and style.

Of course, Afro-Caribbean and Indian students also expressed diverse identities and interests. However, the minority of Afro-Caribbeans and Indians who deviated from the norms of their social groups within the school context did so as *individuals* rather than as *social groups*. White students, unlike their black and Asian peers, had access to multiple *social* identities within the school context. This difference may stem from the lower incentive for advantaged youth to clearly define their school identities and to vie for a position in the peer status hierarchy. That is, because middle-class youth have other resources, especially economic and cultural capital, they may have less interest in gaining status among peers. Hence, they are free to dabble in different identities and styles. Also, whites are the default race group and, consequently, are seen as generic, rather than having specific characteristics and well-defined cultural scripts like minority groups have (Jacobson, 1998; Kimmel, 2002). The invisibility of white racial identity means that white students face fewer expectations in terms of racially authentic cultural practices than their minority counterparts.

Racial authenticity and a popular culture racialized as black together influenced the taste preferences of youth of different ethnic and racial groups. In terms of navigating popular culture, a student asks himself or herself: What styles and music can I make legitimate claim to and still be seen as authentic? Although cultural practices varied in the multiethnic environments I studied, a unitary status hierarchy among students developed, in part based on participation in popular youth culture and in part defined by racial authenticity. Overall, black students had an easier time converting popular tastes into peer status, while South Asians and whites had a harder time, because of peer expectations of racial authenticity. This is a process similar to the way elites in the larger society use cultural tastes and practices to maintain their high status and prevent status mobility (Bourdieu, 1986). To Bourdieu's classic account of social reproduction through status I add an additional layer, in the realm of youth cultures: the role of racial authenticity. In this chapter I have shown how expectations of racial authenticity complicate perceptions of others' cultural practices within urban youth cultures, affecting one's ability to convert cultural practices into status. Race similarly intersects with cultural capital in the larger society among adults, with the effect sometimes of preventing minority Americans from converting cultural capital (e.g., in the form of educational degrees) into economic and symbolic status (Hacker, 1992; Massey and Denton, 1993; Pattillo-McCoy, 1999).

These findings demonstrate the subtle ways in which youth make choices in school about their social identities, which are marked not so much by the traditions of their parents' countries as by more modern, popular forms of culture, albeit influenced to some extent by their ethnic and racial backgrounds (Dolby, 2001; Maira, 2002). The findings show that essentialized understandings of ethnic and racial identities are durable, even while those qualities change over time and across multiethnic settings. Moreover, not only do *coethnics* care about racially authentic cultural practices, but so do peers of other races. And even in multiethnic environments, cultural practices continue to be racially coded so that the link with the historical roots of a taste culture—fabricated or real—continues to define that genre long after the racial identities of its consumers (and producers) have diversified. In spite of the increasingly cosmopolitan ethnicities among teens in multiethnic areas of London and New York City, and despite the softening of boundaries between ethnic and racial identities with the advent of remixed forms of music and style (Alba, 2005; K. Hall, 2002; S. Hall, 1996; Kasinitz, Mollenkopf, and Waters, 2004; Warikoo, 2004a), notions of racial authenticity still play an important role in shaping taste and consumption choices. Second-generation teens respond to their peers' expectations of racial authenticity by blurring the boundaries of music and style, combining interests common to all ethnic and racial groups with "authentic" culture based on their own ethnic and racial identities. This is one mechanism by which teens made cultural choices among the cultural scripts available to them in ways that maximized their peer status.

The findings above can help us understand not only variations in cultural tastes and styles among the second generation but also the process of cultural change and assimilation. Although many have criticized the continued influence of "authenticity tests" as limiting the cultural choices for individuals of particular ethnic and racial backgrounds (Appiah, 1996; Grazian, 2003; Hollinger, 1995; Jackson, 2005; Mahon, 2004; Maira, 2002), the force of racial authenticity today, even among students in ethnically diverse urban schools, is still quite strong. Students expressed loyalty to the boundaries of ethnic and racial identities and the cultural practices they imply, and criticized boundary crossing. Yet identities are themselves continually reinvented, so that a music and style that took root among Caribbean Americans in the South Bronx and grew to symbolize young urban African American life is now perceived as endemic to Afro-Caribbeans in Britain (Gilroy, 1993). New genres with blurred boundaries such as hip-hop–bhangra music, rooted in British Asian identity, are also developing, with new cultural scripts and consequently perhaps new forms of *British Asian* (and South Asian American) authenticity.

Given the different levels of peer status that black and South Asian students have in both school contexts, and given the different ways in which music and style identified as "black," "Indian," and "Punjabi" figured in the peer status hierarchies, how did students experience racial stigma? In the following chapter I turn to students' experiences with racial discrimination. Although peer cultures are most prominently about music and style, they have serious ramifications for adult perceptions of students. Meanwhile, racial stigma *within* a peer culture has its own ramifications for experiences with racial discrimination.

CHAPTER 4

Two Types of Racial Discrimination

Adult Exclusion and Peer Bullying

In the shops, sometimes because we are young and black,
. . . when we go in the shop, security guards like look at us,
and people look at us funny.

—Shivon, Afro-Caribbean Londoner

In this school there is a lot of discrimination. . . . The
kids that wear turbans, they have been so discriminated
against. . . . I think it's some of the black students here
[who pick on them], some Spanish students.

—Kuldip, Indian New Yorker

Given the peer cultures they encounter at school and the racialization in the larger societies in which they live, what experiences with racial discrimination do second-generation teens face? Racial discrimination toward minority children of immigrants in schools, both interpersonal and structural, has been reported on both sides of the Atlantic (Gillborn, 2005; Gillborn and Mirza, 2000; López, 2002; Majors, Gillborn, and Sewell, 2001; Parker, Deyhle, and Villenas, 1999; Sewell, 1997; Solorzano and Ornelas, 2004; Valenzuela, 1999; but see Foster, 1993, for a critique of this literature in Britain). Some scholars of immigration have suggested that certain children of immigrants react to the racial discrimination and racism they perceive in their school environment by developing "reactive ethnicities," rejecting the institution of schooling as racist, culturally white, and hence not for them (Portes and Rumbaut, 2001; Portes and Zhou, 1993; Sewell, 1997; Stepick, 1998). Portes and

Rumbaut (2001) argue that while on a collective level, reactive ethnicity can lead to empowerment through, for example, political mobilization and promotion of group rights, on an individual level, it most often leads teens to reject schooling in favor of ethnic group solidarity: "Youthful solidarity based on opposition to the dominant society yields an adversarial stance toward mainstream institutions, including education. [It] creates a forced-choice dilemma for the young between doing well in school and staying loyal to one's ethnic group" (285). Tony Sewell (1997) has argued that some Afro-Caribbean boys in Britain reject schooling through a "politics of resistance" because they perceive teacher racism; according to Sewell, this leads them to adopt preferences for subcultural music (hip-hop), clothing, and hairstyles. Reactive ethnicity in turn is thought to lead to low academic achievement.

The reactive ethnicity explanation for low school achievement rests not on the assumption that discrimination *exists,* but that students *perceive* racist and discriminatory patterns, policies, and behaviors among adults in school and that these perceptions lead them to reject schooling in favor of particular forms of ethnicity and particular outlooks and behaviors in school. In this chapter I address these underlying assumptions by analyzing second-generation perceptions of racial discrimination in and out of school. I lay out a typology of discrimination that students report. I found that second-generation Indians report much higher rates of racial discrimination in school than do Afro-Caribbeans. However, this discrimination comes not from teachers and the school as an institution, but rather from peers, stemming from Indian students' low peer status. Afro-Caribbeans, on the other hand, report high rates of discrimination *outside* school, from unfamiliar adults, such as shopkeepers, the police, and potential employers who perceive them as dangerous or delinquent. These findings suggest that if experiences with discrimination in school lead to aversion to it, such aversion should be found among *Indians,* who are high achievers on both sides of the Atlantic. Afro-Caribbeans' experiences with discrimination *outside* school are an unlikely explanation for low academic achievement *inside* school. Although more than half of Americans report that they have experienced some form of day-to-day discrimination in their lives (Kessler, Mickelson, and Williams, 1999), all stereotypes and sources of discrimination are not equal, as I will show.

What is racial discrimination? Pager and Shepherd (2008) define it as the "unequal treatment of persons or groups on the basis of their race or ethnicity" (182). In this chapter I focus on *self-reported* experiences with racial discrimination. This is just one measure, and indeed it can under- or overreport actual discrimination (Pager and Shepherd, 2008; Quillian, 2006). For example, students may be unaware of racial discrimination in teachers' perceptions of their behaviors in school relative to students of other races, and this lack of awareness can lead to underreporting. On the other hand, individuals may overreport racial discrimination and assume that a teacher's response is related to race when in actuality the teacher treats students of other races in similar ways. Nevertheless, perceptions of discrimination matter, most importantly because they can have a negative impact on behaviors and academic performance (Loury, 2002; Pager and Shepherd, 2008; Steele and Aronson, 1995).

Previous work on racial discrimination has largely maintained a black-white paradigm. Such a focus, however, takes little account of the divergent (mis)conceptions of ethnic and racial groups in society and the different forms of stereotyping, prejudice, and discrimination that groups frequently face. This oversight stems in part from the American focus on the black-white divide in discussions of racial discrimination. Most studies emphasize white racial attitudes toward blacks, stereotypes about blacks, and racial discrimination against blacks. While anti-black discrimination perpetrated by whites has had devastating and enduring negative consequences for African Americans, the research has not paid sufficient attention to the different forms of discrimination faced by various racial minorities. The lack of emphasis on understanding the nuances of different forms of racial discrimination has led some to argue that whites experience racial discrimination just as racial minorities do, in the forms of affirmative action (D'Souza, 1991; Thernstrom and Thernstrom, 1997) and multiculturalist social policies (Dench, Gavron, and Young, 2006).

AFRO-CARIBBEANS: DISCRIMINATION
OUTSIDE SCHOOL

During interviews I asked students: "Do you ever experience any ethnic or racial discrimination?" Almost half of Afro-Caribbeans in New York reported experiencing discrimination, as did six out of twenty Afro-Caribbeans interviewed in London. However, all of the racial discrimination reported by Afro-Caribbeans in interviews happened outside school—from police, shopkeepers, potential employers, and people on the street. These incidents were based on both racial and stylistic stereotypes. Joy, an Afro-Caribbean girl in London, described an experience on Oxford Street, London's central shopping artery: "We [Joy and her sister] was on Oxford Street and then we was standing by these two women. And then one said to the other, 'Hold on to your bag.' And then, like, my sister said, 'What did you say?' And she's like, 'Nothing, I never said nothing,' and they just ran off. . . . [They were] some middle-aged women." Joy's experience with racial discrimination occurred in a neighborhood far from school.

Experiences with discrimination while shopping also occurred inside stores. Robert, an African American and Afro-Trinidadian student in New York, told me that a shopkeeper treated him and his friends differently from a young Indian customer with different clothing style: "I don't like that people judge you just by the way you dress. Like, I went to Rite-Aid yesterday, and there was a Indian kid and he had on like, like tight-tight clothes, it was really tight. It was like small for him. And then they [the workers] wasn't, they wasn't paying him no mind, but then when me and my friends went in there they started looking at us, like all funny ways." Robert's description illustrates the interaction between style and race that lead to the shopkeeper's scrutiny of Robert and his friends, in contrast to the treatment of an Indian boy in the same store wearing "tight, tight clothes."

Afro-Caribbean students also reported racial discrimination in the labor market. Michelle's observation resonates with Mary Waters's finding (1999) that service sector managers in downtown Manhattan prefer to hire immigrants over African Americans, seeing them as better workers (also see Waldinger, 1996):

N: Do you ever experience any racial discrimination?

M: Oh, yeah, sometimes. It's hard to get a job. . . . I went to Key Food and supermarkets around here, run by Hispanics, and every time I go they tell me that they are not hiring. But my friends are Spanish and they get jobs there all the time, so yeah.

Although Michelle is Afro-Caribbean, the shopkeeper likely registered only her race and her American accent—second-generation Afro-Caribbeans are quickly subsumed into American race categories (Vickerman, 1999; Waters, 1999).

Peers at school sometimes bought into negative stereotypes about black youth. Monique, an Afro-Caribbean girl in London who did very well in school and also was quite popular, explained to me with a sense of humor the irony she perceived. I asked Monique if she'd ever experienced or seen any racial discrimination: "No. In my school it's different, like, I mean, the white kids and the Asian kids are kind of scared of black people. I don't know. So they don't bother running their mouth." I asked Monique why that was true. "They have been watching too much 50 Cent [a popular rapper]. They have been watching too much hip-hop, so some people say, 'Don't talk like that, or you will get shot!' and they will just shut up. They have been watching too much rap music!" Monique astutely explains the relationship between the racial stereotype that blacks are violent and not to be messed with and the lack of discrimination toward blacks among her peers. Tellingly, Monique goes on to pinpoint the source of stereotypes in the music and images of rap that youth consume. In the youth context, among peers the stereotype of blacks as dangerous *prevents* racial discrimination, while among adults outside school it *increases* it. Note that although Monique reports racial discrimination among *peers* at school, she doesn't mention it among *adults* at school.

Police encounters based on race and style stereotypes were all too common. In New York, *all* Afro-Caribbean boys interviewed had been stopped by the police at least once, and the majority had been stopped on multiple occasions. One-third of Afro-Caribbean girls in New York also reported being stopped by police at least once. In London, style mattered more than in New York, a highly racialized context. Half of Afro-Caribbean boys in London, and remarkably, three-fourths of white boys, reported having been stopped by the police. This was probably due to these boys wearing similar styles of dress and living in similar disadvantaged neighborhoods, unlike their Indian peers, whose neighborhoods tended to be slightly better off. Police encounters in London usually took place on estates (public housing complexes), where police were looking for criminal suspects and explained their accusations by suggesting the boy fit a profile of a criminal recently reported. For example, when I asked Thomas, a Sixth Form Afro-Caribbean student, if he had ever been stopped by the police, he told me that it happens frequently: "It's like in my area or if they see you in a hooded jumper [sweatshirt], they will stop you. . . . It's like a regular thing now. . . . They just stop you or search you, say, 'Oh, we have blah blah blah— we have a suspect fitting your description, blah blah.' They go on and search me and when they search me, [they say,] 'All right, go ahead.' [I] walk away, just keep walking." Dressing in a hip-hop–influenced style and living in a poor neighborhood increased this kind of encounter

in London. Note that the number of Afro-Caribbean students reporting police encounters was greater than the number of Afro-Caribbean
students reporting that they had experienced racial discrimination. In
response to my interview question about experiences with racial discrimination, students recounted incidences of explicit, obvious prejudice. It appears that for many, these police encounters did not qualify
as racial discrimination.

The frequency I found of white male police encounters in London
suggests that white males there faced misperceptions quite frequently.
Tim, a tall, muscular, white Sixth Form student in London, told me
when I asked what his style says about who he is: "I don't think [my
style] really says anything about who I am. But often if I am on my
own, I don't know, if I am walking around late [and] I have my hood
up, people can walk past me and be intimidated by me, but there's
absolutely no reason to be. It's just . . . I think how other people see
how I am dressed, how they would think, but I don't think it really
reflects anything." His style and size, more than his race, intimidate
those around him when Tim is out late at night. It is the *intersection*
between race and taste that leads to others' perceptions and misperceptions, and race has less salience in London than in New York. Because
race has more salience in New York in terms of social life, residence,
and even intermarriage (Foner, 2005; Model and Fisher, 2002; Peach,
1996, 2005), it can perhaps more easily influence others' perceptions.

Some parents of Afro-Caribbean boys asked their sons to be mindful
of unfamiliar adults' stereotypes and not to bring on unwanted attention
based on popular styles for boys. Michael, an eighteen-year-old Afro-
Jamaican student in New York, told me that his mother asked him not
to wear do-rags: "She [my mother], she really doesn't care about how I
dress, but sometimes when I wear do-rags . . . she doesn't like it, because
most of the time cops usually see do-rags as a bad thing, especially on
a black male [such] as me." In asking him to exclude some aspects
of popular style in his outfit, Michael's mother tried to prevent her
son's encounters with police who might stereotype young black boys.
Her pleas illustrate the relationship between race and style, which lead
some authorities, like the police who she feared might target her son,
to make associations with delinquency. Although Michael understood
the associations that police make with do-rags worn by black men, he
did not completely give up his style. Recall from chapter 2 that students
themselves—apart from their parents' requests—also sometimes tried to
mitigate these stereotypes through moderations in style.

How did students respond to the racial stereotyping and discrimination they perceived? I asked Afro-Caribbean Michael how he responds to situations in which the police racially profile him. He told me that he shrugs them off:

> N: So does that, do those experiences lead you to not wear do-rags or anything like that or—?
>
> M: No. . . . It doesn't make me, it doesn't really make me rebellious. . . .
>
> N: So how do you react to those situations when the police stop you?
>
> M: Normally I just pass it off as nothing.

Perhaps Michael truly does not react to such situations, or perhaps the situations affect him in ways he doesn't realize. When I asked others how they responded to this discrimination, like Michael and Thomas, they suggested it had little effect on them.

The stereotype of dangerousness and delinquency, most frequently directed via merchant and police suspicions toward Afro-Caribbean boys with hip-hop style, may have serious unintended consequences for future life chances. The assumptions of delinquency can, through a self-fulfilling prophecy, lead young men to live up to the negative expectations that adults place upon them. Furthermore, the stereotype may lead some boys to embrace a heightened masculinity that imparts fear in strangers, in a cycle of promoting *seemingly* oppositional styles. Some boys, through a desire to demonstrate masculinity, may in fact appreciate the hypermasculine stereotype's impartation of status among peers, even though it also leads to discrimination from adults. The stereotype may ultimately prevent them from, for example, acquiring a job or buying or renting property in a desirable neighborhood; it can also lead to a greater likelihood of being arrested and charged by the police. But in the short term it adds to a sense of toughness that garners respect in their peer social world.

INDIANS: DISCRIMINATION *INSIDE* SCHOOL

Nine out of twenty Indians interviewed in New York reported experiencing racial discrimination. Although this is similar to the number of Afro-Caribbean New Yorkers reporting experiences with racial discrimination, seven of those Indians reported the discrimination as coming from *peers in school* (another reported discrimination from kids on a bus), in contrast to all Afro-Caribbeans reporting discrimination to come from *adults outside* school.[1] The easiest targets were Sikh boys who wore turbans, because of their high visibility. Kuldip, a Sikh girl in New York, told me that "in this school, I think there is a lot of discrimination. . . . The kids that wear turbans, they have been so—they have been discriminated against—and that really bothers you. Because it doesn't really make sense, because this is America. It's a free country!" This *cultural racism* (Modood, 2005),[2] based on the notion that Indians (in this case, Sikhs) are culturally different, stands in contrast to the discrimination based on race experienced by black students, described above. When asked to clarify, Kuldip told me it was *students* who picked on Indians: "I think it's often . . . I think it's some of the black students here, some, some Spanish students." In a 2008 report, the Sikh Coalition cited similar harassment and bullying of Sikh students in New York City schools by their peers, often (but not always) based on boys' *patkas*, or turbans[3] (Sikh Coalition, 2008).

Discrimination aimed at Indians, though magnified for boys easily identified by their turbans, was not limited to those with visible signs of Sikh identity. Shamsher, a Sikh boy who was clean shaven and had had short, uncovered hair since birth, told me he had experienced racial discrimination in junior high school:

N: Do you ever experience any racial discrimination?

S: Racial? Yeah, in junior high the people they don't like you. [They say,] "You came from India?" and stuff like that.

Shamsher's response suggests a stigma attached to being an *immigrant* from India (rather than being second generation). He arrived in the United States from India at age nine. However, the number of Indian immigrant students at York High cannot explain their greater likelihood to suffer racial discrimination by peers, because at the time of my research, more immigrant students attending York were from Guyana and Trinidad than from India (New York City Department of Education, 2004–5). In spite of the greater number of Caribbean immigrants at York, Indian students reported significantly more discrimination from peers than did Caribbean students (both Indo-Caribbeans, most of whose families were from either Guyana or Trinidad, and Afro-Caribbeans, whose families were from Guyana and Trinidad as well as other Caribbean islands, especially Jamaica).

Disapproval from peers seemed to lead some South Asian youth to retreat from ethnicity or to downplay their experiences with stereotyping, and sometimes to change themselves in order to prevent harassment from peers. When I asked Gurdaas, a ninth-grade Indian student in New York who covers his traditional long hair with a Sikh patka, whether his Punjabi heritage is a big part of his life, he assumed my question was about discrimination: "[Being Indian] was [a big part of my life] when I was in junior high because mad [a lot of] kids used to make fun of me, so then it was so difficult, but then I got through it. So I thought when I go to high school, they ain't gonna say nothing. But sometimes they do."

Vikram was another ninth-grade Sikh student who covered his uncut hair. I asked him whether being Punjabi would be a big part of his life in the future, and he too reflected on discrimination: "I don't think it's gonna affect me that way, you know, my future profession. Because like I have noticed that the more higher you get in your school or like, you know, the more mature you become, they don't make fun of you. . . . So I don't think it's gonna affect me that much." Later in his interview Vikram told me that in middle school, students harassed him a lot, targeting him because of the turban he wears for religious reasons. He was relieved to see that this changed in high school: "In high school they don't really care about like what race you are from. Like what's your religion and what's your nationality, because you know, they don't mind. They are too mature for that. . . . They are too cool for that."

My questions about ethnic influence were interpreted by Gurdaas and Vikram as referring to the possibility of ethnic discrimination. They both hoped that the teasing they experienced in earlier years would decline as they and their peers grew older, meaning that ethnicity would not be a big part of their lives. Their relief prevented them from cutting their hair, as some Sikh students did in reaction to the racism they experienced among peers. Rajbir, a deeply religious Sikh senior about to start college (first quoted in chapter 2), expressed frustration at the number of Sikh boys he observed cutting their hair, against Sikh religious tenants. "Every year I see two or three Sikhs cut their hair," he told me. "And when they do it, I talk to them and ask them why they did it, and they just say because some kids make fun of them." As Rajbir relates, for some, discrimination among peers leads to a retreat from cultural identity, rather than to identity solidification. This may lead to lower self-esteem; in fact, Portes and Rumbaut (2001) find that Asian children of immigrants report lower self-esteem than their Afro-Caribbean and Latino counterparts. This ethnic distancing did not preclude ethnic solidarity, however: Indians who experienced discrimination maintained strong ties to coethnics while downplaying experiences of racism and prejudice and sometimes diminishing ethnic markers.

Given Indo-Caribbean teens' ties to both Indian and Caribbean identity, their distancing from "Indian" identity in the New York school in reaction to Indian classmates' low peer status is telling, as I note in the previous chapter. There, I show that teens used consumption practices to maximize peer status; they also employed identities and tastes to avert discrimination. For example, recall Richie. Despite looking Indian, Indo-Caribbean Richie identified racially as "black," preferred rap music and style, and expressed distaste for Indian music when I asked him if there was any kind of music he dislikes (he was familiar with Indian music through his parents' preference for it). Richie told me that he gets into fights frequently and that many students get into racially motivated fights with Punjabi students at school.

This was also true of Indo-Caribbean girls. Ellen blamed the racial discrimination she experienced on the misperception that she is Indian:

N: Do you ever experience any kind of racial discrimination?

E: Like, yeah, like, some people think that because you are Indian, like, you know how like some of the Indian people, how they smell, so.[4] And they like to think that you are like the same race. . . . They will talk so and you have to clarify, like, "Oh, I am not that Indian, I am *West* Indian," and they will be like, "Oh." And they'll just leave you alone.

Sadly, but perhaps understandably, rather than confronting the discrimination of her peers, Ellen distances herself from the mistaken low-status identity. Discrimination from peers leads some to a retreat from the symbols and practices that mark their ethnicities (in Richie's and Ellen's cases, Indian), rather than to identity solidification or "reactive ethnicity."

I heard some Indians express disdain for those who wore turbans, perhaps because they believed it led to discrimination that affected all Indians. For example, Abbas, the only Muslim Indian student I met in New York, told me he bullied Punjabi Sikh Indians and described his connections to black and Spanish gangs. When I first met him, I asked Abbas if he had second-generation Indian friends. He quickly told me that he did not socialize with Indians, then said, "I can get you Spanish people, black people, but not Indians." During his interview, Abbas recounted incidents in which he and his friends would encounter a lone Punjabi Sikh in the street wearing a turban; Abbas would tell his friends he wanted to beat the boy up, which they willingly did with him. This was perhaps one way for Abbas to distance himself from the low-status Indian identity in his school. Milner (2004) describes the ways in which youth in other parts of the country also use bullying—albeit not always along ethnic lines—to vie for status. Status being a zero-sum commodity, youth gain status, Milner shows, by bringing down the status of others through put-downs and insults.

Most commonly, both South Asian and Afro-Caribbean students reported that discrimination toward Indians came from black and Hispanic students. Luther, a Jamaican New Yorker, told me when I asked him if he sees discrimination toward other groups:

> L: Against Indians. . . . Like, you know—I don't know if it's like because [they're] Indian or because they just want to beat them up or something like that.
>
> N: Indians, like West Indian Indians?
>
> L: No, not West Indian, like, Talibans [sic].

I asked Luther who "they" were, and he said, "Black people. I saw black people before." He told me that Indians get bullied because they don't fight back:

> N: And do you have a sense of why they are getting picked on?
>
> L: Oh, because, I think because they think they not gon' do nothing back.

When a student is not willing to fight back and defend his pride, he faces continued discrimination. Students commonly perceived Indians to embody this lack of defending self-pride. Note that even non–South Asians like Afro-Caribbean Luther made a distinction in terms of racial discrimination between Indo-Caribbeans and Indians (specifically, Sikhs who wear turbans, whom he calls Talibans).

Sasha, an eleventh-grade 1.5-generation Indo-Caribbean student, cited the dress and way of speaking in peer culture to explain discrimination toward Punjabis: "Well, some, like, some people just don't, like, they don't like Punjabi people, maybe, so . . . I don't know. Because they think they smell, so . . . I don't know, really. Just because some of them do smell and that's probably why. And the way they dress. I don't know, or the way they speak sometimes. They can't speak really good English. So that's why they pick on them." Smells probably associate Indians with foreignness, even though most Indians in the school were either second or 1.5 generation. As mentioned previously, notwithstanding Sasha's citing Indians' inability to "speak really good English" as the reason they are picked on, the number of Indian immigrants cannot explain their higher vulnerability, because more Trinidadians and Guyanese than Indians at York were immigrants (New York City Department of Education, 2004–5).

Although less racial targeting of Indians was reported to me at Long Meadow than at York, Indian students were the targets of bullying in Britain, as well (see also Haywood and Mac an Ghaill, 2003; Modood, 1997, 2005). When I asked Kumar, a tall, quiet Year 11 Indian student in London, whether he experienced or saw racial discrimination, he said he saw it directed at all students, but toward Asians the most:

> K: Like white kids bullying black kids. Sometimes the other way around, black kids bullying white kids, yeah.
>
> N: What about Asians?
>
> K: Asians get bullied by both, both of them! . . . Probably because we are weak or something.

When asked about racial discrimination, Kumar first pointed out that all groups experience some kind of discrimination, but that Asians face it from both whites and blacks. He explained this targeting of Asians as related to their "weak" image.

TWO TYPES OF RACIAL DISCRIMINATION

I found two significant yet different types of racial stereotypes and discrimination. In the larger society, Afro-Caribbeans (and some white working-class males in London with hip-hop style) reported discrimination outside school from adults, based on stereotypes about race and style. These students also held high peer status in school because of their tough image and, to some extent, because of the racialization of hip-hop as black. Indians, on the other hand, faced discrimination within school from peers, because of assumptions of lack of style and toughness. They experienced low peer status in school (and a model-minority stereotype in mainstream society). The different forms of discrimination resulted from two racial stereotypes, especially of minority males: for blacks, one of danger and delinquency; for Indians, one of weakness (see table 9). Haywood and Mac an Ghaill (2003) similarly suggest that in Britain during the 1980s, "Paki bashing," or tormenting of South Asians, was due to "Asian boys being constructed as a weak masculinity, in relation to the tough masculinity of the Afro-Caribbean boys," in the white imagination. Tariq Modood (2005) has also shown that stereotypes

TABLE 9   TWO TYPES OF REPORTED RACIAL DISCRIMINATION

	Afro-Caribbeans	Indians
Site	Outside school	Inside school
Source	Unfamiliar adults	Peers
Stereotype	Dangerous, delinquent	Lack of style, lack of toughness
Ascribed masculinity	Hypermasculinity	Hypomasculinity
Possible consequence	*Future adult exclusion*	*Retreat from ethnicity*

of Asians and blacks in Britain draw from contrasting images: blacks are stereotyped as lazy yet "hard," while Asians are stereotyped as hard workers, culturally distinct people, and pushovers. I found some evidence to suggest that the type of discrimination Asians experienced had the potential to push students *away* from ethnic identity, perhaps in contrast to the type of discrimination most frequently experienced by Afro-Caribbeans leading to *stronger* ethnic and racial identities.

These findings resonate with Kasinitz and his colleagues' research comparing the experiences of Asian, black, and Latino second-generation young adults in New York City (Kasinitz et al., 2008). In this study second-generation Chinese young adults reported experiencing discrimination most *at school* from *other minorities,* while second-generation Afro-Caribbeans more frequently reported discrimination from *whites* in *public* spaces. My findings also resonate with Modood's discussion (2005) of the *cultural* racism and greater discrimination experienced in Britain by Asians than by Afro-Caribbeans. Combined, this research shows that stereotypes of South Asian and Afro-Caribbean identity cross national boundaries and that teens' experiences with discrimination take on distinct forms. Hence, arguments suggesting that perceptions of racial discrimination influence school behaviors and outlooks need to address the *sites* and *types* of discrimination that students experience.

This significant distinction between types and sites has important implications for understanding how perceptions of discrimination can influence school behaviors. My findings run counter to the suggestion of some researchers that perceptions of bias among school staff lead some disadvantaged black youth to reject schooling (Ogbu, 1991; Portes and Rumbaut, 2001; Sewell, 1997; Waters, 1999). The kind of racial bias that Sewell, Portes and Rumbaut, and others describe was much more likely to be identified in my research as occurring *outside* school, and hence is an unlikely explanation for low achievement *in* school among Afro-Caribbeans in either city.

Indeed, discrimination in school (peer based) seemed not to affect schoolwork. I found that in New York, students who reported racial discrimination inside school spent about the same amounts of time on homework as did students who reported no experiences with racial discrimination, of any ethnicity.[5] On the other hand, discrimination outside school seemed to have a *positive* effect on schoolwork: New York Afro-Caribbeans who reported experiencing out-of-school racial discrimination spent significantly *more* time on homework per night (ninety-eight minutes on average) than did their Afro-Caribbean peers who *did not* report experiencing racial discrimination (an average sixty-nine minutes); the same was true in London. This suggests that experiences of discrimination outside school might lead some Afro-Caribbean students to try harder in school. Alternatively, it could mean that more studious students were more aware of racial discrimination in public places. This explanation resonates with political scientist Jennifer Hochschild's (1996) finding that middle-class African Americans perceive more racial discrimination than do working-class African Americans. Unfortunately, these differences did not translate into academic achievement: Indians who reported experiencing racial discrimination still maintained higher grades than their Afro-Caribbean peers who did so.

The very different forms of stereotyping and racism that students reported encountering—both harmful and with lasting effects—have different consequences for students' futures. The Immigrant Second Generation in Metropolitan New York study (Kasinitz et al., 2008) found that different types of discrimination lead to different reactions from the second-generation groups affected. Second-generation Chinese Americans (and upwardly mobile blacks and Hispanics) who experienced discrimination from whites in school reacted by trying harder. In contrast, the study found, second-generation Afro-Caribbeans and Hispanics who experienced discrimination from whites in public spaces reacted with discouragement, anger, and "reactive ethnicity." The teens of my study may yet adopt this type of response as they grow older, enter the workforce, and come up against public institutions that limit their opportunities with more intensity than they have experienced already. Furthermore, as youth grow into adults, the peer social world matters less and holds less weight, and the adult social world matters more; hence, while Indians may rise in status as they move into the adult social world, Afro-Caribbeans may lose status, becoming more vulnerable to racial discrimination and stereotypes that lead to blocked opportunities. Scholars interested in reducing social inequality may therefore be more concerned with the kind of discrimination faced by Afro-Caribbean students, because it is perpetrated by individuals with the power to influence opportunities for advancement. On the other hand, forms of discrimination may change over time; some evidence suggests that for Muslim South Asian young men in Britain, discrimination based on the type described above for Asians is being replaced by hypermasculine images of religious fundamentalism and gang membership (Alexander, 2000).

In this research I focused on the student perspective, so I am not suggesting that racial discrimination on the part of adults does not happen in these schools, but rather that students do not *perceive* it. Students may define only instances of explicit, overt prejudice as racial discrimination, even though more subtle forms affect their academic achievement in ways they do not perceive. For example, recall from chapter 2 the students who recognized that adults often misperceive their styles as delinquent; these students did not mention race in the context of these misunderstandings, and perhaps did not fully grasp the ways in which style intersects with race in terms of adult perceptions of delinquency and attitudes toward schooling. Because of social norms in the school environment, teachers, administrators, and aides may be less likely to overtly express or enact discriminatory views, in contrast to public environments in which there is less familiarity with individual teens. Furthermore, although in my ethnographic research I encountered no instance of explicit racial discrimination on the part of school authorities, nor did students report any in interviews, race did indeed affect adult-student relationships. At Long Meadow, Afro-Caribbean and African boys had much higher rates of school suspension than other ethnic groups (Ofsted, 2004); yet no student mentioned this disparity. In New York one day a very young black (second-generation Afro-Caribbean) male teacher whose dress resembled students' hip-hop style was standing in the corridor, looking out the window. A security guard, thinking he was a student, began to shout at him from behind for being late to class, the buzzer signaling the start of class having already rung. The teacher did not respond, wanting to see what the security guard would do. The shouts grew louder and increasingly harsh. When the teacher eventually turned around, the security guard saw his name badge and realized the mistake. The teacher recounted this incident to me not as one of racial discrimination but rather as one that demonstrates the lack of respect with which the security guards addressed students in his school. Still, it raises the question of whether a young male teacher (or student) of a different race would experience similar antagonism from security guards. The degree to which the person's role (student versus teacher) versus his race, style, gender, or a combination of things influenced this interaction cannot be untangled in an isolated incident. Furthermore, although in the survey I administered a minority of students in *all* ethnic and racial groups disagreed with the statement "Teachers in this school are fair to students, regardless of race," the percentage of Afro-Caribbeans disagreeing (29 percent) was higher than that of Indians disagreeing (18 percent).[6] Lastly, *student* stereotypes of black peers as cool and high in status also led to negative perceptions: on the one hand, for example, black young men were perceived to be tough and the embodiment of hip-hop style, leading to high peer status; on the other hand, this same image led peers sometimes to stereotype them as troublemakers and gang members.

Furthermore, institutional racism in school can adversely affect Afro-Caribbean students in many ways (Dixson and Rousseau, 2005; Gillborn, 2006; Jay, 2003; Parker et al., 1999; Solorzano and Ornelas, 2004). That is, racial discrimination may also result from structural biases in the schools, such as bans on styles associated with particular race groups; a curriculum that ignores the heritage of particular students; expected modes of behavior known to be associated only with particular race or class groups; and tracking systems that invariably place black students in low tracks (Bourdieu, 1986; Bourdieu and Passeron, 1977; Delpit, 1995; Gillborn, 2005; Gillborn and Youdell, 2005; Majors, 2001a; Oakes, 1985). Students are often unaware of the subtle ways in which institutional structures can adversely affect their academic achievement.

CHAPTER 5

Positive Attitudes and (Some) Negative Behaviors

Max (white English) and Rohit (Indian) were kicking each other under the table in their top-track science class. From what I could see, Max was doing more of the kicking. Later, they moved on to punching each other. The punches weren't hard and were somewhat playful, although there was clearly some aggression between them. Eventually, Max left the table to sit by himself. When I asked him why he moved, he told me, "I can't get any work done over there."

—Fieldnotes, London, October 1, 2003

As I left the building of Harrison High in the middle of the school day to pick up lunch, a group of black and Latino students were sitting on the steps outside, one of whom I knew. They were laughing and chatting, and it was unclear whether some of them were supposed to be in class. As we chatted, one of the students asked me if I had taken the SAT test. I told them I had, and they asked me what I got. Embarrassed at what I knew would sound like a high score, I evaded the question. After they pressed me, I started to mumble, "Fourteen . . ." One boy reacted strongly: "What! Fourteen! If that's what I got, I wouldn't be talking like that, I'd be screaming *four-teen!*" He didn't seem to understand why I'd be reluctant to reveal such a high achievement.

—Fieldnotes, New York, June 1, 2004

In the previous three chapters, I focus on tastes in music and style, the meanings those tastes have, their variation between ethnic groups, and the consequences of racial meanings attached to hip-hop music and ethnic identities, both inside and outside school. The global reach of MTV and hip-hop radio led Londoners to express tastes and styles very similar to those of New Yorkers, and students reported these influences as mattering more than their peers' opinions in determining their styles. Still, hip-hop was commonly racialized as black, conferring on black students high status among their peers, even while adults unfamiliar to them stereotyped them as dangerous and delinquent. In contrast, the consequence of hip-hop's black identity for Indian students was low status among their peers. Given that Indian students outperformed their Afro-Caribbean peers in both schools of this research, one might assume that a taste for hip-hop music and style led to lower academic achievement. However, as I show in chapter 2, although hip-hop and rap music were popular among children of immigrants in both places, its meaning to kids differed markedly from what many assume. A taste for rap music and style was not connected to negative school orientations, and in fact teens were concerned that others misunderstand their styles as delinquent and anti-school and so moderated their expressions of style accordingly.

What *are* the students' academic orientations and attitudes, and how *do* they behave in school? Culture is more than just the choices we make about style and music. It also involves attitudes and behaviors. What are kids thinking when they behave in ways that undermine their academic achievement? These are some of the questions that require an analysis of attitudes and behaviors in the face of conflict among the second generation in school. In what follows, I discuss these two aspects of peer culture. I found that teens generally have positive attitudes toward school and believe that they can succeed if they try hard. Those who perceive discrimination or peer stigma toward academic achievement nevertheless have high aspirations and strong beliefs in their ability to succeed in school and beyond. In terms of behavior, I found that considerations of peer status and peer respect drove seemingly anti-school behaviors such as talking back to teachers or fighting with peers in school. In addition to the desire for academic success students wanted status among their peers.

OPPOSITIONAL ATTITUDES?

Popular conceptions of inner-city schools suggest that they are centers of chaos in which kids have little regard for authority, rules, or academic success. Although sociologists of culture have moved away from studying values in favor of worldviews, cultural "tool-kits," "frames," "repertoires," and "narratives" (Lamont and Small, 2008; Schudson, 1989; Swidler, 1986), attitudinal explanations for youth cultures are common. Some researchers have suggested that the subculture among many minority youth can be described as oppositional toward the dominant society and school and that this stance leads to educational failure (Anderson, 1999; Ferguson, 2000; Fordham, 1988; Gans, 1999; Ogbu, 1990, 2004; Portes and Zhou, 1993). These theorists continue a tradition of scholarship suggesting that some youth subcultures explicitly oppose school and adult norms (A. K. Cohen, 1955; P. Cohen, 1997 [1972]; S. Hall and Jefferson, 1976; Willis, 1977). Oppositional culture theory applied to racial minorities, as first described by anthropologist John Ogbu, suggests that children whose families become minorities involuntarily (e.g., former slave populations, indigenous peoples) react to the racism and discrimination they see around them by rejecting institutions of the dominant society such as schools, accusing them of perpetuating subordination and blocking their chances for success (Ogbu, 1990, 1991, 1995). From this follow three implications about youth values and beliefs: (1) that they believe racism and discrimination negatively affect the life chances and school achievement of their ethnic or racial group; (2) that they lack interest in schooling, which they see as racist, and they share this disinterest with peers through a peer culture; and (3) their perceptions of discrimination and the oppositional peer culture leads them to devalue academic achievement and perceive blocked opportunities.

Although Ogbu's original formulation was a theory of *African American* school attitudes (in contrast to what Ogbu saw as more positive orientations among voluntary immigrants and their children), it has had a powerful influence on how scholars of immigration in the United States discuss cultural assimilation. For children of immigrants in certain circumstances, cultural assimilation is thought to involve the influence of disadvantaged African American peers and their participation in an oppositional culture (Portes and Zhou, 1993; Waters, 1999). Sociologist Min Zhou (1997) suggests that "in underprivileged neighborhoods, in particular, immigrant children meet in their schools native-born peers with little hope for the future and are thus likely to be pressured by their peers to resist assimilation into the middle class" (70). Tariq Modood (2004) has suggested that segmented assimilation theory can also explain the trajectories of different immigrant groups in Britain.

My research, however, shows little evidence for oppositional values and beliefs among second-generation youth. This suggests that, contrary to downward assimilation theory, oppositional attitudes and orientations cannot explain the low academic achievement of the schools I studied.

Beliefs about Racism and Discrimination

Recall from the previous chapter that in interviews Afro-Caribbean and Indian teens reported experiencing different types of racial discrimination, and that students of all groups in both cities did not report racial discrimination from school authorities. To further explore the question of student perceptions of racial discrimination at school, I used a set of survey questions to ask students whether they agreed or disagreed (strongly or weakly) with, among others, statements on racism and discrimination. In survey responses, I found minimal evidence of perceptions of racial discrimination affecting school performance. Students surveyed generally thought teachers were fair: 73 percent of New York students and 80 percent of London students agreed with the statement "Teachers in this school are fair to students, regardless of their race."[1] Also, survey respondents did not perceive unequal opportunities for different race groups: 85 percent of survey respondents in both sites agreed with the statement "Young people of my race have a chance of making it if we do well in school," and the majority strongly agreed. However, many did feel that discrimination influenced their schoolwork, even if teachers were generally fair and they could succeed if they tried: 52 percent agreed with the statement "Discrimination affects my achievement in school negatively." This figure is not high if one considers perceptions of discrimination among the general population. Previous research has shown that nearly two-thirds of American adults report having experienced discrimination in their lives (Kessler et al., 1999). When in follow-up interviews I asked students who had been surveyed about positive responses to the question on discrimination, most either cited gender discrimination or said that teachers were generally too hard on them. Thus, as shown in chapter 4, student perceptions of racial discrimination from adults in school cannot explain the overall low academic achievement in both schools.

What about *peer* attitudes? If peers matter a lot to teens, a peer culture that devalues education may also influence achievement behaviors.

Peer Culture's Influence

Teens did not report experiencing peer pressure to demonstrate low academic achievement. Moreover, survey respondents believed that their friends valued education: 93 percent of students in London and 86 percent of students in New York agreed with the statement "Among my friends, doing well in school is important," and a majority in both cities strongly agreed. Students who did well did not experience low social status as a result of their academic performance: 84 percent of youth in the two cities combined *disagreed* with the statement "Among my peers, it is not cool to do well in school," and the majority strongly disagreed. Interview data resonated with these findings. Ajay, an Indian student in London, explained that even the students who misbehave in class prefer to get good grades:

N: Would you say it's not cool to do well in school here . . . or is it cool to misbehave?

A: No, I wouldn't say that. . . . Maybe like joke on the teachers, yeah, but . . . they may mess around here, but they want to get good grades really.

Ajay suggests that "joking on teachers"—an issue I address in the following section—may be acceptable, but students still prefer high grades. Many students in fact expressed annoyance at peers who disrupted class for no reason. When I asked Sophie, an Afro-Caribbean student in London, if misbehaving or talking back to teachers can make a student popular, she explained that it can actually irritate peers: "It don't make you popular; sometimes it makes you stupid. Some students do [misbehave] and people will be like, 'Why you doing that? Why are you being stupid?!'" Sophie's response resonates with the responses of many Afro-Caribbeans as well as students of all other ethnic groups in both cities.

Not only was misbehavior disliked by many, but most youth also preferred to give the appearance of doing well academically. One 1.5-generation Afro-Caribbean student in New York said that high-achieving students do not get bullied for their academic prowess, and he further accused popular peers of suggesting that they do well when they really don't: "They—majority [of popular students], I saw they're fronters, because they put up a front like they, they are doing well in school. Majority of them are doing bad! Like the ones you don't expect to see in like Saturday school [make-up and remedial classes], they are the ones going!" Joe—a self-described popular but low-achieving student—saw popular kids trying to make others think they do well. Thus, rather than making the appearance of low academic achievement, popular students made the appearance of *high* academic achievement; far from masking high achievement, some students actually masked *low* achievement. I also observed many instances in both London and New York of bragging about academic skills. These expressions of pride in academic skills indicate that peers do not stigmatize or devalue high academic achievement and that peer culture supports high academic achievement.

If peer culture does not drive anti-school behaviors and if, as the previous section shows, perceptions of racial discrimination do not, either, then perhaps a perceived lack of opportunity for success drive anti-achievement behaviors among students.

Perceptions of Opportunities

I found little evidence to support the suggestion that urban public school students do not believe in conventional routes to success. Students in both cities expressed strong agreement with the statement "I would like to complete college/university":[2] 100 percent in New York and 91 percent in London agreed. Students also generally believed that they would indeed do so: 95 percent in New York and 86 percent in London agreed with the statement "I believe I will complete college/university."[3] Furthermore, students believed that working hard in school would lead to success in school and in life, with over 90 percent of students in both cities agreeing that "If you work hard in school, you will do well," and almost all agreeing that "Doing well in school and getting an education is important to getting ahead in life." These data show that the vast majority of students believed that their hard work could pay off and that they would go on to higher education. Hence, a lack of belief in the importance of hard work, school success, and a college education cannot explain the overall low academic outcomes in the two schools.

The findings described so far provide little explanation for low academic achievement. Most students do not perceive racial discrimination as a barrier to school success; most think their peer culture supports academic success; and most believe that opportunities for success are available to them. The proportion of students expressing some oppositional attitudes and beliefs is much smaller than the percentages of students failing in both schools; recall from chapter 1 that York High's graduation rate is only 38 percent and that just 43 percent of Long Meadow's students finish school with the qualifications necessary to apply to a university. But what about the minority who *did* express attitudes and perceptions consistent with oppositional orientations? Did these opinions lead them to low aspirations?

To assess whether the minority of students who perceived discrimination and anti-school peer cultures were consequently less likely to believe they would complete an undergraduate degree, I compared their aspirations and beliefs with those of students who did not perceive discrimination or anti-school peer cultures. I found that 89 percent of those who agreed that "Discrimination affects my achievement in school negatively" still believed that they would complete an undergraduate education; this compares to 93 percent of those who perceived discrimination as not to affect them, a statistically insignificant difference. More specifically with respect to race and schooling, 88 percent of students who disagreed that "teachers in this school are fair to students, regardless of their race" still believed that they would complete college; this percentage is not significantly different from the percentage of students who *did* perceive teachers to be fair who believed they would complete college. These findings show no significant difference in terms of aspirations between those who perceived disadvantage and those who did not. They run counter to the oppositional culture hypothesis, that disadvantaged youth's perceptions of blocked opportunities for mobility and achievement lead to stunted educational aspirations and a rejection of formal education. Lastly, even when students *did* feel that their peer culture required poor school performance, this perception did not lead to low educational aspirations: the few students who agreed that their peers think it's uncool to do well in school ("Among my friends, it is not cool to do well in school") still overwhelmingly agreed that they would attend college—just two believed they would not.

Thus, perceptions of discrimination or an anti-achievement peer culture did not translate into low educational aspirations. These findings resonate with a growing number of studies that find little evidence of oppositional attitudes among African American youth (Ainsworth-Darnell and Downey, 1998; Carter, 2003, 2005; Diamond, Lewis, and Gordon, 2007; Lundy and Firebaugh, 2005; Tyson et al., 2005). Here I have extended these findings to the immigrant second generation. My research shows that beliefs about discrimination and peer attitudes do not help to explain academic behaviors and expectations among the

TABLE 10 BELIEFS ABOUT HIGHER EDUCATION: INDEPENDENT OF PERCEPTIONS
OF DISADVANTAGE OR PEER CULTURE

		Agree: "I believe I will complete university/college"	Chi-square
"Discrimination affects my achievement in school negatively."	Agree (n = 91)	89% (n = 81)	0.03
	Disagree (n = 83)	93% (n = 77)	
"Teachers in this school are fair to students, regardless of their race."	Disagree (n = 43)	88% (n = 38)	0.01
	Agree (n = 144)	91% (n = 131)	
"Among my friends, it is not cool to do well in school."	Agree (n = 29)	93% (n = 27)	0.02
	Disagree (n = 147)	90% (n = 132)	

SOURCE: Survey data, n = 191.

majority of students in the schools studied. Moreover, the findings show that attitudes and beliefs alone cannot provide the full picture of the way culture influences the school behaviors (and consequently the academic achievement) of the second generation. Given that attitudes and beliefs do not explain achievement behaviors, and that (as chapter 2 shows) tastes are not connected to oppositional orientations, how *do* students explain behaviors they know will impede their academic success? I turn to this question next, analyzing the motivations for and meanings given to behaviors that get students into trouble in school.

IMPEDIMENTS TO ACADEMIC ACHIEVEMENT: PEER STATUS AND RESPECT

Notwithstanding the positive orientations described above, academic achievement levels in both of the schools in which I conducted this research were low. Roslyn Mickelson (1990) articulated the conundrum of positive attitudes combined with low achievement among certain groups as the "attitude-achievement paradox," suggesting that the paradox could be explained through different measures of attitudes. Mickelson suggests that concrete attitudes better predict academic achievement than abstract attitudes. Ann Swidler (1986), on the other hand, has suggested that studying attitudes, especially values, is not nearly as useful for understanding culture's influence on behavior as studying "tool-kits" of symbols, stories, rituals, and worldviews and how they influence behaviors (see also Lamont and Small, 2008). Given that students expressed such positive attitudes, how did they explain seemingly anti-school behaviors such as engaging in conflicts with peers and teachers and sometimes fighting in school? What leads to fighting in school, and what end does fighting serve, if any? In this section I analyze the narratives that students used to explain their conflicts in school. I focus on conflict because this is where schooling and youth behaviors most often clash—for example, through conflicts with teachers or in physical fights between students that lead to suspension from school.

Self-reported explanations give priority in meaning to the actors themselves (Ewick and Silbey, 1995); in this case, teens' narratives about in-school conflicts counter the common explanation that they signify a lack of value for education (see also Morrill, Yalda, Adelman, Musheno, and Bejarano, 2000). Students employed three narratives when describing how they ended up engaging in physical fights and other conflicts in school: (1) fighting as an *instrumental,* or rational, response to provocation, enacted in order to prevent future teasing or bullying;[4] (2) fighting as a more *intuitive* response to provocation to defend self-pride and respect among peers; and (3) fighting to defend self-pride in response to conflict with a teacher. The data suggest a great deal of concern over maintaining respect and status among peers, and also show how gender norms shape the ways in which peer culture is enacted in conflicts.

Instrumental narratives were common in both cities. Peter, widely reported in the London school to be the smartest student in his year by teachers and peers alike, explained: "If they [bullies] insult you, [and] you insult them back, sometimes it can just work. Because, you know, if you mark yourself out as a victim, you will still be a victim, yeah." Peter's explanation of insulting bullies back as "working" indicates his instrumental use of behaviors to prevent harassment. When I asked Peter who generally gets bullied at school, he said that it's those students who are not good at sports. I knew that Peter did not play soccer with the other boys in his class and instead spent his lunch periods in the library, and hence probably had experienced some bullying at school. Nathan, another high-achieving student in the same class, was petite compared to peers of his age, and he, too, did not play sports at lunch. During his interview Nathan poignantly told me about his recent inter-est with Tae Kwon Do, the Korean martial art. He told me that before starting Tae Kwon Do, he had experienced a lot of bullying, but the sport had helped him to gain enough confidence and strength to stand up to peers. This led peers to stop bullying him, as Nathan explained it. Note that both Peter and Nathan explained bullying via athletic ability rather than academic achievement; if anyone were to be sanctioned for high achievement, it would have been Peter and Nathan, given their widely known academic success.

Another male student, Robert in Queens, explained to me that he engaged in a fight in order to stop harassment at his school. He fought, however, only after repeated attempts to resolve the conflict peacefully and reporting the harassment to his teacher:

> N: Have you ever been in a fight?
>
> R: Yeah, last year. . . . Because the kids here [in high school] were picking on me, and I told the teacher. My mom [told me] never to hit a kid, . . . always tell the teacher. I told the teacher, and the teacher didn't do anything. . . . The next day he [the same bully] was hitting me in class, so then after school he was like, "Oh, we gonna fight right now." . . . And then . . . I didn't do anything at first, I waited. Like he hit me and then I got up and I punched him in his face and his mouth was bleeding. . . . I would never hit anybody just for hitting people's sake. . . . I will only do it to defend myself. . . . Like the result of that was he stopped picking on me. Because when you stand up to a bully, then they stop picking on you. That's what I think.

Robert was growing up with both of his parents, who are African American and Afro-Caribbean. He described a situation in which he first attempted to resolve the conflict using all the other techniques he could think of. However, when he was unable to stop his harassment by those means, he did fight, and he learned the hard way that "standing up to a bully"—that is, defending oneself—can prevent harassment from peers. This skill is crucial given the context in which most urban youth attend school, where the ratio of students to adults is usually much more than sixteen to one, the average for public schools in the United States (Fry, 2005). It is important to distinguish this instrumental fight from a lack of value placed in teacher authority. In Robert's case, in fact, he first turned to teacher authority to resolve the conflict, and resorted to fighting only when appeals to his teacher were ineffective. As demonstrated by the contrast between Robert's and Peter's situations, the pressure to defend oneself to the point of physical fighting was stronger in New York than in London. Gangs were present in the New York school, but not in London.

Many boys in both cities told me about instrumental fights in junior high or ninth grade that "proved" to peers that they were tough and, as in Robert's experience, prevented future harassment and the need for future fights. The *threat* alone that one is willing to fight when necessary—as demonstrated by a ninth-grade fight—was enough to prevent future conflicts. This finding may explain why school violence seems to be more commonly experienced in the early years of high school. A national survey in the United States showed that ninth-grade students are more than twice as likely to report being threatened or injured with a weapon in school than are twelfth-grade students (12.1 percent versus 6.3 percent) (National Center for Education Statistics, 2007, table 4.1).

A fine line divided instrumental narratives that described a student engaging in peer conflict to prevent further bullying and narratives that more explicitly referenced the need to demonstrate toughness and to maintain self-pride in front of peers. Pradeep's story is one example. Pradeep came to New York from India at age thirteen and got involved with local gangs soon after he arrived, which was just three years before I met him. He wore a bandana over his long hair (required by his Sikh religion) rather than a turban—the bandana looked somewhat like the do-rags that many of his peers wore. Pradeep told me that he did not engage in "all that bad stuff" in India. I asked him to explain why he changed when he came to the United States. He told me: "I have to get involved. Because if you don't, they tease you for no reason, like the big boys. Yeah, anyone—like big boys. . . . He's gonna be like, 'You're this and that. You cannot fight.' And you know, I used to be like that in middle school, but when I came over here [to high school], I met boys like him [points to friend], big boys, and that's all." A tall and brawny boy himself, Pradeep later emphasized: "There is no other option; you have to fight, because if you don't fight, you get insulted, you get beaten up by other kids. If you want to stay alive over here, you have to fight."

Pradeep's earnest explanations for his fights demonstrate his perception of the *necessity* of fights to prevent real, physical violence from peers; it is an instrumental explanation. However, in response to his middle school experience, he got involved with a gang as a means of protection. He went from being a victim of bullying in junior high school to a member of a gang that may bully others. During his interview he described with excitement an instance of rivalry between his gang and another, in which he was shot in the leg at a distant park late at night. His reason for participating in fights went from personal safety—instrumental reasons—to gaining respect and status among peers.[5] Far from simply preventing further violence and attacks from peers, Pradeep now seemed to enjoy his new life: he had the respect of peers, and others at school would not attack him. Unfortunately, his participation in delinquent behaviors affected his academic achievement and future options. Pradeep's grade-point average was just above passing, and he lamented to me that he has recently been skipping classes too often, even though he also expressed a desire to become an engineer in the future.

Others more single-mindedly described their conflicts with peers as means of defending self-pride, rather than responses to fears of bullying or violence. When I asked John, an Afro-Caribbean boy in London, whether it makes a student cool to misbehave in class, he replied: "It's normally just sticking up for yourself, that's all. . . . Like, if someone tries something on you, tries to beat you up or something, you stick up for yourself. That's what people normally would respect." John clarifies misbehavior as having to do with "sticking up for yourself" and maintaining respect in the eyes of peers. Knowing how to behave and interact with peers so as to maintain their respect was an important part of youth culture in both cities. Larry, an Afro-Caribbean student in New York, told me that an older student had picked on him and later became his friend, impressed by Larry's willingness to defend himself. When I asked him if he had ever been in a fight, he described the situation: "He [the boy he fought with] threw something at me. Since he is older than me . . . he thought that he just gonna push me around. . . . Yeah, we fought, but then after that we just started chillin'. . . . Because he realized that, you know. . . . Like some people if they find a victim, they gonna fuck, they gonna mess with you. And, you know, they find out that you . . . are true to yourself or you ain't gonna let them just mess with you." Being "true to yourself" not only convinced peers not to push Larry around and to give him respect but also gained him a friend. Larry found that peers liked him more after he had proven his toughness, his willingness to respond to provocation. Maintaining respect in the eyes of others required demonstrating toughness when necessary.

Maintaining pride in front of peers, as with keeping to a certain style, reinforced norms of masculinity and femininity. Engaging in physical fights was twice as common for boys in both cities as it was for girls—overall, one-third of girls I interviewed had been in a physical fight in high school, compared to two-thirds of boys. Thomas, a Sixth Form (grade 11 equivalent) Afro-Caribbean student in London, told me his most recent fight had happened after another boy's encounter with Thomas's sister: "Recently I beat up a boy because he barged [*sic*] my sister, but that's about it. . . . We was walking on the street and some boy barged my sister, and I asked him to say sorry and he said no and started again. . . . I was like, 'No, you didn't do that.' And then he pushed me, so I pushed him back. He tried to swing, so I had to beat him up. . . . That was two days ago." When the admonishment turned into a fight, the conflict between the boy and Thomas's sister became a challenge to Thomas's masculinity—that is, to eye a girl who clearly is walking with Thomas is to challenge his protection of her.

Although boys expressed more concern about physical posturing and overt gestures of aggression, narratives about the need to defend one's pride and maintain respect were not unique to boys. Jennifer, a twenty-year-old Afro-Caribbean mother in New York who was about to graduate when I met her, explained to me: "I feel if you don't put your foot down and let them know where you stand, then they are just gonna try and take advantage of you. . . . If you don't say anything, then they will be like, 'Oh, yeah, I could push and boss her around because she is not gonna say anything to me about it. So therefore I am gonna pick on her and keep picking on her until she says something to me.' You have to be tough to a certain extent." Jennifer employed her defensive skills to prevent others from targeting her. By maintaining her respect by "putting her foot down," she would not be victimized.

Just as many boys reported fights in ninth grade that established others' respect for them, many girls reported major conflicts in ninth grade, as well, even if these did not always escalate into physical fights. Murray Milner (2004) finds that girls use secrets as markers of boundaries: they share secrets to express intimacy and trust, and withhold secrets to keep others at bay. Similarly, in my research girls' conflicts were often over gossip and negative comments spoken in whispers among other girls or over dirty looks. For example, when I asked Sharon, a white English working-class Year 11 (tenth-grade) student, if she had ever been in a fight, she told me yes and proceeded to describe a fight one year prior with a girl she had encountered on an estate (public housing complex) close to her own. Sharon believed that the girl was talking to friends about her, so Sharon confronted the girl aggressively: "She was standing there. . . . She was looking at me, and I didn't like the way she was looking at me. So I went over to her, you know, 'Why you looking at me like that?' That was it, really, so we started fighting." Although the girl did not overtly confront her, Sharon's simple feeling that the girl might be whispering about her served as a challenge to her dignity and respect. Hence, Sharon decided to settle the affront with physical conflict.

Many girls in New York described their ninth-grade conflicts and physical fights as lessons in independence and reported learning that trusting others by sharing their "secrets" would lead to loss of respect, because others would inevitably "talk behind their backs." For example, Jasmine, an Afro-Caribbean ninth-grade girl in New York, explained to me that she learned not to trust certain friends after she was betrayed:

> Yeah, like don't tell them [friends] certain things. Like don't depend on them for things because for all you know they can turn on you and say something about you behind your back, and [also] you know, not to really worry about what they say. Just do what you have to do. . . . Ever since I heard what my friends Kim and Stacy told me, you know, I stopped. Well, I still hang out with them, but it's like, I won't tell them all the info no more. And when I come after class, it's like, "Hi" and "Bye." Go straight to class, no conversation, it's a "Hi-bye" thing, that's it.

As a result of Jasmine's friend betraying her, they had a fight, and both wound up suspended from school. Jasmine's demonstration of toughness combined with her new reservation and distancing from friends were her way of maintaining her symbolic status among other girls.

Ranjit, an Indian girl in New York, also felt betrayed by peers. I asked her whether she had ever been in a fight:

> R: I've been in two fights. Last year and this year because girls, they like to say something, but when you say something to them, they don't say nothing. . . . If you got something to say something, say it to my face. It's better than saying it behind my back; and I don't like liars.
>
> N: So girls were talking behind your back?
>
> R: Yeah, and then my best friend told me . . . and I went up to her face [the girl talking about Ranjit] and she goes, "Oh, I didn't say that." She was like, she was mad [very] nervous! And I said, "Why you being nervous?" . . . I was like, "You tell me, tell me right now that you said that!" . . . And that's just how we started fighting.

To resolve the affront to her pride and respect among peers (especially those who were told negative things about her), Ranjit had to confront the source of the rumors aggressively. She later explained the difference between immigrants from India and Indians "born here" (like herself): second-generation kids stick up for themselves and respond to challenges and attacks, unlike recently arrived immigrants, who ignore affronts. The implication was that she commanded respect and that soon enough immigrants would learn that they, too, needed to demonstrate their willingness to fight back. Soon after I met her, Ranjit changed her hairstyle into small braids, and her nails were often painted with designs on the tips, both African American–identified styles. Protecting oneself by choosing friends carefully, not divulging personal information, and ensuring that others do not make critical comments behind one's back are important aspects of girls' lives at school.

The third type of conflict narrative involved conflict with teachers, and here, too, students showed the need to maintain respect in front of peers. Mary, a Year 10 white working-class girl in London, told me: "They [teachers] are not fair sometimes. Because . . . you don't do anything and then they pick on you for no reason. But if they will be rude to me, I will be rude back because I don't take rudeness from teachers." Mary's response to injustices she saw in some teachers led her to "rude" behaviors that could impede her academic achievement. Mary identified her family as English (she is white), illustrating the nonracialized nature of feelings about "not taking rudeness" and bias. Still, Mary's attitude did not coincide with a lack of conventional aspirations and goals. When I asked about her future plans, she told me that she aspires to get an education as a beautician and obtain a steady job with a good income:

> N: Would you say education is important to you?
>
> M: Yeah. . . . Because I want to have a good job when I am older. And that's—I don't want to be on the streets and everything. Just want to have a good job and have lots of money. . . . I want to be a beautician or hairdresser. . . . I want to carry on in Sixth Form.

Hence, occasional defiance of teachers did not lead to nonmainstream aspirations and goals for Mary. An Afro-Caribbean classmate of Mary's described similar interactions with teachers as related explicitly to *respect*: "To me, yeah, actually everyone is the same. If you don't give me respect, I won't give you respect. That's how it is. I won't treat a boy different from a teacher. They are both the same—what's the difference? To me, I think, yeah, well, I ain't gonna actually act rude, because they [teachers] are actually older—respect your elders and everything. But, like, if they are actually proper disrespecting you, you just gotta talk."

Terry's emphasis on respect suggests its importance in peer culture. His understanding that to maintain respect, he had to respond when others were rude or disrespectful—despite also believing in the importance of respecting elders—demonstrates an important behavioral element of culture among the youth I encountered in both cities. These observations were not unique to Londoners. Michelle, a sixteen-year-old Afro-Caribbean student in New York, told me: "I respect my teacher only if they respect me. [If] [t]hey want to get loud, I get loud." In other words, if an opponent raises the level of a conflict to shouting, Michelle must, in order to maintain respect in the eyes of peers, shout back or "get loud." Unfortunately, standing one's ground in this manner will likely be interpreted by school authorities as defiance and academic disinterest.

These demonstrations of pride, however, did not preclude high aspirations; students separated their conflicts with teachers from the desire to learn. One day I tagged along on a class field trip to London's Museum of Natural Science and made the following observation:

> After lunch at the museum's student cafeteria (1:30 PM), 4 kids had gotten in trouble and were separated while others lined up (Ben later told me that although the teacher thought they had defiantly wandered off, they actually had gotten lost). When the teacher asked the four to line up at the end, Ben, still visibly upset at the injustice of being punished for a genuine mistake, retorted, "Oh so now you want us to line up!" As a consequence, the teacher barred him from the museum visit. She asked me to sit with him while the others toured the museum.
>
> After going off to get some food (chips, chocolate bar), Ben came and sat with me. He wore his sweats low, has a peach fuzz moustache, was light-skinned black. His father is Irish, and his mother is Jamaican. He told me he thinks it's important to learn something new every day. When I asked what he learned today, he said, "Not to go on science trips." He later told me that that's what his parents say, and they ask him every evening what he learned in school that day. He wants to go to college after Year 11. When I asked him if teachers in the school are fair, he said, "I don't care. I don't pay any mind. I just come to learn, I want to learn something every day." He asked about what I was doing in his school, and when I mentioned graduate school he asked what my plans were for after. I mentioned something about research influencing social policy, to which he queried, "How does one get elected?"

Around 2:30 the other students came back. Many gravitated toward Ben, trying to distract him from our conversation about how people get into politics. But he told them to "shut up, I'm having a conversation!" He was listening intently—looking at me with serious eyes. Eventually, the conversation ended and he was back with his crew. Posture slightly changed, laughed a bit more, swagger walk. (Fieldnotes, September 24, 2003)

Ben's conflict with his teacher does not preclude a desire to learn. His and the other narratives above describe peer conflict in two ways: as undertaken for the instrumental purpose of preventing harassment and physical violence, and as undertaken with peers or teachers to maintain respect among fellow students. The sometimes unconscious nature of these fights, when youth describe them as natural events, are similar to the ways in which the *habitus* (Bourdieu, 1986; Bourdieu and Passeron, 1977) of (dominant) cultural capital seems natural and not constructed or deliberately chosen by those who embody it. The "right" responses to conflicts with both peers and teachers in class can lead to symbolic status among peers, just as the "right" tastes and behaviors in school can lead to school success and elite status in the dominant society (Bourdieu and Passeron, 1977). The line between these two goals was sometimes unclear. Recall Pradeep's explanation of joining a gang in high school to end the common harassment he had faced in junior high. Joining the gang probably led to its own symbolic status for Pradeep, at a time when he no longer feared others' attacks. Similarly, sociologist Paul Willis, in a study of British youth (1990), describes fighting as "maintaining honour and reputation whilst escaping intimidation and 'being picked on'" (103). Youth in Willis's study engaged in fights as little as possible but as much as they felt was necessary in an environment in which they felt unsafe.

Toughness and sometimes physical fights are cultural resources that allow youth to survive and to maintain respect in their peer social worlds. Having the "right" reaction to provocation can make the difference between future bullying and recognition of status. Rather than valuing fighting per se, youth in my study adhered to a system of expected behaviors (see also Morrill et al., 2000). The respect associated with defending one's pride does not always represent what youth *aspire* to, but rather serves as a *cultural resource for survival*. Elijah Anderson (1999) recorded similar behaviors among young men in inner-city Philadelphia who adhere to what he calls a "Code of the Street" that compels them to maintain a tough stance to prevent others' attacks.

Pradeep's and others' experiences point to the physical, not just symbolic, threats that youth in the schools contended with.

The findings in this chapter suggest that strong pressures exist among teens to sometimes engage in physical fights with peers, despite their positive aspirations, a desire to do well in school, and a belief that they can make it if they try. The desire to maintain pride and respect among peers sometimes leads, despite their best intentions, to behaviors that conflict with their academic objectives and desires. Given the findings that low achievement in inner-city schools among children of immigrants cannot be explained by the influence of oppositional popular or peer cultures, and that fighting in school does not signal anti-school attitudes, what might be a more promising explanation for culture's influence on the school behaviors of children of immigrants in urban areas? In the following chapter I synthesize the findings of this and the previous chapters to develop a theory of how peer cultures in their multiple dimensions influence behaviors related to academic achievement. What leads teens to the tastes, behaviors, and types of responses to peer conflict that I (and others) have observed?

CHAPTER 6

Balancing Acts

Peer Status and Academic Orientations

The findings on youth cultures that I have presented in this book so far suggest that second-generation youth living in disadvantaged areas do not hold oppositional attitudes, that perceptions of discrimination do not influence their aspirations, and that a taste for rap or hip-hop music does not lead to oppositional attitudes. Furthermore, I did not find evidence that academic success leads to social failure. What, then, explains the aspects of youth cultures that *seem* oppositional? Why do kids—especially but not exclusively boys—fight in school, when they know it will lead to suspension? Why are students with the stereotypical accoutrements of academic success—unhip clothes, heavy backpacks, and the like—teased and bullied? And why do teens wear clothes that they know mark them as delinquent in the eyes of many teachers and other authority figures? Given the low academic achievement in both schools of this research, how *does* peer culture influence academic achievement, if not through oppositional orientations?

The finding discussed in chapter 2 that second-generation youth in London, too, prefer African American–rooted music and style suggests that hip-hop is now a globalized taste culture for urban youth, rather than something that is unique to disadvantaged neighborhoods in urban America and that signals rebellion. The idea that an oppositional youth culture influenced by African American peers can explain certain tastes and behaviors does not resonate with the findings on attitudes described in chapter 5. Furthermore, the finding in chapter 5 that despite positive school orientations many second-generation teens still engage in physical fights and other confrontations detrimental to academic success suggests that teenagers are quite concerned about maintaining pride in front of their peers.

In the world of youth culture the quest for *peer status* is paramount. That is, teens' behaviors and styles can better be explained by the desire to gain status—to be "cool"—among their peers. Murray Milner (2004) has analyzed peer status among students from diverse high schools in the United States and concluded that teens are preoccupied with peer status because they spend the vast majority of their waking hours with other teens, not adults, and because they have little power or say in the other spheres of their lives. Youths' class and status within mainstream society is determined by their parents. However, children engage in their own status hierarchy, based on their own youth culture. Their peer social world is one domain in which kids, not adults, determine who is on top and who is below.

Academic achievement has little bearing on peer status among kids. Rather, it is the accoutrements of hipness that matter to them—as illustrated by students' explanations of bullying as stemming from comportment and style, rather than from academic achievement. *Academic achievement is simply not relevant to youth culture and the peer status hierarchy.* This finding suggests a shift in understanding of the mechanism by which peer culture can lead some second-generation minority youth to fail academically and consequently to experience downward assimilation. It is not for want of aspiration, as these findings show; rather, academic failure results when the quest for peer status comes into conflict with academic achievement and, for example, a student responds to provocation by fighting to defend his or her pride. Second-generation teens thus are attempting to navigate, and succeed in, two distinct social worlds—the world of conventional school success and their peer social world. These worlds are distinct but, crucially, *not in opposition to one another.* Previous theories of downward assimilation suggesting that second-generation teens attending urban, disadvantaged, low-performing schools adopt an oppositional culture from their African American peers have overlooked this important aspect of the cultural lives of the second generation. They are, indeed, adapting culturally and assimilating into American and British cultural life. However, this adaptation leads them on a different pathway from what previous scholars have suggested.

TABLE 11 CULTURAL EXPLANATIONS FOR DOWNWARD ASSIMILATION

	Oppositional Culture Explanation	Peer Status Explanation
Rejects mainstream goals and norms?	Yes	No
Values academic success?	No	Yes
Relationship between peer social world and adult social world	Oppositional by design, conflictual	Distinct, but not by design
Source of low peer status	Academic achievement	Fashion, music, racial authenticity, not responding when provoked
Source of taste culture	Neighborhood, African American peers	Globalization, media
Source of ethnic/racial inequality (culture)	African American peer influence	Emphasis on peer culture (fashion, music, respect)

What does it take to gain peer status? Wearing stylish clothing, listening to popular music, and defending one's pride all lead to peer status; conversely, "nerdy" clothing and lack of toughness in conflicts lead to low status and, sometimes, bullying. In the most disadvantaged neighborhoods, defending one's pride can prevent not just symbolic censuring but real, physical violence—having "street smarts" is a matter of survival (Anderson, 1999). The similar taste cultures in New York and London suggest that the source of popular music and style among urban youth is global culture rather than the local neighborhood. Recall the remarkable similarity in favorite artists between New York and London teens.

Prudence Carter (2005) identifies the resources that lead to status among a disadvantaged group as *nondominant cultural capital*: "a set of tastes, appreciations, and understandings, such as preferences for particular linguistic, musical, and dress styles, and physical gestures used by lower status group members to gain 'authentic' cultural status positions in their respective communities" (50). In other words, nondominant cultural capital buys status in a nondominant social world, such as those inhabited by black youth or second-generation youth. Carter's formulation borrows from Pierre Bourdieu's (1986) definition of cultural capital. According to Bourdieu, knowledge about the dominant culture can lead higher-status children to higher academic achievement and subsequent high social status as adults through cultural capital—an unwritten set of skills and preferences, including ways of speaking and interacting with teachers, comportment, and tastes (Bourdieu and Passeron, 1977). Whereas Bourdieu and Passeron show how an upper-class culture at school maintains the status quo and prevents disadvantaged children from achieving academically, Carter's analysis shows that an unwritten set of cultural rules for behavior leads to status *among minority youth*. That is, particular styles, ways of interacting, and taste preferences lead to status *within* groups that have low status in the larger society.

Here I apply Carter's theory to second-generation urban youth cultures. In this case, showing toughness, maintaining self-respect, adopting hip-hop tastes in music and style, and observing racial authenticity all lead to high peer status. Crucially, nondominant culture is not *in opposition to* mainstream culture but rather outside of it. If there is a cultural influence on downward assimilation, the quest for peer status, not opposition to adult expectations, explains it.

Black identity increases a teen's authentic claim to nondominant cultural capital (and hence peer status), especially in the realm of popular culture. The relationship between black racial identity and nondominant cultural capital is similar to the relationship between white racial identity and Bourdieu's cultural capital in the U.S. context. In American society, members of racial minorities who have cultural capital—for example, in the form of a higher-education degree—may not always be read by others as "authentic," because of the perceived incongruence between minority racial identity and the habitus of the upper classes. This makes it harder for minorities to convert certain forms of capital, such as an education degree, into economic and symbolic status (Hacker, 1992; Massey and Denton, 1993; Pattillo-McCoy, 1999). Similarly, nonblack students in both the cities I studied had a harder time converting cultural accoutrements into status among peers. As I show in chapter 3, nonblack students could sometimes be accused of "acting black" in their hip-hop styles and music preferences, and hence could not convert tastes for hip-hop into peer status as easily as black peers (African American and Afro-Caribbean alike) could.

WHAT TEENS *DO* REJECT

Although students were not rejected by their peers for high academic performance, other cultural accoutrements led to low peer status.

During interviews many teens told me explicitly that an individual's racial authenticity, tastes in music and style of dress, and interactional styles all have ramifications for status among peers. In chapters 3 and 4, I describe how expectations of racial authenticity and racial identities affected peer status and discrimination in the multiethnic school sites of this research. In what follows, I discuss teens' distaste for peers who lack the "right" tastes and styles, seem weak, or seem introverted. These characteristics could lead to low peer status regardless of a teen's academic achievement level.

Along with the need to socialize and to be tough, the "right" style of dress and "right" tastes in music were important for status among peers. Students dismissed peers who did not adhere to the popular dress code. Jason, a fourteen-year-old white student in London, explained to me that

> people think if . . . you try to tie your trainers [sneakers] up all the way to the top and don't have your [sneaker] tongue out; or have your trousers all the way up; never wear your hood up—people think . . . you don't really like the music and stuff, like hip-hop and stuff. . . . 'If you are clever and like, dress like hip-hop and stuff, that is good. It's like you are clever and, but since you dress as well, that's good. But people that's geeky, like people that dresses like different, I dunno.

Jason clarifies that it is one's clothing style rather than academic achievement that matters for symbolic status among youth at his school. Irfan, an Indo-Caribbean boy in New York, also distinguished between academic achievement and style of dress. He explained that

> the people that do good and come out of here [high school] in four years, they are highly respected. But, like, the people that come with big bookbags for no reason whatsoever, those are considered geeks. . . . Like certain kids they do good and . . . they won't act like abnormal from everybody else. But the kids that, like they are by themselves, they bring every single book they have, and they do good, they are considered geeks. . . . But if you are able to juggle everything, . . . then you are highly respected.

Irfan's words suggest that academic success can add to a high level of peer social status for a teen, though the more important measures are style and socializing with peers—being "quiet" or carrying the wrong accessories decreases symbolic status among peers.

The quest for peer status led some students to hide tastes considered uncool by their peers. In London, Niko, an Afro-Caribbean student, was introduced to rock music by his cousin. He grew to like it and, as a result, listened to a variety of styles of music regularly. Niko told me that his three favorite artists or groups are The Darkness (a rock group), 50 Cent (hip-hop), and Justin Timberlake (pop). When I asked Niko if the music he listens to relates to his identity, he replied that he keeps his appreciation of rock to himself: "I would never, ever tell you [a peer] what I like. I am afraid I might get laughed at or something like that. I try to cover it up—no, not cover up, but I try to hide some of it because I feel that most of it is unnecessary to tell to other people." I asked Niko about which tastes he would cover up: "The rock 'n' roll, because most of them will laugh at that." Niko, an extroverted student who played soccer with his classmates during school breaks, explains the importance of demonstrating the "right" music taste for maintaining symbolic status. Among his peers, a taste for hip-hop and rap, not rock music, was popular. Peer sanctioning had a conforming influence on teens, as they used signals of popular tastes in order to gain status.

Similar to Niko, though perhaps more confident in his unconventional tastes, Roshan, an Indo-Caribbean boy from Queens, told me that although some rock listeners hide their tastes from peers, he did not worry about others' judgments:

> If I play rock around here, then some people would be like, "Oh, that's crappy." They don't want to hear it. And if I play rap around here, everyone might like it. That's the thing—some people just like stick to like one genre of music. . . . I, like, open myself to everything. And you know, some people just don't wanna accept other kinds. They probably do go home and like listen to it, but in like secrecy. They don't wanna tell anyone that they actually like it. And I just come out and say it. I am not afraid of what people say.

For both Niko and Roshan, rock music did not gel with the peer culture at school. Unless one wanted to be associated with the minority rock group, listening to rock music was a solo matter. But unlike Niko, Roshan had the confidence to make public his taste for unpopular rock music.

The "wrong" response to being teased or picked on could also lead to low peer status. The lack of a strong response to bullying could lead to symbolic and even real violence from peers, as described in chapter 5. The bullying targeted those who did not respond as expected according to peer culture. Abbas, an Indian boy in New York, told me that toughness was needed to prevent harassment at his school. He told me that it was the "nerdy types" who got picked on. I asked him to explain what a nerdy type is. He told me, in a menacing tone of voice: "Like nerdy type, like if you don't got the looks, you don't got the courage, you don't got the guts, then you are a nerd! . . . Yeah, you got to be tough, yeah. If you are not tough, then forget it. You are not going to be able to survive in Queens." Abbas's words demonstrate that nerdiness is defined by behaviors unrelated to schoolwork. Instead, he emphasized "courage" and "guts," important features for peer social status.

Finally, reclusive behaviors led to low status among peers. Baljit, an academically weak 1.5-generation Indian student in New York, clarified that students make fun of some students who do well not for their academic success, but because they do not socialize:

N: If you do well in school, do kids make fun of you?

B: Sometimes they do when you, they think you always in studies and you don't go out or hang around with anybody.

Baljit points out that the taunting results from a lack of attention to peer culture and a sole emphasis on academics, rather than from academic performance itself. Jake, a sixteen-year-old white English student who did well academically, similarly told me that loners, rather than smart students, are teased: "Some people, they are smart, but they, they don't go outside [during lunchtime] at all. They just stay inside the library and they don't, . . . they sort of, uh, how do I say it? They segregate themselves, and they don't try and integrate at all and so therefore they get picked on, which is a shame." Jake went on to contrast himself with the academically strong but socially introverted individuals he described; he was a student with high grades who nevertheless had many friends, listened to hip-hop music, wore brand-name clothing, and played soccer with his friends during school breaks. The above statement shows Jake's disdain for high-achieving students who do not also engage peer culture, as he does.

Anish, an Indian Year 11 student in London, had a similar perspective and added that quietness, *especially* when teased, would lead to further teasing:

N: In general, do kids get made fun of because they are doing well in school?

A: Not really, but the thing is, it's not by doing well in school, but it's just that they are quiet—that's why some people take the piss out [make fun]. They just sit there instead of saying something.

Anish's answer identifies two qualities that bring lowered social status among youth: being quiet and showing weakness—not sticking up for oneself when provoked. The comments of Kim, a white student in London, resonate with Anish's: "There is a boy who I saw get bullied once. . . . They bullied him because he just sort of, he is quiet . . . and he is not gonna fight back or say anything back. . . . They . . . just pick on the kids they know are not gonna fight back."

The above discussion demonstrates that teens have a strong sense of who has high status among peers and who does not. Cultural markers and status are quite important to teenagers, though the cultural codes they employ are markedly different from mainstream adult cultural capital. The culture among them differs from mainstream adult culture, but not because it opposes mainstream adult culture and academic achievement. Rather, peer cultures are less concerned with what dominant cultural capital earns than with what nondominant cultural capital can buy: peer status. The peers whom teens encounter constitute their primary source of social acceptance and status, so it is no surprise that peer influence is quite powerful.

BALANCING ACTS: TWO SOCIAL WORLDS

Schools have two social fields operating simultaneously. One is the official school culture, put forth and reinforced by adults—administrators, teachers, and security guards. This culture has its own status system and expectations, involving grades, positive relationships with teachers, and cooperation with authority. This social field expects students to defer to authority, deal with peer conflict through adult intervention, and don non-hip-hop styles. Mainstream cultural capital leads to success in this social world. The other social world in schools is that of youth, which pays little attention to grades and relationships with teachers (either in the positive or negative sense) and instead emphasizes toughness, peers, and familiarity with music and styles that are hip among youth. This social world expects teens to maintain self-respect, to deal with peer conflict by responding when provoked, and to consume popular music and style (in the case of urban schools, hip-hop). *Nondominant* cultural capital leads to success in this social world.

These two sets of cultural expectations are different cultural tool-kits aimed at different goals. That is, they lead to different kinds of status, earned through different cultural practices. Some students succeeded in balancing these two social worlds. Others prioritized one social world over the other, some by emphasizing peer status to the detriment of cultural tools necessary for school success, and others by emphasizing adherence to adult cultural expectations in school to the detriment of peer status.

TABLE 12 BALANCING ACTS: TWO SOCIAL WORLDS IN SCHOOL

	Adult Culture	Youth Culture
Conflict resolution	Deference to authority	Self-respect
	Adult intervention	Personal response when provoked
Style	Not hip-hop	Hip-hop, urban
Culture for success	Mainstream cultural capital	Nondominant cultural capital

When I asked teens what makes for a successful person, most gave answers consistent with what conventional adults might say: material wealth, education, achieving one's goals, having encouraging friends, and adopting highbrow speech and dress. What they seem to want most is both peer status *and* success in terms of work, education, and material well-being; furthermore, they link success to doing well in school, and they believe that they too can do well if they put their minds to it.

The most successful students (in both peer and adult social worlds) were savvy about when to employ their nondominant cultural capital and when to employ their dominant cultural capital. Successful minorities have long been known to be skilled in code-switching—indeed, this skill is necessary for success (Carter, 2005; Mehan, Hubbard, and Villanueva, 1994). Recall from chapter 2 the students who did their best to signal hip tastes yet moderate their styles of dressing. Prudence Carter (2005) has described students who manage to balance success in both worlds as *cultural straddlers:* "Characterized by bicultural perspectives, they are strategic movers across the cultural spheres" (30).

Other students found the balance more precarious. Although peer culture is not opposed to academic success, concerns with peer status can sometimes overshadow participation in the culture expected by adults in school. This sometimes leads to conflicts with academic achievement, despite students' best intentions to both do well in school and maintain high peer status. Peer culture may sometimes impede academic achievement, not through explicitly oppositional attitudes, but through behaviors that prevent learning. For example, as discussed in chapter 5, when repeatedly provoked, one is expected to fight to maintain respect. Yet engaging in fights can lead to school suspension if a student is caught. Furthermore, standing up for oneself in the face of harassing peers or a teacher perceived to be unjust can also lead to punishment at school, especially when a student continues to argue when a teacher asks him or her to quiet down or to discuss issues calmly and in private. Striking the right balance is not easy. During my first week of ethnographic research in London, I followed a Year 9 class for a day and observed the following:

> Howard, an Afro-Caribbean boy, was misbehaving, as I had observed him do in prior classes. His young, stern English teacher asked him to leave the room, which he felt was unfair, given that other students had also been chatting and misbehaving. The teacher insisted, and soon there was a stand-off. She took his bag as if to move it out of the room, and Howard held on to it. Their eyes locked for at least 15 seconds. Eventually, Howard let go of the bag and followed his teacher and bag out of the room. (Fieldnotes, September 17, 2003)

Howard seemed caught in a bind between standing his ground and getting into more serious trouble, and backing down and facing embarrassment in front of his peers. I wondered what would have happened if he had not let go of his bag. The teacher, perhaps understanding Howard's peer culture, might have also felt that she could not back down, for fear of her other students thinking she could be easily dominated.

Tastes in clothing also came into conflict with school authorities. For example, in London one day I witnessed a heated argument between a teacher and a student that arose because the teacher asked the student to pull his pants up over his exposed underwear; the boy refused and went on to insult the teacher. In New York, many posters around the school described what clothing was not allowed in school, including hats, do-rags, and bandanas for boys and, for girls, clothing that exposed midriffs or shoulders. As I walked down the hall one day toward the end of the school year, I saw a security guard writing up a "violation," much like a parking ticket, for a boy wearing a do-rag. Michael, an Afro-Caribbean student, explained to me that the school was cracking down on do-rags and that after three violations a student would be automatically suspended. Although many students took pains to signal moderation in their clothing styles, this subtlety was sometimes lost on adults—especially outside school—who, unlike peers, could not distinguish between extreme and moderate participation in style. The coding of rap and its concomitant hip-hop style as oppositional makes some adults *perceive* certain aspects of peer culture as delinquent, especially among boys (particularly black boys), despite students' own attribution of different meanings to their styles.

Still, the importance of music and style did not have a strong correlation to achievement behaviors overall. When I compared high with low academic achievers in both cities, I found that high achievers were just as likely to say that music is an important part of their identities as were low achievers. In terms of style, high achievers were marginally more likely than low achievers to say that style is an important part of their identities in London; the opposite was true in New York. However, I found that in both cities those for whom style is an important part of identity did similar amounts of homework per night compared to those who felt style is not central to identity. Students who told me it is important to have name-brand sneakers spent slightly more time on homework on average than those who attached less importance to footwear. These findings show that an emphasis on music and style did not coincide with poor academic achievement, or with behaviors less conducive to academic achievement, especially outside school. In what follows I provide three snapshots of students and how they balanced these two social worlds.

STACEY: SUCCESS IN THE BALANCING ACT

Stacey, an Afro-Caribbean student in New York, was successful at the balancing act between maintaining peer status and meeting adult cultural expectations for school success. I met Stacey at Harrison High School, the site of my secondary interviews in New York. When we met, I quickly noticed that Stacey spoke to me using standard English, saving slang and urban cadence for conversations with her peers, during which her speech style noticeably changed. For our interview I met Stacey after her Latin class in one of the trailers in the schoolyard. She was taking honors and Advanced Placement classes at school; had a 94 grade-point average; and on a scale of 1 to 10, rated school 10 without hesitation (in contrast to music being a 6). She already knew where she would be going to college and that her major would be history. Her long-term plan was to earn a Ph.D. in history. Nevertheless, Stacey told me that we would need to finish her interview in one sitting, because she would be skipping school the following two days. The next evening was the school prom, and she would be spending the day preparing for the big night; the day after that, Friday, she and her senior friends would be off to Great Adventure, an amusement park in New Jersey, together.

When I met up with Stacey for her interview, she wore two sets of earrings that looked like diamonds, a black T-shirt, and a very short skirt. During the interview I was surprised to hear her contrast her style at basketball games versus at school:

> [At basketball games] I dress a little bit more casual, and when I am in school I dress more popular [*sic*] because I care what teachers think about me. Because, you know, when you dress the wrong way, they might get a bad impression about you or something. . . . Like if you come to school in like a little belly shirt or something, they might not take you as seriously. They might think you are not smart or something.

She mentioned that some peers describe her style as "preppy" and "white," but she does not see it that way:

> N: Does anyone ever misunderstand you based on the way you dress?
>
> S: Yeah. People tend to think, like—they are like, "white girl," or whatever. . . . They don't think I can hang out with the black people and be, for lack of a better word, "down," so.

Stacey's description includes a cautious translation of urban slang ("down"—hip, part of the group) for me. As I noted in chapter 2, many students, like Stacey, took great pains to signal hipness yet moderation in style. And moderation in one context may signal something different in another—hence the contrast in meaning that Stacey and I ascribed to the length of her skirt. She explicitly describes code-switching in her style between the environment where teachers will be evaluating her academic skills—the classroom—and the environment where peer culture dominates—the basketball court.

Stacey described herself as a popular student with a diverse array of friends and tastes: "I hang out with a lot of West Indian people and, like, Guyanese Indians. Hang out with a lot of them, and they listen to like reggae and soca and Indian music. And when I hang out with my white friends, we listen to pop and rap and stuff. And when I hang out with my Spanish friends, we listen to Spanish music and rap and stuff, so hip-hop."

Stacey demonstrates cultural flexibility not only in her ability to balance high achievement in school with popularity but also in her music tastes. She also maintained her pride and stood up for herself when she perceived a teacher to be unfair. When I asked her if she ever had conflicts with teachers or friends, she told me that two weeks prior she had called a teacher a "tyrant" because "it's that time of year when everybody's coming to class late—so he started yelling at the class: 'I will not allow this! Senioritis is not going to set in yet!'" After calling her teacher a tyrant and "using the F-word," she was sent out of class. Because of her solid record in school, however, school officials looked the other way and did not punish her. The incident, as well as her missing school for social activities like the prom and the trip to Great Adventure, shows an investment in her peer social world, while her high academic achievement shows her emphasis on school success as well. Still, she never crossed the line of physically fighting with another student in school, in contrast to the other Afro-Caribbean girls I interviewed in New York, two-thirds of whom had been in a fight in high school. Stacey had figured out ways to succeed in the adult social world and in school while also maintaining popularity and status among her peers.

TERRY: TIPPING THE SCALE TOWARD YOUTH CULTURE

In contrast to Stacey, Terry was one student who emphasized his peer social world over adult cultural expectations. Terry was growing up with his second-generation Jamaican mother in London and saw his Ghanaian father on occasion. He lived in one of London's most disadvantaged housing projects. Energetic and popular, Terry seemed to get along with most of his classmates when I observed him in the classroom. One classmate, when describing the Form Class's social groups, placed Terry in the "rude boys" group (in contrast to "the geeks," "the grungers," and "the normal kids"). My first observation of Terry when I visited his class was that he seemed always to be smiling and often staring off into the distance when teachers were giving directions. Terry was late to our scheduled interview over lunch. He explained that his soccer game ran past the start of class during the first school break and hence he came late to science class; as a result, his teacher held him back from his second break period, when we were meeting, as a punishment.

Although he was successful with his peers and maintained status among them, Terry's academic achievement was weak, placing him in the bottom third of London students I interviewed. A new program at his school allowed low-achieving students to participate in an apprenticeship program in which, once a week, they worked with a skilled professional; Terry spent his Mondays honing his carpentry skills. This avenue, if he continues, may provide a safety net from downward assimilation. Terry told me during his interview that he spent his time after school and on weekends playing soccer and basketball and making music with his friends. Since basketball was unusual among London students, I asked Terry how he had developed his interest, and he described the influence of a cousin. He told me of his interest in the L.A. Lakers, whom he follows on satellite television, and specifically Shaquille O'Neal (O'Neal has since left the Lakers) and Kobe Bryant. Terry told me that he got into rapping from MTV Base, the British MTV station that plays exclusively hip-hop and R&B music videos. He named Chingy, Ludacris, Wayne Wonder, and 50 Cent as singers and rappers whose music he especially liked. These artists were all popular on mainstream hip-hop radio in the United States and Britain at the time, and all are African American rappers except for Wayne Wonder, a Jamaican-born singer who now lives in the United States. When I learned that Terry loved music and rapping so much, I asked him if he had taken a music class in school: "In this school I take music classes, but not rap ones. We don't do stuff like that. We do stuff from the past like Beethoven and whatever." During a school assembly, Terry played "La Bamba" on Trinidadian steel pans as part of a group performing with his music class. It seemed that this was his school's attempt to connect with its student body through the music of many students' ethnic heritage, but not of their youth culture. Terry enthusiastically defined his way of dressing as hip-hop and stylish and told me that it's important to wear nice clothes and sneakers, lest his peers make fun of him. Only after some probing did he mention homework at all as among his after-school activities.

Terry named Jason, a student in his form class, as his closest friend. A teacher told me that Jason had been switched into Terry's class because of his misbehavior in the early years of secondary school. I often saw Jason ignoring teacher directions in class and surrounded in the halls with friends and admirers. A charming young man, Jason won his school's MC (rapping) competition and had friends across the entire school. Terry admired high academic achievement. When I asked him if peers make fun of those who do well in school, he reacted strongly: "No! Nobody takes the mick out of [makes fun of] Peter [the highest achiever in his class]! They all think he is smart. They are like, 'I am as smart as Peter!'" Relatedly, he did not think his peers find it uncool to do well in school. Furthermore, he spent thirty to ninety minutes on homework every night, the most common amount students reported to me on both sides of the Atlantic. Terry also agreed that "young people of my race have a chance of making it if we do well in school" and that teachers in his school are fair. Hence, although Terry engaged popular culture and did not always focus on his schoolwork, this was not a result of anti-school attitudes or a critique of racial inequality in his school environment.

KULDIP: TIPPING THE SCALE TOWARD
ADULT CULTURE

Some students prioritized success in the adult social world of school success to the detriment of status among peers. Kuldip was one such student. Having moved with her parents and older siblings to New York City from India at a very young age, she has no memories of life in India. I first met Kuldip in the school library during her lunch period. She sat with rigid posture, a long braid running down her back. I noticed an Indian-looking gold necklace tucked under her shirt when I met her in school. A soft-spoken girl, Kuldip eventually opened up during our interview. She took Advanced Placement history, and she told me she had an A average in math, science, and English. The first thing she did when she came home from school was to complete her homework.

Kuldip told me that although she enjoyed playing basketball, she did not play for the school team because

> I don't really like spending so much time in school. . . . I don't think going on the basketball team here is sort of important. . . . I don't like the students here, either, because they are from the neighborhood and some of them are really disrespectful. Most kids in this school, they don't respect the teachers and other classmates. It's really not right, so that's why I don't join any teams. I am not so—so much into the school.

Kuldip complained that her teenaged cousin was under the negative influence of U.S.-born peers who smoke and cut classes. She preferred to steer clear of her peer social world, focusing instead on academic achievement and her family. She told me that her family is extremely important to her: "I am totally different in school than I am at home. At home I talk much more. In school I am much more shy and I just—I don't really care about the way I look in school. And at home I do—I make sure I dress properly." When I asked Kuldip about the difference between her school and home personas, she told me that at school "I have an objective. I have a goal. I want to get my education. . . . I study a lot, and that's what I come to school for and that's why I don't really care about friends." She seems to have made a conscious decision to engage only the adult social world at school, through academic achievement, and to ignore the peer social world around her as best as she can. Kuldip's family may substitute for the social relationships that her peers have with one another. She told me that "I am not too much into friends and, you know, hanging out with them and stuff. I really—I'm really a person who likes my family. I am really homely."

Still, Kuldip was not following the model of womanhood that her mother demonstrated, and her emphasis on family did not stop her from rejecting a traditional Indian model for marriage. She planned to complete college and become an accountant, and was critical of her older sister being engaged to be married—through a traditional Indian arranged introduction—at age twenty-three, which Kuldip felt was too young. Her emphasis on academic achievement, too, did not preclude her from critiquing her teachers: in her survey Kuldip agreed that teachers sometimes discriminate against students in her school on the basis of race. She expressed very American tastes in actors and music: Nicole Kidman, Jewel, and Shania Twain. She did not talk about the bhangra that many of her Indian peers in Queens enjoyed.

The examples of Stacey, Terry, and Kuldip show different emphases and priorities. Moreover, the contrast between Stacey and the others shows that some students are more skilled than others at the balancing act between pursuing academic achievement and maintaining peer status. Kuldip seemed to have consciously chosen to focus exclusively on academics, while Terry seemed unwilling to sacrifice peer respect and status for academic achievement. None of them, however, saw her or his peer culture as opposed to mainstream society; indeed, almost all students I met expressed conventional desires to do well in high school, attend college, and build successful careers. Furthermore, students admired peers who had high peer social status yet also did well academically. This is what most youth aspired to, though they often found it difficult to make the choices most conducive to achieving all of their goals.

It is not a coincidence that Terry is an Afro-Caribbean young man and Kuldip an Indian young woman. Black students had more to gain by engaging in their peer social worlds, because of the identification of black racial identity as cool, hip, and high-status and because of hip-hop's identity as "black." On the other hand, Indian students could incur peer accusations of racial inauthenticity if they engaged too closely with black-identified popular culture, and their own ethnic identities were stereotyped as weak and foreign. Hence, black students' engagement with peer culture led to greater status gains, perhaps encouraging them to emphasize it more. In addition, for boys, defending one's pride and self-respect not only gained peer status but also served to maintain masculine identities; this was not true for girls' gender identities, and it may explain boys' greater overall emphasis on peer status, sometimes to the detriment of meeting adult cultural expectations in school.

Nevertheless, I found that Afro-Caribbean, Indian, Indo-Caribbean, and white students seemed to behave similarly with respect to homework. On the survey, each group's median response to the question about how much time they usually spend on homework was "30–90 minutes." However, ethnicity did seem to impact behaviors affecting academic achievement *within* school, aside from peer and teacher conflicts. When asked on the survey how frequently they skipped school, 44 percent of Afro-Caribbean students admitted to sometimes skipping, in contrast to just 18 percent of Indian students.[1] This evidence suggests that peer status considerations may have a stronger impact on in-school behaviors that negatively impact academic achievement than they do on out-of-school behaviors, supporting the proposition that peer status considerations drive seemingly anti-school behaviors among the teens I encountered.

WHITHER DOWNWARD ASSIMILATION?

In chapter 1, I outline the predominant theory of immigrant assimilation in the United States today, segmented assimilation theory (Portes, Fernández-Kelly, and Haller, 2005; Portes and Rumbaut, 2001; Portes and Zhou, 1993, 1997). This theory gives both structural and cultural explanations for the divergent paths into American society taken by the second generation. The problem with existing theories of youth cultures among the second generation is their lack of attention to the *meanings* teens themselves make out of their cultural choices. That is, the theories treat cultural products and behaviors as unitary in meaning rather than polysemic and dynamic. It is easy to draw conclusions regarding negative orientations toward school when teens fight in school, come late to class, and wear clothes that commonly create fear in adults; however, I have shown that the quick assumptions made by many adults are often wrong and too simplistic. I urge that social scientists interested in youth cultures spend more time on how particular cultural tastes and practices figure in the larger picture of children's lives and understandings.

The proposition that proximity to inner-city culture leads to adversarial cultures among some second-generation youth is a weak explanation for the downward assimilation trajectory. Second-generation teens are picking up on more *global* than *local* popular cultures, as evidenced by the influences on their styles and the strong similarity between New York and London second-generation teens; their interests in black-identified music and style do not coincide with anti-achievement orientations; and they express positive outlooks and attitudes toward school.

If not oppositional peer cultures, then, what *does* explain downward assimilation? What leads to the poor academic outcomes in both schools of this research? Evidence in this chapter suggests that conflicts between peer culture and academic achievement may impact some teens, despite their best intentions. In addition to these cultural factors, the *structural* factors outlined by downward assimilation theory influence the poor outcomes that Portes, Rumbaut, Zhou, and their colleagues have found among certain second-generation groups, and indeed, these may have the greatest impact (Portes et al., 2005). It may be the case, for example, that the organizational structure of schools (e.g., tracking and lack of personal support) and school rules and curricula that exclude minorities impede achievement for certain minority youth (see Chin and Phillips, 2004; Conchas, 2001; Flores-González, 2002; Gillborn, 2005; Gillborn and Youdell, 2005; López, 2002; Majors, 2001a; Mehan et al., 1994; Valenzuela, 1999); that an implicit code of conduct unfamiliar to minority youth is expected but not articulated in schools (Bourdieu and Passeron, 1977; Delpit, 1995); or that the behaviors of youth of different ethnic, race, and class groups are similar but the consequences of certain behaviors are different for different groups (see Kasinitz et al., 2008; Waldinger and Feliciano, 2004). A recent formulation of segmented assimilation theory does suggest that predominantly structural factors determine outcomes for the second generation: "Downward assimilation does not emerge . . . as a deliberate path, but as an outgrowth of a web of constraints, bad luck, and limited opportunities. . . . Results [from the Children of Immigrants Longitudinal Study] are almost frightening in revealing the power of structural factors—family human capital, family composition, and modes of incorporation—in shaping the lives of these young men and women" (Portes et al., 2005, 1031–1032). Perhaps, then, scholars should rethink the oppositional culture explanation for downward assimilation.

CHAPTER 7

Ethnic and Racial Boundaries

More of the black people [are popular], because . . . black
people stand up and all the Indians that get joked on, they
. . . just keep it aside and go on the next day.

—Kevin, Afro-Caribbean New Yorker

[The popular kids] are the hottest group. . . . They have the
latest styles, latest fashions, and they wear the latest trainers
and the latest hairstyles, mostly like that.

—Nicole, Afro-Caribbean Londoner

In previous chapters I have described a youth culture in which peer
status looms large, in addition to high academic aspirations. I have
shown how wearing the right clothes, listening to hip-hop music,
observing racial authenticity, adopting black racial identity, and maintaining one's respect can all lead to peer status. In this chapter I move
from cultural products, behaviors, meanings, and identities and how
these influence peer status to how youth culture organizes itself in the
realm of *social groups and relationships*. Given that peer status matters
so much to students, what social divisions do we see in their schools?
Who has high peer status, and who has low? In chapters 3 and 4 I
describe how black racial identity sometimes led to higher peer status
and, conversely, how Indian identity could lead to low peer status
and even racial discrimination from peers. In this chapter, I take a closer
look at how students saw the boundaries of their social lives and how
these boundaries differed between New York and London.

The relationship between cultural and social life is complex. I draw
from sociologist of culture Michele Lamont's analysis of the *symbolic
boundaries* between social groups—that is, the "lines that people draw

to categorize people" (Lamont, 1992; see also Lamont and Molnár, 2002). To better understand what constitutes cultural capital in particular social worlds, Lamont analyzes the criteria by which social groups define who is "in" and "out" of their respective groups. I wanted to understand how teens in multiethnic environments divide themselves, what criteria they use to determine status in their peer cultures, and how these criteria compare between New York and London. I paid particular attention to the degree to which race and ethnicity played a role in dividing up the student bodies into social groups. Previous studies have analyzed the "boundary blurring" of ethnic groups in the realms of citizenship, language, religion, and skin color (Alba, 2005; Alba and Nee, 2003; Wimmer, 2008a; Zolberg and Long, 1999). Zolberg and Long (1999) define boundary blurring as "the tolerance of multiple memberships and an overlapping of collective identities hitherto thought to be separate and mutually exclusive" (8–9). Here I integrate Lamont's emphasis on investigating the distinctions that people make (for example, ethnic boundaries versus boundaries based on taste preferences) with Alba's (2005), Zolberg and Long's (1999), and Wimmer's (2008b) discussions of state institutional influences on specifically *ethnic* and *racial* boundaries. I do so by considering the kinds of boundaries drawn by teens in multiethnic schools rather than focusing solely on *ethnic* boundaries, and by looking at how not only national-level dynamics but also *school structures* influence those boundaries.

The school contexts of this research provided an interesting laboratory for an analysis of ethnic and racial boundaries among the second generation in school, because both are ethnically diverse and neither is dominated numerically by any particular ethnic or racial group. We know that racial integration in school can have dramatic positive effects on the academic achievement in school and college of minority students, especially African Americans (Crain and Mahard, 1978; Dawkins and Braddock, 1994; Hallinan and Williams, 1990; Massey and Fischer, 2006; Trent, 1997; Yun and Kurlaender, 2004). Furthermore, the classic "contact hypothesis" of reducing racial prejudice holds that interracial contact leads to less prejudice between groups, assuming that the groups have equal status, that they share common goals, and that any prior prejudice was not extreme (Allport, 1954; Hewstone and Brown, 1986). Given the contact hypothesis's suggestion that integration decreases prejudice under the right circumstances, we might expect that school integration weakens the symbolic boundaries between ethnic and racial groups, as well. I found, however, that not only the ethnoracial makeup of the student body but also the organization of schools affects the degree to which students of different ethnic backgrounds interact, form relationships, and distinguish "us" from "them" along racial lines. The cross-national comparison of this research demonstrates the ways that school structure promotes or prevents full racial integration and, more generally, speaks to institutional influences on the symbolic boundaries in a society.

Up to this point I have described remarkable similarity between the youth cultures of London's and New York's second generation. In terms of popular culture, hip-hop has become a global currency for hipness and status among urban teenagers, in contrast to the local, race-based underground culture it started as more than thirty years ago. Still, there were differences between New York and London youth. Race and ethnicity were much more significant in New York's social life than in London's, but not in the spreading of countercultures or popular culture. Although the multiethnic environment in both cities led to some boundary blurring between ethnic and racial groups, the highly anonymous structure of York High School, in addition to the unique history of race relations and migration in the United States, led New Yorkers to define their in- and out-groups much more in terms of race and ethnicity than did students in London, whose symbolic boundaries were more diffuse.

MAPPING THE SOCIAL LANDSCAPE: SCHOOL SOCIAL GROUPS

Rather than assume a salient boundary marker such as ethnicity, I asked youth themselves about the social groups at their schools, to elicit what boundaries they themselves see. Sixty-six percent of students interviewed in New York described *race* groups when asked to describe the social groups at their school, in contrast to just 20 percent in London. Although the New York City Board of Education compiles school statistics by the race and ethnicity categories commonly used by U.S. social scientists, students defined their race and ethnicity categories quite differently from those used in official statistics. They called themselves and each other African American, black, Punjabi, West Indian, Guyanese (sometimes "Guyanese and Trini"), Indian, Spanish, Puerto Rican, and white (sometimes Italian). "Black" meant African American and Afro-Caribbean; "Guyanese" or "Guyanese-Trini" usually meant Indo-Caribbean ("Trini" being short for Trinidadian); "Indian" could mean parents or ancestors (in the case of Indo Caribbeans) from India; and "Spanish" meant Hispanic. When I asked students to describe the different social groups at school, these were the labels they most frequently used. Many responses were similar to Indo-Caribbean Irfan's:

> N: If you had to describe the different social groups in school, like who hangs out with who, what would you say they are?
>
> I: There is the Guyanese groups, like . . . mostly by where you come from. All the Spanish people hang out together here. Everybody where you have come from.

Like many of his peers, Irfan interpreted a question about social groups to be about ethnicity, which suggests that ethnicity was the most salient group boundary in New York. Note that "where you have come from" probably means ancestry, not birthplace, given that more of Irfan's peers are second generation than are immigrants.

An incident in New York in the school auditorium illustrates the high salience of ethnicity there:

> The class met in the auditorium today to practice for their upcoming skits on *Of Mice and Men*. Before class started but after the late bell rang, students were milling about at the front of the auditorium seating area. Richard, who is Dominican, was running around, smiling. He went by jokingly yelling, "Don't ever mess with a Puerto Rican! Don't ever mess with a Puerto Rican!" He was running away from a Puerto Rican friend. And then he stopped and looked around, asking, "Who's Dominican? Who's Dominican? You're Dominican, right [to a boy from another class sitting in the audience]? Come help me!" (Fieldnotes, April 29, 2004)

Richard's joke about whom he could rely on when threatened by a peer of a different ethnic background illustrates the primary affinities and divisions related to race and ethnicity in New York.

Responses in London to the question about school social groups were more diffuse. Teens in London reported three main categories of social groups at school: gender, proximate groups—their Form Classes (similar to American homeroom classes) and what they did during lunchtime, and consumption groups—tastes in music and style. Twenty-four percent of London interview respondents named gender groups when asked about their school's social groups. I was struck when I began my research in London by the gender segregation in students' social patterns. When they could choose seats, inevitably boys would end up on one side of the room and girls on the other. In the schoolyard during lunchtime, many boys played soccer in exclusively male games, while other boys played handball on the school wall. In contrast, girls often socialized on the picnic benches, in the hallways, or at other female-dominated areas. Even students who insisted that their school had no social divisions said that students did separate by gender. For example, Vimal told me, "Everyone hangs out with each other, like, but mostly separated by, boys hang out with mostly boys and girls with girls."

Perhaps this separation resulted from their social groups having developed at an early age, in Year 7 (age eleven), when the class first comes together at the start of British secondary school, in contrast to when American high schools start, at age fourteen, grade 9. Also, I never saw girls playing sports during school breaks in London—neither girls' groups nor individual girls among a group of boys—so leisure activities during school downtime could also have led to greater gender separation at Long Meadow than at York High.

In addition to gender, one-third of London students identified Form Classes, or groups within their Form Classes, as social groups. Members of a Form Class spend their whole school day together until Year 10 (age fourteen), when science classes become tracked and students begin to take electives. After Year 10 students still spend most of the day with peers from their Form Class, and even Year 11 students have English class with their Form Class, which most have known since Year 7.[1] Hence, students in most Form Classes grew to be quite close and fond of each other, even if the inevitable occasional fights developed. One Year 11 Indian girl, Angela, explained how close her Form Class was: "My class is like, [we] love each other. I mean really tight. I don't know, we just click. All of us just click with each other. . . . When we are in trouble, our class always . . . stick up for us." This closeness formed in the course of being together for five consecutive years. A talkative girl with high grades, Angela enjoyed sharing her Indian culture with peers and learning about their ethnic backgrounds. On Diwali, one of the most significant Hindu holidays, as her class left afternoon registration to go home for the day, Angela shouted happily, "Happy Diwali, everyone!" Another day during gym class, I sat with Angela and some other girls from her Form Class, including Sharon, a white working-class girl I also knew. As Angela and Sharon were chatting, I suddenly heard Angela exclaim loudly, "You mean I've known you for five years and I don't know your roots?! Now, tell me, I want to know about you!" Angela told me in her interview that she was going to be very sad at the end of the school year because her Form Class would be breaking up and everyone would be going their separate ways—some to Sixth Form, some to work, and some to college.

When mentioning the Form Class, some (like Angela) used it as the unit of analysis, and others, such as Frank, spoke of within-class social groups. Frank was a white Year 10 student. When asked to explain his school's social groups, he said:

> F: I don't know, really don't how to explain it, but you know Jason? . . . Yeah, his table sit like at the back. And then you got my table sitting like right next to his. . . . And then we got all the like people who—geeks, sort of. [They] sit along near the window, near the front of the board. . . . And then we have got the girls' tables there, and then, like Lucy, Habiba, and Lisa would sit in the middle.
>
> N: How would you describe those groups?
>
> F: My group is just the people who play football [soccer]. . . . Depends what classroom it is. Say if it's in maths. I will probably sit with the people who play football, like Derek and John and Vimal. But if I was in a different class, like sociology, I would sit next to Jason.

Frank's description shows that his social world at school is his Form Class—all of the students he mentions are from his Form Class. Frank bases his social group on his lunchtime activity (soccer), but when he sits in an elective class and not all of his classmates are with him (sociology), he sits with the one student who *is* from his Form Class, Jason. I observed this seating arrangement in many elective classes—students usually sat with peers from their own Form Class, regardless of taste preferences, ethnicity/race, or other kinds of social divisions.

As Frank explained, in addition to identifying with their Form Classes, students in London formed social groups during school breaks, according to their activities during those times—20 percent described lunch activities when defining the school's social groups. The entire school had two breaks during the school day (one thirty minutes, the other forty minutes), during which time all students were free to eat a snack or lunch in the cafeteria, play in the large schoolyard, sit in the library, use a computer in the computer lab, or even roam the school's hallways since no classes were in session. One's activity during breaks was quite important to defining one's social identity.

Finally, some London students (24 percent) described taste groups at school. Abe, a seventeen-year-old white Sixth Form student who

TABLE 13   STUDENT IDENTIFICATION OF SCHOOL SOCIAL
GROUPS *(Percentages)*

	Social Groups
New York	Race/ethnicity (66)
	Popularity (16)
	Taste (16)
London	Form Class divisions (33)
	Gender (24)
	Taste (24)
	Lunchtime activities (20)
	Race/ethnicity (20)

NOTE: Although there were 120 interview respondents, because of time constraints, some were not asked the questions on social groups and popularity because preliminary interviews with a range of students addressed questions regarding school social groups and peer hierarchies. I did not include preliminary interview data in the final results. Percentages do not add up to 100, because many students mentioned more than one kind of group and others gave infrequent responses not listed here.

SOURCE: Interview data, *n* = 86.

had moved to London from the north of England a few years prior, described the school's social groups in terms of music:

> I would say you could almost separate it with like music. You have got, like, people that like more Americanized music like hip-hop and stuff like that. Then you have got people that like garage, proper English garage. And then you have got people who like rock music and like [a] couple of people that like classical music. And you probably could go to the different groups because you can obviously—you can see them even when they are wearing [school] uniform, you can still see them. People would—there is one girl I see and she wears like big boots and she has got pink hair, stuff like that. She likes rock music, and there is, like, kind of people who wear their trousers a bit baggy, even if it's uniform and stuff like that, you can see. So I'd say that's how you could separate it.

Recall that in Sixth Form (ages sixteen to eighteen) students no longer had to wear uniforms and so could more clearly mark their music preferences. Abe points out the congruence in London between style of dress, music tastes, and social groups. After Form Class groups, taste groupings were, along with gender, the most common groups described by London youth in interviews.

Although identified much less than in New York, race and ethnicity were significant for social groups in London in two ways. First, as in New York, some students named racial or ethnic groups (20 percent).

Second, race was frequently a part of the taste categories named by 24 percent of London youth, in that groups based on taste preferences were often racialized. For example, although many white and Indian students listened to hip-hop music, hip-hop was seen as "black" music, for its African American origins. On the other hand, rock and punk were seen as "white" music, because of their association with white artists. Grace, a Year 11 student who lived with her Nigerian mother and English stepfather but spent a lot of time in the United States with her Afro-Caribbean father, told me:

> It's like, there is all black in my group. . . .There is one mixed-race person and there is one white person, but the white person . . . she is more, like, you know, black. The way she behaves is like a black person, and she likes black things. . . . And then you have the all white girls group. It's a mixed— it's got, oh, you might get one black girl in it. She behaves like more like a white girl. . . . But then you can get white people that act like black people, black people who act like white people.

Students like Grace defined racial categories in terms of taste and behaviors, rather than by the race of individuals in the group. These socially defined groups are labeled "black" and "white" *because of the cultural heritage of the genre's contents*, in contrast to New York groups, which were defined *by the race or ethnicity of their members*. The "black" behaviors Grace alludes to are aspects of popular youth culture, including tastes, speech patterns, and interactional styles.

Fuzzy Lines on the Map: Blurred Boundaries in Social Groups

In addition to the specific responses described above, more than one-third of respondents in both cities described loose social categories in their schools or said that they themselves did not adhere to existing social groups. Thirteen percent in New York and 22 percent in London said that in fact there were no firm social groups in their schools. For example, when asked about her school's social groups, Rukshana, a Muslim 1.5-generation Indo-Trinidadian girl in New York, said:

> It be like, Hispanics hang out with Hispanics, blacks hang out with blacks. Indian people hang out with Indian people. They don't mix and match that much. . . . I mean, they talk—I mean everybody talks. But just that they mostly keep to their culture, that is. They would socialize with everybody. This school is very diverse and everybody talks to everybody, but mostly they would, like, you know, feel comfortable talking to their [own group]—but it's mixed, everybody is with everybody. It's just hectic. You cannot go,

TABLE 14 FLUID SOCIAL GROUPS

	New York	London
Percent saying the school had no firm social groups	13	22
Percent saying that they themselves did not belong to any of the social groups	24	13
Total	37	35

SOURCE: Interview data, $n = 86$.

like, on third floor you don't see like only black people there, no. It's black, Indian, everybody. Everybody's there.

Rukshana played on the school's tennis team and always covered her head with a *hijab*. On the day I interviewed her, she wore track pants, boots, and a loose-fitting short-sleeved T-shirt, and she told me that on a scale of 1 to 10, sports are a 9 in her life. When discussing dating, she admitted to having stayed away from black men for a while, based on her experiences with racial discrimination from black peers when she was younger; this attitude had recently changed, however, when she met a young black man whom she described as "nice, handsome, and black." At first, Rukshana, a high-achieving student, seems to contradict herself in the above quote, suggesting that students are both segregated and integrated. However, her words resonated with my observations at York High School. Students congregated in the cafeteria and in the school's neighborhood in single-race groups, but in the hallways and even sometimes in public spaces near the school I also often saw students in mixed-ethnicity groups. Often, just when I started to despair at the level of segregation by ethnic group in New York, I would observe interethnic friendships and social groups. The opposite also happened: when I would start to feel that students' cosmopolitanism and diversity of friendships and trust crossed ethnic boundaries, I would notice the opposite. When I looked more analytically, however, I found both phenomena—ethnicity played an important role in students' lives, and they talked about race and ethnicity a lot. However, they were flexible enough in their identities to draw upon the cultural tools they learned from their peers' ethnic backgrounds. Many reported that they enjoyed learning about other cultures from their peers. Ethnicity thus had a strong presence, but teens were also quite cosmopolitan in their relationships to other cultures (see also Warikoo, 2004a).

Like students in New York, students in London were quick to point out that the school social groups were fluid. Beatrice, a white Sixth Form student (age sixteen), explained:

> I think one of things I quite like about this school is that it's not like . . . really obvious defined groups of people who, you know, are labeled in certain ways and they only hang out with certain people and things like that. It's not like that at all. I mean, obviously there are friendship groups and things like that, but not to the extent where it's like, "Oh, I won't talk to you." . . . I think everyone is kind of mixed and I think that comes a lot from the different ethnic groups as well. . . . It's nice, I kind of like it.

Beatrice points out that the social boundaries between groups are quite loose and not based on ethnicity.

In addition to the students reporting fluid boundaries between social groups, others reported that they themselves did not fit into the social group typology they had described to me. During interviews, after students named the different social groups, I asked them to tell me which group they belonged to. Twenty-four percent in New York and 13 percent in London said that they themselves did not belong to a particular group. For example, Jennifer, a twenty-year-old senior in New York whose parents are Puerto Rican and Afro-Trinidadian, told me:

> In this school, from what I have noticed, a lot of Puerto Ricans hang out with each other. A lot of Italians hang out with each other. And a lot of African Americans hang out with each other. And it's like, it's crazy because everybody should just hang out with everybody, that's the way how I feel. Everybody should just branch out. Even though you don't know the person, get to know everybody. It doesn't make any sense to just be in your own little group and laugh and having fun. I feel everyone should branch out, get to know everybody.

I asked Jennifer which group she was in: "Well, I would be in all of them. It really doesn't matter to me, just as long as they don't stink and they have a good sense of humor." Jennifer's sentiments suggest that reaching out beyond one's ethnic group is the morally correct thing to do.

Boys echoed these sentiments. Sanjay, an Indian ninth-grade student in New York who helped his mother run the convenience stores his father had left them when he passed away, described a similar situation when I asked him about his school's social groups: "Some Punjabi people hang out with Punjabi, blacks with blacks, Spanish with Spanish. I like hanging out with mixed, not like all Punjabis, but all others, everybody mixed." Dan, an Afro-Guyanese student who had come to the United States at age six, explained to me that the difference between his cosmopolitan tastes and his friends' boundary maintenance sometimes led to conflicts:

N: So which groups at school do you feel most comfortable with?

D: There's not really one group that I feel comfortable with at school. Sometimes I might hang out with the goths or I might hang out with the thugs or what not. Every time they ask me a question, I try and blow it off because it might be racist: "Oh, why you hang out with these people? Man, they are crazy! Those white boys are nuts!" . . . And my white friends are like, you know, "Why you hang out with those thugs?" I am like, "What are you talking about? They are my friends, just like how you are my friends! It doesn't really matter."

Like Jennifer, quoted above, Dan sees being open to myriad cultural influences and a diverse set of friends as the morally correct mode of interacting with peers. It may be the case that although most youth prefer diverse friendships, the New York school structure creates a situation in which students gravitate to their own ethnic groups for security and connection.

In London, when I asked Terry, a Year 10 Afro-Caribbean, about school social groups, he told me of his wanderings during lunchtime: "There is groups, but people, me personally, I don't just hang around with one person. Me, I like to move, like, so I keep in touch with all my friends. So I might be with one group that'll be speaking, then I go to another group speaking, might play football with some of my friends. . . . I don't like stick with one particular people." I asked Terry how the groups are different: "Some might be just sitting down, talking. Some might be playing football. Some might be doing different stuff, like in music room." Terry, like many of his peers, defines the social groups by break-time activities. Yet he sees himself as transcending group boundaries, and he perceives peers to have more rigid cultural boundaries than him. Youth like Terry valued omnivorous social networks and preferred to see themselves as transcending group boundaries—both in New York and in London—rather than being confined to one group. They felt a sense of self-worth in their willingness to engage with noncoethnic peers, and expressed frustration with others' lack of understanding of other groups. This finding is similar to research suggesting that contemporary elites value "cultural omnivorousness" over single, elite taste preferences in such things as opera or high art (Bryson, 1996; B. Erickson, 1996; Peterson and Kern, 1996; Peterson and Simkus, 1992; Warde, Wright, and Gayo-Cal, 2007). These findings suggest value placed in omnivorous *social networks* by the (non-elite) students I met.

As demonstrated through my mapping of social life above, the multiethnic school setting led to blurred ethnic boundaries—fuzzy map lines—and a cosmopolitanism among teens in both schools (see also Warikoo, 2004a). Many respondents drew a moral boundary around the willingness to engage peers of diverse ethnic backgrounds, and in spite of the boundaries they saw around them, many youth preferred a diversity of friendships.

MAPPING WHO IS ABOVE AND BELOW: PEER STATUS

Another way to understand symbolic boundaries is to ask about the status hierarchy (Lamont, 1992, 2000; Lamont and Molnár, 2002). I asked students to assess the status hierarchy of their schools and then to identify where in the hierarchy they were located as individuals. The difference between London's and New York's peer status hierarchies further illuminates the subtle difference in the salience of race and ethnicity between the two cities.

What is a good measure of peer status? Max Weber (1968) defined status in mainstream society as *prestige* or *social honor,* and he differentiated status groups from class groups by pointing out that status groups share a *lifestyle.* In a more recent study, Murray Milner (2004) found that youth define status as popularity. In his study of the status systems of high school students, Milner asked college students to describe the status systems of their high schools; in doing so, many operationalized status as popularity, indicating that popularity is, in lay terminology, synonymous with status among youth. For example, one boy from Massachusetts explained in an essay:

> The social scene . . . was split broadly into two extreme groups commonly called the "jocks" and the "freaks." . . . The jocks were not necessarily all athletes . . . rather they were the "cooler" and more popular students. . . . Although the different cliques were not openly ranked, most people would agree that the jocks were the more prestigious, popular, and "cooler" students by the traditional high school standards. (Milner, 2004, 41)

Because I was concerned with students' perceptions of status among peers, I asked them about popularity. I asked students to describe the most popular and least popular groups at school and to explain why those groups were popular or unpopular.[2] My findings diverge from previous scholars who have written about what influences status among youth and who suggest that participation in sports for boys and cheerleading for girls play an important role in popularity and peer status (Adler and Adler, 1998; Coleman, 1961; Eder and Kinney, 1995; Merten, 1997). This divergence is likely due to the infrequency of extracurriculars in British as compared to U.S. schools; the great difficulty of scheduling after-school activities at York High given the staggered scheduling (necessary because of school overcrowding); and the great ethnic and racial diversity in both schools, in contrast to the settings of most previous research on peer status.

Peer Status in New York: The Continuing Salience of Race and Ethnicity

When I asked New York students to tell me about the popular groups in their school, 43 percent mentioned one or more race or ethnic groups. Most commonly, the popular race group was black students, followed by Hispanics. The high peer status of black students stemmed in part from popular hip-hop being racialized as black. Black students who prioritized defending self-pride and being tough along with having hip-hop tastes and style occupied the top of the status hierarchy, according to all ethnoracial groups and both boys and girls. Black identity's popularity was sometimes related to the perception that black students engaged in delinquent behaviors. For example, when I asked Maurice, an Indo-Trinidadian student who had come to New York at age ten, who was most popular in his school, he told me: "Black students are the most popular, because they think they're hard, they like to fight. They make people scared of them . . . by the way they dress. It's different, extremely big clothes—pants down to their knees, they smoke weed, carry knives and guns. . . . Also cigarette behind ear. People are scared of them, so they want to hang out with them so they don't get beat up." Maurice points out that peers look to those who are feared for protection from bullying.

Black identity also had privileged status among girls. Nikki, a ninth-grade student whose African American mother is from the South and whose father is Afro-Trinidadian, told me that the social groups at school were the "popular group," "middle group," and "unpopular group." Nikki placed herself in the "middle group." I asked her what behavior was typical of the popular group: "They're disrespectful. Like if they see you in the hallway and they don't like you, they will push you. Or if they just see you, they will still push you no matter what. Or sometimes, like, say you bought something before them [e.g., the latest sneakers], they will fight you. Or it's like, if you sit near them on the bus, they will be like, 'Oh, she mad [very] ugly!' " I asked Nikki what race the popular students tend to be: "Oh, mostly black."[3] Although Nikki did not use race to describe the popular students, she quickly responded to my query about it. Despite being black, Nikki identified herself with the "middle group." Both David and Nikki imply that most of the popular students are black, not that most black students are in the popular group.

Many students, like David and Nikki, put a negative spin on their descriptions of the popular students at school. This perhaps is due to the practice of according popularity and status not to those whom peers *like,* but whom they *respect.*[4] It resembles the ways that working-class men express disdain for upper-class men, as Michèle Lamont (2000) has documented in her study of the ways working-class men in the United States and France draw boundaries between "us" and "them." Popular youth have the power to enforce conformity to peer culture norms through, for example, not befriending those perceived as wearing uncool clothes or not comporting themselves in a "cool" way. Even the most disliked individuals can still be seen as popular and high-status through a collective respect for their status among peers.

"Spanish" (Hispanic) fell just below "black" in the peer status hierarchy. Simone, a Jamaican student in New York, succinctly explained the groups and the relationship to ethnicity and status:

N: If you had to describe the different social groups at school, what would you say they are?

S: It would be the popular group, nonpopular group, and like in between.

I then asked Simone which students fell into the groups she described.

S: Well, most of the Indians . . . [are in] like the nonpopular group.

N: And what about the African American kids?

S: Yeah, they would be, like, in the popular group.

N: And the Spanish kids?

S: They will probably, probably be in between.

Here, Simone places the categories of Indian, Spanish, and African American in a clear status hierarchy. Like Nikki, although Simone is

Afro-Caribbean, she describes herself as being in the middle group, rather than the popular group she later described to me as "bullies."

When I asked students in New York to describe the *unpopular* students in their school, 46 percent mentioned race groups, and of those the majority mentioned Indians or Punjabis—this was more than half of the students who gave a specific answer to the question (other than "I don't know" or "No one is unpopular").[5] The other group mentioned more than once (but half as much as Indians) was whites. Some joking banter I recorded in school illustrates the stereotype of whites as uncool:

> At the start of class Lucy walked in late. She sat down across from Indo-Caribbean Amy, and Amy yelled, "Ew, you got the pink Jordans [Air Jordan sneakers]?!" Lucy, who participates a lot in class and has stylishly long curly hair, said, "Ye-ah! I wear pink all the time, so why not the pink Jordans?!" Amy said, "I know, but still! Ew!" The boy who yesterday told me he is Colombian said jokingly, "She got no style, because she white!" The girl didn't seem fazed by them, and it seemed to all be a joke. (Fieldnotes, May 14, 2004)

Although a friendly joke, the comment illustrates the association of white identity with lack of style, which leads to low peer status.

Questions about discrimination made the low status of Indians clearer, as described in detail in chapter 4. When I asked Khaleed if he ever experienced or witnessed racial discrimination, the Indo-Guyanese student told me that he didn't experience it himself, but he observed it at school: "Right in school, right here, the Punjabi kids, the Indian ones who respect their culture and are abiding by it and wearing whatever they are wearing, they are being discriminated [against], which I think is a very sad thing." I asked Khaleed who is picking on them: "You find a lot of kids, like ignorant kids. You find from all different racial backgrounds, all different. You find a Spanish kid, you will find some Africans and even some Indian kids who know about the culture, they would pick on them, which is really sad." Khaleed's response resonated with my own observations. I heard some Indians express disdain for those who wore turbans, perhaps because they felt it led to discrimination that affected all Indians. Youth gain the zero-sum commodity of status by bringing down the status of others through put-downs and insults (Milner, 2004).

Twenty-three percent of New York students described as unpopular those students who do not speak much, who have no friends, or who do not socialize outside school hours. As with popularity, this behavior was racialized by some, in this case as Indian. For example, Gwen, an Afro-Caribbean girl in New York, told me that Indians are unpopular at her school because they leave right after school and do not participate in after-school activities: "[The] Indian group . . . are not that popular. Because they kinda like keep to themselves. They don't really become involved in sports and stuff, and they, like, after school's done, they are out of here. They are not involved in anything." Gwen told me that many of her friends were Indian and that she didn't have many black friends. During a different part of her interview, she mentioned that she ran on the varsity track team and that many of her friends were athletes and also were popular. This apparent contradiction illustrates the dynamism of social groups and the degree to which students racialized groups yet saw individuals as exceptions to the patterns they perceived. Gwen may have seen the unpopular group as mostly Indians, even if she thought that not *all* Indians were in the unpopular group.

Descriptions of popularity and unpopularity in New York illustrate the interplay of race and peer culture in determining peer social status. Peers might, for example, assume an Indian student does not socialize outside class and hence label her unpopular, unless she demonstrates otherwise. This is the converse of the mechanism for popularity, whereby black students were stereotyped as having the toughness and correct style and tastes to earn high peer status, unless they demonstrated otherwise. Students in London, as shown in the next section, demonstrated a similar interaction between race and other aspects of peer culture. As with social groups, however, race mattered relatively less in London.

Peer Status in London: Diffuse Responses

Londoners were twice as likely as New Yorkers to say that their school did not have popular groups or that they did not know what they would be. Those who did mention groups most commonly attributed popularity to students who were "known" or "loud" or were part of a large social group in school (31 percent); those who made popular taste and consumption choices (20 percent); individuals in their Form Classes (16 percent); or misbehavior or bullying (15 percent). Being sociable and well known was the most common response. For example, Tanya, a Londoner whose mother is Indian and father white English, told me that the popular students "might have loads of friends. Then they have friends from the other Years, which make them even bigger." She later

TABLE 15 HOW STUDENTS DEFINED POPULARITY *(Percentages)*

New York	Race/ethnicity (43)
	Misbehavior or bullying (37)
	Don't know or There are no popular groups (17)
London	Don't know or There are no popular groups (35)
	Known, loud, or in big social group (31)
	Taste (20)
	Form class individuals (16)
	Misbehavior or bullying (15)

NOTE: Percentages do not add up to 100, because many students mentioned more than one kind of group, and others gave responses not listed here.
SOURCE: Interview data, *n* = 86.

pointed out that some popular students are smart: "Some of them are clever ones, really clever. . . . As long as they have, like, mouth, which they could . . . chat a lot and they hang around." Tanya pointed out that some popular students were successful at academics but what mattered most for high status was being well known and loud.

Race was related to status in that hip-hop style had high status, and hip-hop was associated with black racial identity. In London, however, taste was more salient than race and ethnicity in determining peer status, as it was for delineating social groups there. Terry, an Afro-Caribbean Year 10 student, told me when I asked him what makes a student popular in his school: "That they are getting with the trend. They know about things. They know about the latest music. They know about the latest clothes. They know about the latest trainers. They know about slang. Just the way they—it's mainly about what they wear, and the way they act. Just like people might know more slang. People might dress more slick." Terry identified popular tastes, language, and behavior as leading to popularity. I then asked him about how race factors into popularity. He was of two minds: "I'm not sure. . . . Tend to be, because there is some that are white and—no, I think—I am not sure. I think black, I think black, because most people in this school, most people I know that seem to be popular, they are black. . . . Jason [a mixed-race student] is popular. But Chris is popular, and he is white. So there is some people that are white and popular too."

Although the popular students tended to have black-identified styles, race did not determine one's level of popularity. Rather, the mechanism by which most (but, crucially, not all) popular students were black was the greater propensity of black students to consume hip-hop style,

TABLE 16   HOW STUDENTS DEFINED WHO IS UNPOPULAR
(Percentages)

New York	Race/ethnicity (46): • 38% (of New York respondents) said Asian group • 19% said whites (including 1 Russian) Quiet, loner, no socializing (23) Don't know (19)
London	Quiet, loners (36) No one is unpopular (28) Don't know (19) Grungies (9) Race/ethnicity (4)

NOTE: Not all students were asked the questions on status and social groups at school. Furthermore, those who said, "I don't know" in response to the question on who was popular at school were not asked about who was unpopular. Hence, I show data from 73 students here. Percentages do not add up to 100, because many students mentioned more than one kind of group and others gave responses not listed here.

SOURCE: Interview data, *n* = 73.

because of hip-hop's black identity. Still, unlike New Yorkers, Londoners did not mention race when first asked about who was popular in their school.

In terms of low status, students in London most frequently described unpopular students as loners: 36 percent of students said that the unpopular students at school were the *quiet* ones or the students who were *alone* most of the time, or both. Aside from these responses, "grungies" (students preferring rock and/or punk music and the associated styles) were cited by 9 percent. Here also, London students emphasized race and ethnicity less than their New York counterparts did: only two students in London (4 percent) mentioned a racial or ethnic group when asked to describe the unpopular groups at school, in contrast to 46 percent in New York.

As with social groups, then, I found that ethnicity and race were more salient in New York than in London in determining the peer status hierarchy. In both cities black students were identified with popular tastes through hip-hop's African American roots and hence had higher status via taste preferences. However, race was the salient marker in New York, while a taste for "black" music and style (hip-hop) mattered more in London.

Coda: The Question of Subcultures and Peer Status

Does a singular status hierarchy explain the social relationships in these schools? Murray Milner (2004) found that large, racially diverse schools tend to have pluralistic status hierarchies, with race groups forming independent status hierarchies within the same school. In contrast, I found that a definitive status hierarchy encompassing *all* students existed in both cities. When I asked students about who was popular and unpopular in their schools, they pointed to this overall status hierarchy, rather than to popularity within a subgroup or subculture. Perhaps the large number of different groups in the schools I studied, in contrast to schools with two or at most three main groups, led to this difference from Milner's research.

Of course, subcultures and status hierarchies within those subcultures did exist to some extent. For example, the students who consumed punk and rock music and styles often rejected hip-hop and criticized it for being violent and misogynistic. In the overall school hierarchy, "grungy" was identified as low-status. However, internally a status hierarchy within the grungy subculture could develop, so that those with the most distinctive grungy style might have very low status in the overall school status hierarchy yet high status within the grungy subculture. I found evidence of this in London, where a Year 11 girl with pink and black–dyed hair who often dressed in black with big combat boots told me of her admiration of Lisa, a Sixth Form student she did not know personally but who had a similar style. When I interviewed Lisa, she told me of problems she had had with hip-hop–identified students who bullied her in school and who did not appreciate her unconventional style.

In contrast to students who rejected hip-hop in favor of punk and rock music and style, low-status Indians seemed to desire status in the overall peer hierarchy. On the one hand, knowledge of the latest bhangra music and styles would confer status in the Indian subculture but not in the overall peer status hierarchy. On the other hand, as detailed in chapter 3, Indians engaged the overall status hierarchy by, for example, consuming not only Indian but also hip-hop music and styles, most commonly opting for the hybrid hip-hop–bhangra genre of music. Perhaps this hybrid genre that blurred boundaries offered Indian students a forum to engage both popular culture and racial authenticity, while white students had no such forum and hence had to choose between "black" hip-hop, "white" rock and punk, and weak omnivorous tastes.

INTERACTIONS ACROSS RACIAL AND ETHNIC BOUNDARIES

The findings above suggest that the ethnoracial boundaries were stronger at York High School than at Long Meadow Community School. This was not just true of students' descriptions of school social groups and status groups. Race and ethnicity were also more likely to be a barrier to *individual social interactions* among students in New York than in London. Seventy-four percent of London youth surveyed said they "agree a lot" with the statement "In my school, students feel comfortable talking with students of other racial and ethnic groups." In contrast, just 42 percent of their New York counterparts agreed strongly. During in-depth interviews, I probed further into this question, asking respondents about themselves rather than about how their peers behaved. I asked students, "What groups in school do you feel most comfortable with?" and "What groups in school do you feel least comfortable with?" In New York more than one-third of respondents named ethnic or racial groups as those they are most comfortable with, and 20 percent of groups New Yorkers were uncomfortable with were ethnic or racial groups. In contrast, just one respondent in London named an ethnic or racial group in response to either question. The most common response in London to the question of which groups the respondent felt most comfortable with, after "none," was to name specific individuals in the student's Form Class (see table 17).

Dating preferences also illustrated New York youth's stronger ethnic and racial boundaries on the individual level: 54 percent in New York listed their own race, ethnicity, religion, or national origin in response to the open-ended question, "If you were to date someone, what race/ethnicity would you like him/her to be?" In contrast, just 35 percent in London listed coethnics as a preference for dating. The greater salience of ethnicity in New York led to same-ethnicity couples in New York consisting of two people with quite distinct styles and music tastes but the same ethnic background. For example, Indo-Guyanese Tina wore pink and black Converse sneakers to school every day, with black and hot-pink jelly bracelets and nail polish to match, signaling her taste

TABLE 17 "WHICH GROUPS AT SCHOOL DO YOU FEEL COMFORTABLE/
UNCOMFORTABLE WITH?" *(Percentages)*

	New York	London
Comfortable	Race/ethnicity (34)	None (29)
	None (31)	Form Class individuals (20)
		Race/ethnicity (2)
Uncomfortable	None (43)	None (56)
	Students who misbehave/ gangs (23)	Race/ethnicity (2)
	Race/ethnicity (20)	

NOTE: Percentages do not add up to 100, because many students mentioned more than one kind of group and others gave responses not listed here.
SOURCE: Interview data, $n = 86$.

for punk and rock music as well as skateboarding, all of which she described to me in her interview. I often saw Tina in the hallway with a boy who wore baggy jeans in a hip-hop style. During her interview, I asked Tina about this boy and learned that he is Indo-Guyanese, like her. She told me that she liked punk and rock music, and disliked "ghetto" music, in contrast to him, whom she identified as her boyfriend. I asked Tina why she preferred rock: "I like the beat and I like that it doesn't talk about, like, you know, the ghetto music, rap, it talks about killing and about girls, and they use girls in a negative way. In rock music they don't do that. . . . I don't really like rap and hip-hop and all that stuff." Although Tina felt strongly about the portrayal of women in rap music, it seemed not to matter to her that her partner had different taste in music:

N: And so is your boyfriend into punk, too?

R: He is half. . . . He is like, he is like both. He is both, a mixture, like ghetto and punk. . . . He is like half punk and half ghetto. Like he listens to rap, but he listens to rock.

Tina's connection to her boyfriend goes beyond their taste preferences, and she shares with him her ethnicity rather than her taste preferences.

New York students were also more likely to have close friends of their own ethnicity: when I asked students in interviews to name their closest friends, 82 percent of those named in New York were of the same ethnic group, compared to 68 percent of those named by London interview respondents.[6]

TABLE 18   SOCIAL INTERACTIONS

	New York	London
Agree a lot: "In my school, students feel comfortable talking with students of other racial and ethnic groups."	42%	74%
Prefer to date own race/ethnicity	54	35
Percentage of closest friends who were of same ethnicity	82	68

SOURCES: Survey data (*n* = 191) and interview data (*n* = 86).

Blurred Boundaries in Social Interaction

Although New Yorkers expressed greater barriers to interethnic social interaction, teens in both cities were overall quite comfortable with peers of different backgrounds. Ninety-four percent in London and 84 percent in New York agreed (either "a little" or "a lot") that "in my school, students feel comfortable talking with students of other racial and ethnic groups." In interviews, although New Yorkers were more likely to refer to racial barriers in describing the social groups at school with which they felt most or least comfortable, the most common response overall in both cities to the questions "What groups in school do you feel most comfortable with?" and "What groups in school do you feel least comfortable with?" was "none" (see table 17). Finally, in response to the open-ended survey question "If you were to date someone, what race/ethnicity would you like him/her to be?" more than one-third of respondents in both cities wrote in "Doesn't matter."

In fact, in London many who had an out-group preference for dating in fact preferred ambiguous ethnicity: 41 percent of survey respondents in London who did not put their own group or "Doesn't matter" in response to the open-ended question on race and dating wrote in "mixed race"; this was 11 percent of all the respondents in London.

TABLE 19   BLURRED BOUNDARIES IN SOCIAL INTERACTION

	New York	London
Agree a lot or agree a little: "In my school, students feel comfortable talking with students of other racial and ethnic groups."	84%	94%
Dating preference: doesn't matter	33	38

SOURCES: Survey data (*n* = 191).

Being quite literally between two cultures made mixed-race looks quite popular. Stan, a working-class white student who dressed in hip-hop style, was one who wrote "mixed race" in response to the open-ended survey question. In his interview, I asked Stan to explain his answer. He said: "I don't know. I just got something for mixed-race girls. I don't know. It's like I never said I am gonna like them, it's just something about them. . . . If I had my ideal girl, you know, [she would be] Alicia Keys or something like that."[7] Stan's answer resonates with the responses of many peers in London, including other whites as well as Afro-Caribbeans. The preferences of these youth resonate with a growing trend in popular culture in favor of mixed-ethnicity looks, called "ethnically ambiguous" in articles in Britain's *Observer* and the *New York Times* during the time of this research (Arlidge, 2004; La Ferla, 2003).

What explains the much greater salience of race and ethnicity in the symbolic boundaries drawn by New York teens than in those of London teens? Turning to this question in the following section, I identify three possible influences: (1) differences in school structure, (2) different histories of racial formation and segregation in the two cities, and (3) different histories of migration. Qualitative comparative research presents the problem of disentangling multiple causes of a particular outcome; that is, how can we identify with certainty which of these factors matters most, given that we cannot control for any of them between London and New York (Lieberson, 1992)? Although all three factors are likely to have an impact, the evidence I show strongly suggests that school structure plays an important role in the contrasting symbolic boundaries between students in the two sites.

THE IMPACT OF SCHOOL STRUCTURE ON SYMBOLIC BOUNDARIES

Recall that London students often used the Form Class as their social unit of analysis: 33 percent named Form Classes or subgroups thereof as their school's social groups; 16 percent named Form Class individuals as those who were popular in their school; and the Form Class was the most commonly cited group in response to the interview question "Which social groups in school do you feel most comfortable with?" Another 20 percent of Londoners identified school social groups by lunchtime activities. These findings suggest that the school structure at Long Meadow—specifically, students following a Form Class for the whole school day for five years and taking two daily schoolwide lunch breaks—has an influence on symbolic boundaries. Below I describe in more detail the contrasting school structures of Long Meadow and York High, both typical for their respective cities.

Secondary schools in Britain, which serve ages eleven to sixteen, are structured around a Form Class. First coming together in Year 7 (age eleven, the first year of secondary school), a Form Class has most subjects together for the whole school day, and for the next five years until its members at age sixteen finish secondary school. Although some members do have elective and tracked classes for particular subjects, the Form Class still dominates the educational experience for most British secondary students. Outside physical education, Long Meadow students encountered non–Form Class peers in tracked classes for the first time at age fourteen (Year 10), and in that Year, just one class a day was tracked (science). It was only in Sixth Form (ages sixteen to eighteen) that students were sorted by academic and vocational interests (and skills to the extent that some required remedial classes before starting college-track classes). The five years with their Form Class peers established the weak ethnic and racial boundaries before tracking could separate them by race and ethnicity at age sixteen. Indeed, when students were in non–Form Class classes, they tended to sit with their Form Class peers, as described earlier.

The Form Class structure led London students to bridge ethnic differences. Nathan, a white English student, explained that racial separation happened only in the early years in secondary school, before students got to know peers of other groups: "People, sometimes people do gang together with skin color. Though I don't really find that the case very much. That's only in Year 7, when people are just getting to know each other. So in this school, you quickly learn to become friends with all, all nationalities. Or you begin to go into the group which has very few friends." As Nathan explains, once students have a chance to form close relationships within their Form Class, they no longer feel the urge to cling to same-race peers. Nathan's description contrasts with the New York context, in which students never had the same chance to form those close bonds and hence more often stayed in the same-race groups that Nathan observed when his class first came together, in Year 7.

In addition, Long Meadow, with just more than one thousand students in a building with ample space, could offer lunch to all its students simultaneously. The school had two schoolwide breaks during the day, during which time students could eat in the cafeteria, play in the school-yard, roam the halls, or sit in the library or computer room. Finally, the school day began and ended with a morning fifteen-minute and afternoon five-to-ten-minute registration period with a form tutor, who usually followed the Class through its years until Year 11 (age sixteen). During morning and afternoon registration, the form tutor would take attendance, sometimes check students' school supplies, make announcements, and when necessary, reprimand students (especially at the end of the day). Every day, a different student in the class was entrusted with the Daily Record Sheet, which the student took to all his or her classes for teachers to write a short description of how the class had behaved that day; if a particular student was troublesome (or excelled, which was less frequently reported), his or her name would appear on the Daily Record Sheet. When bad behavior was so reported, the form tutor would make individuals or the class stay after school. The Daily Record Sheet created some self-policing and peer policing by students, especially when a teacher threatened to write negative comments on the sheet. Crucially, however, morning and afternoon registration was a time for most classes (except those with the strictest teachers, or on days when the class got too loud) to socialize and chat among peers.

In contrast to British secondary schools, urban public schools in the United States usually house thousands of students, and many are overcrowded, especially in neighborhoods of high immigration. The large schools are a result of the bureaucratization of U.S. schooling at the turn of the twentieth century, instituted in part to deal with large-scale urban growth, predominantly through immigration (V. E. Lee, 2000; Tyack, 1974). Large schools were thought to be more efficient in offering multiple tracks (e.g., academic, vocational) under one roof and one administration. As a result, American high schools traditionally move students from class to class with different peer groups for most subjects, in order to achieve high specialization and tracking made possible through large school size (V. E. Lee, 2000; Tyack, 1974). However, research has shown that tracking systems in the United States often lead to within-school racial segregation in which black and Latino students tend to be in bottom tracks and white and Asian students in upper tracks (Oakes, 1985; Roscigno, 1998; Solorzano and Ornelas, 2004). Most classes in the New York school were separated based on skills or perceived abilities and motivation. Expressed student interest, an application form, test scores, English Language Learner status, grades, and teacher recommendation are just some of the criteria used to place students in their classes at York High. This separation can reduce inter-ethnic contact and, hence, strengthen racial and ethnic boundaries. I found this to be the case most prominently at York High with immigrant English Language Learners (ELLs), who spent nearly the entire day with other ELLs of the same linguistic background.

New York City's public schools also operate on a semester system, so that classes change both every September and every February. There are no set "home room" or "registration" classes that travel from subject to subject together; rather, students encounter different configurations of peers in every subject. In addition, as with most public high schools in Queens, York High is vastly overcrowded, serving more than three thousand students in a building designed for less than two thousand. As a result, the school is forced to educate students in shifts, so that although individual students attend school only for seven to eight periods a day, the school runs for twelve periods. Some students start school before 7:30 A.M., and others finish after 4 P.M. Related to the overcrowding problem is the lack of a morning or afternoon homeroom period: students need to arrive and leave the building as quickly as possible and so have little downtime at school. Hence, the school structure is such that students spend little nonacademic time in school, and they also do not see many peers for long periods—those who share a class often do so only for one class, and in that class only for a semester.

Lunchtime poses a great challenge for overcrowded schools. York High School solved this problem through a staggered, optional lunch period. The cafeteria served lunch starting at fourth period (starting at 9:45 A.M.) and continued through eighth period (ending at 1:35 P.M.). When scheduling their classes, students could state a preference to have a lunch period or not (and have seven consecutive classes instead). But this preference was not guaranteed, and the schedule would change (along with the peers encountered during that lunch period) twice a year, with the start of each new semester in September and in February. Some students who preferred to have lunch did not get one. More commonly, students told me they preferred to go straight through the day with no lunch break—perhaps partly because the food was not particularly tasty, but probably more to avoid the social anxiety of not knowing anyone during the assigned lunch period. One teacher told me that she allowed a few students she knew well (because they were in a rare, special English class that stayed together and had the same teacher for two years) to come to her classroom and sit in the back quietly during their lunch break while she taught other students. I observed three to four students regularly taking her offer. When I was trying to schedule an interview with one Indian student, he told me that I would not find him in the cafeteria during his lunch period because he went home every day for lunch (against school rules).

Many New York students spent their lunch period in the library when they could get in (besides often being closed, the library had space limitations). The library was a safe space for students who did not share their lunch period with any friends, because they could sit quietly and read a magazine, or chat with someone who might sit at their table. One day in the library I met Tasha, a black student who had arrived at York High School one week prior. Tasha was in the library during her lunch period. She confidently told me of her mixed ancestry: "Well, I'm a mixture of everything. . . . I'm Dominican, Trinidadian, Jamaican, St. Lucian . . ." Soon after I met her, I recorded this in my fieldnotes:

> I bumped into Tasha in the hallway at the start of her lunch period. The library was closed—as was frequently the case, because meetings were sometimes held there or teachers brought classes in to use the library's resources. Tasha asked me where she could go, since the library was closed. She insisted that she didn't want to go to the cafeteria, and seemed intimidated by the prospect. She asked Dave, the boy I was talking with when I encountered her, where he goes during his lunch period. He told her he goes to help his guidance counselor. (Fieldnotes, May 13, 2004)

Tasha had not yet figured out a strategy for dealing with her lunch period, the cafeteria not seeming to her a viable option, at least at that time. Students were not permitted to wander the halls during their lunch period, since classes were in session during all lunch times. There was also no outdoor space for them to play in, since the schoolyard was taken up by trailers that served as makeshift classrooms—another solution to the problem of overcrowding.

Lunchtime illustrates well the dilemma faced by students in large urban high schools in the United States: how to deal with anonymity and the lack of opportunities to form strong, trusting friendships, especially with peers who on the surface seem quite different from oneself. The large size (York's three thousand students); the class structure that mixes students up every period for seven periods and again every September and February; no homeroom time; and limited lunch breaks, if any, together create a situation in which students have little opportunity—whether downtime at school or extended interaction with particular peers—to develop close relationships with peers with whom they do not immediately identify. Some recent immigrants from India

I met at York High explained to me that when they arrived in the school, other Punjabi students noticed them and approached them in the hallway, asking many questions and befriending them. It was an attempt to show the new arrivals the ropes, perhaps because they knew the new students would find little guidance or make friends easily on their own. In this anonymous environment, not only immigrants but also U.S.-born students gravitated toward what felt most familiar—their own ethnic and racial groups.

The overall structure at Long Meadow involving the Form Class, form tutor, and schoolwide breaks contrasts with York High's highly anonymous structure. Daily registration periods and two daily school-wide breaks in the London school provided time for students to socialize outside their classes. In contrast, the schedule at York, at most, provided students a period for lunch in which to socialize (albeit the students in that lunch period changed twice a year) and, at the least, provided no nonacademic time at school (for those who had no lunch period). These findings contrast with previous theorists' arguments that urbanization and industrialization help to break up traditional ties of birth membership (e.g., religion, ethnicity, family) and consequently lead to self-realization as an individual process, achieved through consumerism (Zukin and Maguire, 2004). In fact, I found that the more atomized, bureaucratic school system in New York strengthened the salience of race and ethnicity. In the absence of opportunities to form lasting relationships, New York students clung to those who on the surface look most like themselves—their same-group peers. Previous scholarship has documented the positive influence of reducing school size on academic achievement at urban public schools, and the ill effects of large anonymous school structures on academic achievement (Lawrence, 2004; Sizer, 1984; Tajalli and Opheim, 2005). The research presented here suggests that large school size and an anonymous structure can also lead to more rigid ethnic and racial boundaries between students.

The evidence above suggests that the most promising explanation for the greater salience of race and ethnicity in the U.S. context of this research is the highly anonymous school structure of urban America, especially when compared to the British context. Given that children spend about one-third of their waking hours in school (Hofferth and Sandberg, 2001), opportunities for them to socialize in school can make the difference between developing comfort with and distancing oneself from other groups.

Of course myriad differences aside from school structure distinguish the United States and Britain. I turn now to two commonly cited differences between Britain and the United States in terms of race relations, and evaluate their possible impact on the stronger ethnic and racial boundaries I found at York High: racial segregation and identity, and patterns of migration.

RACIAL SEGREGATION AND IDENTITY

Previous scholarship has documented the degree to which U.S. society is racialized, in contrast to British society, where class defines social groups and even political mobilization more than race and ethnicity do (Foner, 2005; Katznelson, 1973; Modood, 1996). The U.S. history of slavery and racial segregation and the African American–led Civil Rights Movement have shaped discussions of social difference and disadvantage in the United States, leading to an emphasis on race. This history has shaped U.S. discourse concerning ethnic groups. For example, Richard Alba (2005) has suggested that race is the one major realm in which Mexican Americans encounter powerful boundaries with mainstream America. Others argue that ethnic groups have sometimes taken advantage of hard-won policies achieved during the Civil Rights Movement, such as affirmative action and anti-discrimination policies (Alba and Nee, 2003; Kasinitz et al., 2008; Massey, Mooney, Charles, and Torres, 2007).

Although Britain's colonial history preceded the immigration of South Asians and West Indians to Britain, and although black identity has been excluded from British national identity (Gilroy, 1987), the legacy of racialization is weaker in Britain than it is in the United States. For example, racial intermarriage between Afro-Caribbeans and whites is much more common in Britain than in the United States. Model and Fisher (2002) find that second-generation Afro-Caribbean men in Britain are four times more likely to marry whites than are their U.S. counterparts, and second-generation Afro-Caribbean women in Britain are three times more likely to marry whites than are their U.S. counterparts.[8] Not surprisingly, residential segregation patterns correlate with intermarriage rates and can at least partially explain low intermarriage rates for American blacks. Urban America is significantly more racially segregated than London, especially for blacks (Peach, 1996), and Afro-Caribbeans in the United States tend to live near African Americans

(Foner, 2005). The highest percentage of Afro-Caribbeans in a single British Ward is 30 percent (Peach, 1996), in contrast to the hypersegregation of the American inner city (Massey and Denton, 1993).[9] British schools are also significantly less racially segregated than American schools (Burgess and Wilson, 2004). The greater racial segregation in New York relative to London means that even if New York students attend school with multiple ethnic groups, their neighborhood lives are more likely to be mostly with coethnics. Ellen, an eleventh-grade Indo-Caribbean New Yorker, told me that her diverse school meant that students mingled across ethnic boundaries, yet outside school they socialized with their own ethnic groups, because ethnic groups lived in segregated neighborhoods:

> [D]ifferent races hang out with different people. But like mostly you get, like, your own race hanging out with your own race. And not because, like, when you walk around the school you say, like, "Oh, I won't talk to this person," like of the different race. But like after school and stuff you just see, like, one group. . . . I guess because, it's like the different areas that you go to, it's where you hang out. I think that if [my neighborhood] had different kinds of people, then we would all hang out with different people. It depends, like, where you live.

Ellen attributes the after-school ethnic segregation to living in different neighborhoods. However, given the opportunity in school to foster lasting relationships across ethnic and racial lines, students might bridge those boundaries outside school as well.

On the other hand, the United States also has historically been a nation of immigrants, both in its demographics (with waves of immigrants since its inception) and in its national identity; this is not the case for Britain (despite significant immigration to Britain and periods of low U.S. immigration [Zolberg and Long, 1999]). Foner (2005) has documented the historical and contemporary construction of the ideal immigrant forefathers of the United States, in contrast to European erasure of immigration history in the popular imagination. The popular understanding of the United States as a "nation of immigrants" should have made the softening of ethnic boundaries smoother than in Britain. In addition, Alba and Nee (2003) have argued that U.S. changes after the Civil Rights Movement such as anti-discrimination laws have decreased the social distance between minority groups and the majority, leading to the blurring of ethnic boundaries. New research has also shown that second-generation teens and young adults in New York City engage and prefer cosmopolitan tastes and friendship networks

(Kasinitz, Mollenkopf, and Waters, 2004; Kasinitz et al., 2008). In contrast, the British government's policies of multiculturalism have recently been blamed for fostering separation and preventing integration—that is, for encouraging stronger symbolic boundaries between ethnic and racial groups (Giddens, 2006; Goodhart, 2004). Moreover, compared to other European countries like France, Britain does have strong race-conscious policies such as anti-discrimination laws (Bleich, 2003; Favell, 1998). Some have argued that British social policies on immigration and unemployment have been guided by racism, resulting in greater racial division and inequality in society (Solomos, 1988). Hence, the different roles of race and ethnicity in British and American society seem not to fully explain the findings described earlier in this chapter.

PATTERNS OF MIGRATION

The current wave of immigration to the United States began in 1965, whereas Britain experienced significant immigration from the Caribbean and South Asia during the 1950s, a period of low immigration to the United States. Consequently, a greater percentage of New York City's population is foreign-born compared to London's (36 percent versus 27 percent) (U.S. Census Bureau, 2000b; Office for National Statistics, 2001a). The parent populations at my research sites reflected this difference. At Long Meadow in London, 72 percent of survey respondents' mothers were foreign-born, in contrast to 81 percent of mothers of York High students. Although most mothers in both cities were foreign-born, just 6 percent of London survey respondents were first or 1.5 generation (born abroad and having immigrated before age eleven), in contrast to 27 percent in New York. This relative recency and larger proportion of immigrants might account for the greater salience of ethnicity in New York, assuming that ethnicity's salience will decrease over time for an ethnic community. Many scholars have found that, for example, native language usage drops sharply between the first and second generation (Portes and Rumbaut, 2001; Rumbaut, 2004; Rumbaut, Massey, and Bean, 2006; Zhou and Bankston, 1998). Similarly, in Portes and Rumbaut's (2001) study of children of immigrants in Miami and San Diego, U.S.-born youth and U.S. citizens were more likely to call themselves some form of American or ethnic American, in contrast to their foreign-born and foreign-national peers, who were more likely to define their ethnic identities in terms of their (foreign) nationalities or with pan-ethnic labels.

On the other hand, some research suggests that many in the second generation may lean more toward ethno-religious identity than their parents: 75 percent of forty-five- to fifty-four-year-old Muslims polled in Britain said they felt that "I have as much in common with non-Muslims as I do with Muslims," and that percentage *decreased* with every age group down to fifteen- to twenty-four-year-old British Muslims, 62 percent of whom agreed with the statement (Mirza, Senthilkumaran, and Ja'far, 2006). In the United States many second-generation Afro-Caribbeans identify more strongly as black or African American than do their immigrant parents (Vickerman, 1999; Waters, 1999). Lastly, immigrant respondents in the school surveys I administered were *more* likely than U.S.- and U.K.-born respondents to agree with the statement "In my school, students feel comfortable talking to students of other racial and ethnic groups" (96 percent versus 87 percent), which suggests that in these school contexts being U.S.- or U.K.-born can actually mean *stronger* perceptions of racial division. Hence, the longer history and smaller presence of immigrant communities in London do not fully explain the weaker ethnic and racial boundaries of London youth compared to New York youth.

In this chapter I have demonstrated two aspects of the urban multi-ethnic schools I studied. First, multiple ethnic groups in the same school led to the blurring of ethnic and racial boundaries in both the United States and Britain. Second, the traditional urban high school structure in New York impeded greater ethnic and racial boundary blurring, compared to the London school's structure, typical for Britain. Although York High served a multi-ethnic school population, that multi-ethnicity was not enough to ensure strong interethnic ties; rather, students needed structural opportunities to bridge racial and ethnic boundaries in school, like those that students had at Long Meadow Community School. This finding resonates with Gordon Allport's (1954) original conceptualization of the contact hypothesis; specifically, that reducing prejudice (and in this case, blurring the boundaries between ethnic and racial groups) is aided by institutional supports such as customs of racial interaction and by "true" rather than "casual" contact—as exemplified by the London Form Classes in contrast to the constant shifting of peers in the New York school.[10] Although the contact hypothesis is commonly understood to mean that "contact equals less prejudice," Allport astutely pointed out that the right conditions are necessary for contact to lead to less prejudice. Similarly, research on school integration should take into account segregation not only across schools but also *within* schools. The latter form of segregation takes place via not only systems of tracking (Oakes, 1985; Solorzano and Ornelas, 2004) but also, as I have shown, through school size and lack of peer continuity, preventing students from reaching out to peers who do not seem like them on the surface.

Other research in the United States has shown that a small, intimate school structure can improve academic achievement (Lawrence, 2004; Sizer, 1984; Tajalli and Opheim, 2005). This has led to a vigorous small-schools movement. The findings I present here suggest that in addition to improved academic achievement, small and intimate schools can also improve race relations. Specifically, schools that provide time for students to socialize and to get to know a small group of diverse peers can foster the blurring of racial and ethnic boundaries. This of course depends on whether schools host students of diverse ethnic and racial backgrounds; schools of any structure that host only one ethnic or racial group (most commonly in the United States, predominantly white or predominantly black students) do not provide opportunities to bridge ethnic and racial boundaries.

The analysis of youth culture among the second generation through the lens of their social lives and, specifically, their symbolic boundaries, provides a useful tool for further understanding the intersection of ethnicity and race with youth culture. It illuminates how institutions can shape the distinctions that groups make in a society (or in this case, the social world of second-generation youth in school) and how these distinctions consequently can vary cross-nationally (see also Lamont, 1992, 2000). Furthermore, it illustrates how teens reproduce some of the same social processes of status differentiation among themselves that may be found in the larger society (Bourdieu, 1986; Bourdieu and Passeron, 1977). Finally, the research presented here extends previous discussions of how state institutions influence processes of ethnic assimilation via boundary crossing and blurring among ethnic groups (Alba, 2005; Alba and Nee, 2003; Wimmer, 2008b; Zolberg and Long, 1999) to the ways by which school structures influence the symbolic boundaries of students' social lives at school. I have shown how not only national institutions but also local institutions influence ethnic and racial boundaries.

CHAPTER 8

Explaining Youth Cultures, Improving Academic Achievement

During the week that I was putting the finishing touches on this manuscript, a group of students from a Boston public high school gave a presentation at Harvard. They had worked with a doctoral student on a study of social justice at their school. As they presented their three key findings, I was struck by one in particular. The student reading from the group's PowerPoint presentation prefaced her comment by saying, "Okay, this is big," to laughter from the audience. Then she read: "Student choices don't always match their vision for themselves. Don't interpret on the basis of what you see. Ask. And remind them if there is a disconnect between their actions and their hopes for themselves." It struck me that it took these urban high schoolers just three months to come to the conclusion that I drew after many more months of intensive research. I am glad I asked, and I hope that researchers and teachers will continue to ask teens much more about their styles, music choices, and behaviors for the purposes of understanding what drives their behaviors and, more important, for pushing them to be their very best.

In addition to asking teens, the students who presented their findings at Harvard asked adults to remind kids of their hopes if they see a disconnect. Perhaps this is what York High's school principal meant when she addressed students on the purposes of schooling: "We are here to prepare you for the world after high school and that includes how you treat one another, what you say, how many academic requirements you have been able to meet, and even what you wear, including how you wear your pants" (school website). Hopefully this preparation with respect to style entails explicit direction for code-switching, rather than a simple attempt to drive youth culture from students' lives—an impossible feat even if it were desirable.

In this book I unpack the elements of second-generation youth cultures and their meanings to teens in order to understand the relationship between second-generation youth cultures and youth orientations toward school. In chapter 1 I describe segmented assimilation theory's explanation for poor outcomes among certain ethnic groups—minority children of immigrants with low skills living near poor African Americans. I argue that the cultural part of this theory—that ethnic minorities living among disadvantaged African Americans adopt anti-success behaviors, outlooks, and tastes, in part because of the influence of their African American peers (Portes and Rumbaut, 2001; Portes and Zhou, 1993)—does not hold up against empirical observations. A small minority of the students I studied did express oppositional attitudes. However, oppositional beliefs did not lead to lower aspirations and, conversely, a taste for a putatively oppositional music and style— rap and hip-hop—did not lead to oppositional attitudes. Furthermore, the small minority of students with some oppositional beliefs cannot explain the overall low levels of academic achievement in the schools I studied. Researchers, parents, and school authorities alike have been too quick to assume that a taste for hip-hop and rap music and style implies rebellious outlooks and attitudes. In fact, the culture ascribed to the American inner city is available to anyone who has a television, a radio, or Internet access, as demonstrated by the immense popularity of American hip-hop in London.

The similarity between youth in New York and London with respect to taste preferences, attitudes, and interactional styles suggests that local contexts and individuals are not always the purveyors of youth cultures. Downward assimilation theory's premise of poor African American youth influencing the cultural outlooks of second-generation youth in urban disadvantaged schools cannot be the only explanation for teens' consumption of hip-hop and rap; if it were, youth culture in urban America would look different from youth culture in London, where there are no African Americans and where the indigenous poor are white. Instead, hip-hop has become a global currency for status among youth, and this global media influence has more weight than local and peer influences on taste preferences in New York and London, as I show in chapter 2. African American peers cannot be blamed for any "contaminating effect" on downwardly mobile second-generation teens. By taking an in-depth look at the cultural lives of children of immigrants in New York and London, I have more clearly unpacked the process of cultural incorporation. I offer some reason for optimism, in spite of the low academic performance in the schools I observed: low academic achievement is *not* attributable, as some have feared, to lack of aspiration or belief in mainstream success through doing well in school.

In fact, previous research has shown that the strongest critiques of the ideology of the "American dream" often come from those minorities who have had some success—for example, the black middle class (Hochschild, 1996) and working-class students attending a successful Puerto Rican nationalist school (Ramos-Zayas, 2003). Sociologist John Diamond and his colleagues (Diamond, Lewis, and Gordon, 2007) find that African American students attending a high-achieving suburban high school are critical of racial inequality in their school; nonetheless, their critiques do not lead to oppositional orientations toward school. In the world of rap music, a successful African American rapper from Chicago, Kanye West, became popular with the album *The College Dropout,* in which he critiques the dominant ideology that inner-city youth will succeed and make decent money by going to college rather than dealing drugs. West grew up in a middle-class Chicago neighborhood with his mother, an English professor at Chicago State University. Despite his mother's Ph.D., an interlude in West's album sarcastically suggests that a college degree will not necessarily bring the good life:[1]

> So now you get your [college] degree tattooed on your back, you're so
> excited about it
> If you continue to work at the GAP, after several interviews, Oh my
> god!
> You'll come in at an entry level position

West sarcastically questions a college degree's ability to lead to high status work and financial rewards. His lyrics stand in contrast to those of more popular rappers from poorer backgrounds about their belief that hard work and dedication can lead anyone to success. Jay-Z, a successful rapper-turned–actor and music producer who was raised in Brooklyn public housing, told *USA Today:* "People want to see some type of struggle [like mine]. . . . Nobody cares about people who wake up to money their pops left them. . . . They want to see a person come from nothing and work his way up so they can be like, 'Yeah, *he deserved that*'" (Barboza, 2001). Unlike Kanye West, Jay-Z puts forth a belief in the American dream that hard work leads to success and that those who deserve success will attain it. When I asked low-performing students whether they would like to do well and why they had not done well in the past, they expressed quite conventional views, such as wanting to make a change and to improve in the future; and they believed that they have ample opportunity to succeed in life (also see Carter, 2005; Hochschild, 1996).

This does not mean, however, that peer cultures have no relationship to educational stratification. As I describe in detail in chapter 6, striving for *peer status* can sometimes conflict with behaviors conducive to academic achievement, despite teens' best intentions. I suggest in this book that a better way to understand youth behaviors and tastes is to examine youths' peer social world, which is distinct from the dominant, school-endorsed social world at school. This peer social world has its own culture with particular scripts for behavior, language, tastes, clothing, and interactional styles. Here again I depart from the conventional downward assimilation explanation in that I show that many behaviors in school that are detrimental to academic achievement—fighting with peers, talking back to teachers, wearing clothes that a teen knows signal delinquency to adults—do not in fact stem from disinterest in academic achievement. Rather, they show that being cool in front of one's peers is extremely important to most teens, including second-generation teens. The quest for peer status, rather than a rejection of mainstream institutions and norms, drives these behaviors. What most students desire is success both among their peers—peer status—and in academics. This theoretical intervention in explanations for low achievement among some children of immigrants leads to different policy implications for improving their academic achievement, implications to which I turn at the end of this chapter.

In this book I extend Pierre Bourdieu's theory of social status and culture to youth culture. I show how the social world of youth parallels the social world of adults, in which high-status individuals, too, employ culture to maintain and reproduce their status (Bourdieu, 1986; Bourdieu and Passeron, 1977). Youth in both cities spent much energy vying for symbolic status among their peers, much as adults do in the dominant social world. An overemphasis on symbolic status, however, could interfere with an individual's goals within the dominant, "adult" social world of academic achievement if the student did not have the skills to balance his or her peer social world with the dominant social world of school success and academic achievement. Some teens were better than others in the balancing act of success in both. Others prioritized success in one over the other.

Previous scholarship has described the value for minorities and children of immigrants of maintaining bicultural identities (Gibson, 1988; Mehan et al., 1994; Portes and Rumbaut, 2001; Suárez-Orozco and Suárez-Orozco, 1995). However, these studies have emphasized combining *ethnic* culture and *American* culture through "code-switching"— that is, employing different languages, comportment, and even styles in different situations. The findings in this book suggest that children of immigrants should learn how to move not only between their parents' and the mainstream adult (whether American or British) cultural worlds but also between their peers' and adults' cultural expectations, in order to promote school success. As one articulate New Yorker, Jamal, put it:

> See, I know the difference between when to act like this [points to his hip hop clothing] and when not to act. . . . And another thing is that, what if you are going for a job, how is [your clothing] gonna portray you to the man that's interviewing you? . . . They might think that, you know, "Okay, he looks like he is going to steal one of my items. He looks lazy. He looks like he's not gonna come to work. He might come to work late."

Jamal's awareness of the need to change his style in different situations, given others' prejudices, is a pragmatic approach to a world in which adults often misread teen styles.

For boys, symbolic status among peers was tied to masculine identity, especially in the realm of interactional styles and defense of self-pride. Vying for peer status may lead boys, especially minority boys, to more conflicts with behaviors conducive to academic achievement than it does their female counterparts through engaging in fights with peers and confrontations with authorities. Also, elements of cool among peers may (wrongly) signal disaffection to adults who are unable to discern "style from substance" (Foner, 2005, 58). This likely affects boys more than girls, since boys expressed greater preference for music and styles associated with rebellion in the larger society (namely, rap music and male hip-hop style).

Although youth cultures were quite similar for all students in the schools of this research, I did find differences in the two cities related to stereotypes about race and ethnicity and influenced by the organization of schools. I show in chapter 3 how different ethnic groups access peer culture differently and how peer culture leads Afro-Caribbean teens to high and Indians to low peer status. Having more to gain in terms of status via popular culture, Afro-Caribbeans placed more emphasis on style than did Indian, white, or Indo-Caribbean students. This difference may partially explain Afro-Caribbean students' lower academic achievement compared to native whites and second-generation Indians, because placing a greater emphasis on youth culture without code-switching skills can lead to low academic achievement, despite a student's best intentions. This was especially true for Afro-Caribbean boys, perhaps leading them to a gap with their female counterparts larger than the degree to which boys of other ethnic or race groups fall behind their female counterparts in academic achievement (Coley, 2001; Donahue, Voelkl, Campbell, and Mazzeo, 1999; Knapp, 2005; López, 2002; U.K. Department for Education and Skills, 2004). Finally, the organizational structure of schools impacts how students define status groups at school. Although ethnicity mattered a great deal in both cities, York High School's structure provided few opportunities for students to develop lasting relationships across ethnic and racial lines as easily as Long Meadow students did. This finding suggests that race does indeed still matter in a unique way in the United States, even among youth attending multi-ethnic schools in cosmopolitan New York City. It also shows how the organizational structures of schools impact racial integration.

YOUTH CULTURE AND THE LIFE COURSE

The unfortunate irony of youth culture is that its scope is limited. By the time kids grow older, youth peer status buys them less and hence matters less to them. In fact, engaging in youth cultures may even impede economic success through employers' stereotypes about popular styles of dressing, walking, and speaking, especially if the young adults have not learned to code-switch between their peer cultures and the dominant culture. Teens told me of changes as they grew older, or changes they planned to make in themselves as they grew older, to focus more on academic achievement than on peer culture. For example, Jagdish, an Indian student in London, told me that what's "cool" changes as one grows older:

N: Would you say it's cool to do poorly in school?

J: No, because everyone knows that . . . their education is most based on their future [sic], so. But I think most of the people like, they know, but they also act cool.

I asked Jagdish to clarify what he meant by "act cool": "Try to, you know, try to show off, like sometimes back chat [talk back] to teachers and stuff like that. . . . Like when you are kids, like you just want to have fun. Just have fun, that's it. But as you get older, I think you realize that you need education or something like that to get good jobs." Jagdish was an average student. His words suggest that peers desire both to "act cool" and to do well academically. He speculates that as they grow older, they will emphasize school success more and peer status less.

Pradeep had a similar plan to focus on education as he grew older. A sixteen-year-old Sikh student in New York involved with gangs, Pradeep attended many South Asian club parties in New York and New Jersey. When I asked him about what his life would be like in ten years, he told me that he planned to change his ways:

> Ten years [from now], I'm gonna be a gentleman. . . . Like, I am gonna leave everything after high school. Like, all the stuff that I am doing right now. I am gonna leave everything. . . . I am gonna get a nice job, you know, like I am gonna go to college. Study hard. . . . Because all that stuff what I am doing right now, you know, it's not going to help me after college or, you know, after high school. It's not going to help me. Like I see my big boys, they are all in jail. Like three, four people. They were like, you know, good students. They are like, and they went to jail twice, and I don't want that.

When I asked Pradeep why he said he is going to change his ways after high school rather than right now, he pointed to the life course:

> N: And so why do you say that you're gonna do it in a year or after high school, as opposed to, say, right now?
>
> P: Not right now. Because I know that's my age.

Pradeep's reported average in school was in the bottom third of respondents in New York and was just above passing. He had come to New York from India as an adolescent, and he went on to explain that at this age he has to fight and to be tough, lest he be continually harassed by peers. Unfortunately, his current behavior probably limited his future options. Earlier in the conversation, Pradeep told me that he would like to stop cutting classes, as he has been doing, to secure his future:

> N: What do you plan to do after high school?
>
> P: I want to be an engineer or something. Like, I am going into biotech. That's what my dad wants me to do. So, yeah, but [up to] today I am like cutting a lot, so I am just trying to avoid . . .

I asked Pradeep why he cuts classes so much:

P: I don't know. I have no idea why I am cutting. Maybe I am sleepy, or I don't know.

N: What do you do when you cut?

P: Hang around, hang around with my friends. . . . Sometimes playing with my peers. . . . But not anymore.

In other words, Pradeep wanted to focus on his education and believed he could have a successful career, but understood that certain behaviors might prevent him from doing so. I hope he will learn to balance his desire for peer status and academic achievement before it is too late for him. His thoughts poignantly illustrate the contradiction between good intentions and bad behaviors on the part of him and many students like him, and they show that delinquent behaviors do not necessarily stem from oppositional attitudes toward mainstream society and norms. Still, the unfortunate reality is that many students like Pradeep will not realize their goals and their current behaviors will close future doors to them. Unlike teens with more advantages, Pradeep and his peers have little cushion to help them bounce back from mistakes made at a young age. Instead, his disadvantage is likely to compound itself for every wrong turn he makes.

As Afro-Caribbean students grow older, the implications of peer cultures and racial stereotypes may become even more dire. Recall from chapter 4 that Afro-Caribbeans were most likely to report experiencing racial discrimination from adults in public spaces, compared to Indians, who were most likely to experience racial discrimination in school from their peers. As they leave school and enter adulthood, job interviews, housing searches, and shopping for life's necessities all become important tasks essential to livelihood. These spheres, however, are precisely those in which Afro-Caribbean young men and women are likely to continue to face barriers and racial discrimination, perhaps impeding their chances for success. This may lead them to a greater awareness of and frustration with racial discrimination, as shown by Kasinitz and his colleagues (2008) in their study of second-generation young adults in New York. They found that Afro-Caribbean experiences with racial discrimination in public spaces from unknown adults could lead to reactive ethnicities, in contrast to second-generation experiences with discrimination at school (and at work) from familiar individuals, which led students of diverse ethnicities to try harder.

WHO AND WHAT DEFINES YOUTH CULTURES?

In this book I have focused on the reception side of youth culture and have not discussed the construction of youth culture. This leads to important questions: what and who define youth culture? How do teens influence or decide what is cool? Of course, the media play a powerful role in shaping the music and style preferences of youth, through the carefully crafted music industry as well as the production and marketing of pop artists and of styles and brands such as Nike (Klein, 2002; Pattillo-McCoy, 1999). This role was evident in the strong media influence on the styles of the students I encountered in both cities.[2] Still, individuals create their own meanings and understandings, so that the significance of particular tastes lies not only in what the taste is popularly thought to mean (or what the makers intended) but also in how consumers use the taste preference and create meanings by using it in their daily lives (Davis, 1992; Liebes and Katz, 1990; Radway, 1991; Watson, 1997). Willis (1990) suggests that one way youth express their agency is through "commodity-related expressive consumption, or common culture." In other words, teens express their ideas and attitudes through particular choices in music, style, and so forth. In my study, students described going to great lengths to signal hipness without delinquency, style without opposition in their clothing—so as best to send the right message about their participation in peer culture and also in oppositional cultures (lack thereof, mostly). Hence, the study of youth culture requires the inclusion not only of tastes and behaviors but also of cultural meanings, outlooks, and worldviews (Schudson, 1989). In terms of behavioral expectations, urban ethnographer Elijah Anderson (1999) has suggested that a minority of youth in the inner city set a tone in which toughness is expected and necessary for survival among all. These expectations may exist among more advantaged teens, as well (Pattillo-McCoy, 1999).

AN URBAN SECOND-GENERATION OR UNIVERSAL PHENOMENON?

In chapter 6 I describe the phenomenon of "preppy punks": youth in New York City who consume punk music, go to concerts at the famous punk venue CBGB's, and don Mohawks, yet go home to middle-class and even posh neighborhoods like Manhattan's Upper East Side and Brooklyn's Cobble Hill and attend the city's elite private schools like

Fieldston and Packer (Stapinski, 2004). These students do not reject mainstream society; an article in the *New York Times* tells us: "Unlike the punks of the 70s, punk rockers today feel no compulsion to do badly in school." (1) A worker in a punk store reports that he tells his young customers: "Become an Iggy [Iggy Pop—a punk artist who stood the test of time], rather than a Sid Vicious [a punk star who died young of a drug overdose]" (1). The accoutrements of punk aside, these youth sound remarkably similar to the youth in my study: they consume styles and music previously associated with a counterculture and they value mainstream success.

My point in describing this scene is to demonstrate the importance of the elements of youth culture among other groups in society (see also Chin and Phillips, 2005; Davies, 1995). As the example above demonstrates (and as, I am sure, many readers' recollections of their own high school experiences can attest), peer cultures look countercultural on the surface for many youth, and most promote defending self-pride and being "cool," as well. Students in most schools, in the United States and around the world, face choices regarding the degree to which they want to engage their peer cultures versus focusing solely on academic achievement. And disadvantaged areas are not the only places where acting tough and engaging popular styles lead to peer status, sometimes to the detriment of academic achievement. This peer culture, then, cannot fully explain differential outcomes between race groups. There exists in fact a long tradition of scholarship on youth cultures and peer status and on the relationship between academic orientation and peer status among youth in general (Brown, 1990; Coleman, 1961; Rigsby and McDill, 1975). In this book I extend this work by analyzing the relationship between peer cultures and peer status among children of immigrants in New York and London schools.

Because my research was conducted in schools whose student populations were majority minority and that have low socioeconomic status levels, the research itself cannot demonstrate the influence of disadvantaged status on youth culture and the degree to which my findings are unique to urban disadvantaged second-generation youth, or whether instead I would find similar results among more privileged youth. Other research has shown that in schools serving more middle- and upper-class families, the most popular students are those who are skilled in sports and use sports participation to signal a willingness to have fun, while the least popular are the ones who spend too much of their time in the library ("too much" as defined by their peers, of course) (Adler and

Adler, 1998; Coleman, 1961; Eder and Kinney, 1995; Milner, 2004). My findings resonate with the ways nonacademic aspects of culture influence peer status in other types of schools; they differ, however, in that hip-hop music and style are perceived by many adults as delinquent and oppositional, especially when consumed by urban minority students. The findings in this book also resonate with the research observations of Katherine Newman and her colleagues (Newman, 2004) made in small, predominantly white U.S. towns that had experienced rampage school shootings. Newman and her colleagues found that most school shooters have experienced bullying, questioning of their masculinity, and having low peer status; in these cases the status hierarchy and norms of masculinity at school had devastating effects on those with low status.

The importance of authenticity, too, is not unique to second-generation youth. Michèle Lamont and her colleagues (Lamont, Kaufman, and Moody, 2000) found that winners of the prestigious Presidential Scholarship for high school students define authenticity, or "being true to yourself," as an important part of the ideal self and a moral imperative. Even adults place importance on authenticity. Thomas Frank (2004), in a book on American politics, suggests that Kansas and other "red state" voters reject the Democratic Party and northeastern liberalism in favor of the "authenticity" of the heartland. Frank writes: "What divides Americans is authenticity, not something hard and ugly like economics. While liberals commit endless acts of hubris, sucking down lattes, . . . the humble people of the red states go about their unpretentious business, eating down-home foods" (27).

Hence, I caution readers against assuming that urban minority youth are unique in their cultural worlds. Middle- and upper-class youth, too, participate in their own youth social worlds distinct from those of the adults in their lives. Milner's research (2004) on peer status focused on the experiences of college students when they were in high school, and his conclusions are somewhat similar to mine. College students in Milner's study reported that when they were in high school, peers placed a great deal of emphasis on status; he suggests that this is because they have little power in other spheres of their lives. The worlds of middle- and upper-middle-class youth might look quite similar to that of urban poor and working-class youth, especially given the increasing hipness that familiarity with urban poor culture has (Bryson, 1996; Jackson, 2001). Still, the *consequences* of certain behaviors and styles may differ for minority youth, who may be seen as more menacing by authorities than middle-class youth in similar clothing or with similar dispositions. Furthermore, middle- and upper-class families have more resources with which to steer their children away from danger if necessary—for example, by enrolling them in private schools with smaller class sizes and with more supervision if they go astray.

Economically advantaged youth may also feel less compelled to engage in competition for peer status at all—especially when it comes into conflict with academic achievement—because they have more access to other forms of capital through their families, including (mainstream) cultural, economic, and social. Hence, middle-class youth might engage with peer culture, but when it comes into conflict with school success or academic achievement, they may back out more easily (also see Anderson, 1999). Similarly, other research has shown that norms of masculinity (toughness, resolving conflict through physical fights, and the like) are stronger among working-class young men than among those with greater economic advantages (Coleman, 1961; Davies, 1995; Martin, 1996). Future studies of disadvantaged groups should include nondisadvantaged groups as well, to understand which findings are unique to disadvantage, and which are not.

STRUCTURE MATTERS, TOO

Finally, we should not forget that structure also matters for academic achievement. Although vying for peer status impacts school behaviors and can thus impact academic achievement, peer culture alone cannot explain the very low academic achievement overall of students in both schools of this study. The recent emphasis on youth cultures as explanations for academic achievement among the second generation belies the importance of *structural* influences on school outcomes. We know that myriad inequalities between the schools and home environments experienced by students like the ones in this research and those experienced by students from more advantaged backgrounds affect academic achievement: parental income, parental education, migration status, school funding, teacher quality, school and residential segregation, neighborhood poverty, and many others (Bowles and Gintis, 1976; Kozol, 1991; Massey and Denton, 1993; Menjívar, 2006; Neckerman, 2004; Portes and Rumbaut, 2001; Wilson, 1996). Some, in the tradition of critical race studies, have suggested that institutional racism is embedded in the organization and structure of schools and their "hidden curriculum" (Dixson and Rousseau, 2005; Gillborn, 2006; Jay, 2003; Solorzano and Ornelas, 2004). These scholars reveal seemingly "race-neutral" practices that have a disproportionate adverse impact on minority students, such as lower-level exams given to "low ability" students in Britain that predetermine a lack of high achievement (Gillborn, 2006). Although this book is concerned with explaining culture and its potential impact on school success, these structural impediments are certainly significant drivers for stratification in school outcomes.

THE STUDY OF CULTURE, RACE, AND EDUCATION

My findings suggest a need for more in-depth studies of ethnicity and culture, defined more broadly than just ethnic culture from the sending country. Many scholars have studied how second-generation children relate to and draw from their parents' ethnic cultures (Gibson, 1988; Kasinitz et al., 2008; Louie, 2004; Zhou and Bankston, 1998). However, this book has shown how that lens is incomplete as long as it does not take into consideration how second-generation teens engage *youth* cultures. Studies of culture should also be careful not to conflate the different aspects of culture, which may not coincide as we assume they do; in the case of my research, consumption of music rooted in critiques of the dominant society (music that has now become mainstream among youth) did not coincide with a rejection of mainstream norms and folk theories about getting ahead in life. Rather, cultural products are polysemic, so that, for example, a particular rap song may be consumed as a form of rebellion for one individual in a particular social context, while being consumed in another as a way of conformity to popular youth culture. This means studying not only cultural products, tastes, and practices but also the *meanings* that those preferences and practices have for individuals and how they relate to attitudes and understandings of the world (Schudson, 1989).

In addition, besides youth cultures, other aspects of culture affect school achievement. For example, in an ethnographic study, sociologist Annette Lareau (2003) has shown how children of different class backgrounds experience strikingly different *family* cultures, with implications for their future success. Also, much research has shown how *school* cultures advantage upper-class and white children over their working-class and minority peers, through a code of expected conduct familiar only to middle- and upper-class children (Bourdieu, 1986; Bourdieu and Passeron, 1977; Delpit, 1995); through rules targeting minority styles (Majors, 2001b); through school curriculum bias (Valenzuela, 1999); through lack of personal support (Conchas,

2001; Flores-González, 2002); and through lack of open discussion of racial stratification (Pollock, 2004). Finally, it may be the case that the behaviors of youth of different immigration, race, and class groups are similar, but that the *consequences* of certain behaviors are different for different groups (Kasinitz et al., 2008; Waldinger and Feliciano, 2004). The details of youth culture in this book constitute just one piece of a complex web of structural and cultural influences on academic achievement among the immigrant second generation.

POLICY IMPLICATIONS: HELPING STUDENTS "MAKE GOOD CHOICES"

Public schools in the inner city are tough. Academic achievement is no small feat when the student's school lacks resources, sufficient qualified teachers, and space for the total number of students. And, when compounded with many immigrant families' lack of financial resources, education, and access to the culture of the dominant American society, there are many obstacles faced by the children of immigrants in the kinds of schools I have described in this book. Still, many manage to succeed. Of those who do not, what has failed them? This question has perplexed academics, teachers, and of course parents. In this book I put one small piece of the puzzle of academic achievement into place—the role of peer cultures among children of immigrants. Drawing on the research presented in this book, I outline below some strategies for improving academic achievement among urban second-generation youth.

1. *"Make good choices": Schooling should help students' balancing acts between their peer social worlds and academic achievement via code-switching and decision-making skills.*
A major finding of the research presented in this book is that most second-generation teens *want* to do well, though their behaviors do not always support this desire. Their participation in two social worlds—that of the dominant society and that of peer culture—leads to sometimes-competing interests. I have shown how teens sacrifice peer status to varying degrees in order to achieve academically. Schooling that promotes open discussion of these competing pressures, rather than simply repeating mantras such as "no fighting in school" without engaging students about *how* to avoid fighting while maintaining pride, can enable youth to strike a balance between their different cultural worlds. Perhaps this is the traditional role of school counselors; unfortunately,

urban American guidance counselors are overextended. York High School's nine guidance counselors were responsible for more than three thousand students—that is, well more than three hundred students per counselor. Explicitly teaching students code-switching skills for moving between cultures (e.g., adult versus peer culture) and engaging different cultural tool-kits in different situations will help them to balance their two social worlds.

The teacher I observed most at York High ended every class period by asking students as they walked out of her classroom to "make good choices." This daily plea struck me as a touching reminder of the most important levers that determine students' academic outcomes: the daily choices that they make, which often unconsciously prioritize peer culture over academic success, despite students' dreams and goals. Students often paid no attention to the consequences of the quotidian choices they made in their lives. For example, in our London interview, Carl earnestly told me that he wanted to improve his school behavior and to do better in school. Later that day I saw him getting up in class at an inappropriate time; when I asked him in a nonauthoritative way about what he had said in his interview, much to my surprise, he looked at me sheepishly and sat down. I was shocked; I had expected Carl to tell me to mind my own business, or at best ignore me. Instead, he got back to work. This incident suggested to me that Carl did indeed *want* to do well, but that he often acted without paying attention to the choices he was making that would imperil his academic success. When I pointed out to him that his behavior did not match the goals he expressed, he actually changed his behavior immediately. Empowering students to make good choices and to be aware of the daily choices they make and the cultural tool-kits necessary for academic success is one step toward helping them make those good choices.

2. *Schools should engage youth cultures. Disciplinary codes should incorporate an understanding of peer culture.*
The previous recommendation emphasizes how *students* can bridge the gap between different cultural expectations in their lives. *Schools,* of course, play a significant role in facilitating or preventing academic achievement. Previous research has suggested that student oppositional cultures lead to underachievement; the implication of this hypothesis is that to improve academic achievement, schools should steer students away from peer culture. However, I found that peer culture and academic achievement were not, in fact, at odds. An important implica-

tion of the research in this book is that decreasing the social distance between the adult social world and the youth social world—exacerbated in predominantly minority, disadvantaged schools—will improve academic achievement. That is, integrating teens' social worlds with their academic learning can help bridge the cultural divide. This could mean, for example, introducing a poetry lesson by analyzing rap lyrics. Teachers and administrators should carefully engage and understand students' social worlds so that they do not misread youth culture as anti-school, for example, by subscribing to the misguided "baggy pants theory" that the baggier a boy's pants, the less focus he has in school.

Disciplinary codes should also incorporate an understanding of youth cultures. In the preceding chapters I show how defending one's pride in front of peers serves not only to maintain peer status but also, for boys, to demonstrate masculine identity. This pressure led girls and especially boys to engage in posturing—whether with peers or with teachers—to maintain self-pride in front of peers, sometimes resulting in punishment at school. Nancy López (2002) has similarly pointed out that school discipline for Dominican boys in New York asks them to behave in ways inconsistent with the masculine selves that they are trying to maintain. Hence, disciplinary codes should engage students when defining appropriate behaviors, responses, and punishments. I am not suggesting that students be permitted to fight and bully others in school. However, engaging students' social worlds when drawing up a set of rules and consequences could mean, for example, suggesting that a student take a five-minute break and walk out of the classroom rather than verbally responding when she or he is upset with a teacher; in this case, walking out would be viewed as a means of anger management rather than a cause for punishment.

I learned of just such a conflict during my research. Ms. McDuff, a teacher in New York, told me of a problem with Lina, an eleventh-grade student in one of her English classes. One day in class, Lina became very upset with Ms. McDuff and walked out of the classroom in a rage. Later, Lina told Ms. McDuff that she had left in order to prevent herself from reacting loudly and behaving inappropriately; she knew herself well enough to know that if she stayed in the classroom, she would say something that she would later regret. After the incident, Ms. McDuff's superior required that Lina be punished with school suspension for three days for walking out of class, in spite of the action having been Lina's best effort to prevent a further confrontation between her and the teacher, in defense of her bruised pride in front of peers.

When students help to define the punishments for particular behaviors and agree to respond to conflicts in particular ways, there is less chance of trouble. The engagement with discipline should be realistic on both ends: the code must be strict enough to create positive learning environments, yet should not systematically exclude and punish certain groups—especially black boys in both the United States and Britain—as codes do now (Gillborn and Gipps, 1996; Sewell, 1997; Skiba, Michael, Nardo, and Peterson, 2002). By engaging youth in techniques for balancing their peer and adult worlds, schools can expect less disengagement from students.

3. Teachers should be recruited who are familiar with students' cultural repertoires and skilled in engaging student challenges.
Many students I encountered—especially black students with hip-hop style—expressed frustration with adult misunderstandings of their styles, especially outside school. The most common description of what a student's style meant was that others *mis*understood their styles as signaling oppositional outlooks. Although these misunderstandings were reported outside school, at least one teaching assistant in London expressed misconceptions of student styles as signaling delinquency. Furthermore, teachers with backgrounds similar to their students' are more likely to understand and hence have the skills to engage students' peer cultures.

By definition, college-educated teachers in a school whose student body has low rates of parental education will have less in common with their students than teachers serving areas with higher rates of college education. Still, recruiting teachers with similar backgrounds— from similar neighborhoods and similar class, ethnic, and racial backgrounds—will aid in student achievement. Although teacher-student matching is no guarantee, it helps teachers to better understand the cultural choices that youth make, what motivates those choices, and how to consider the pressures of peer culture (see also Warikoo, 2004b). Hence it can help teachers improve student achievement. Also, individuals tend to trust those who seem more familiar; this trust can make the difference between engagement and disengagement for some youth.

The most successful teachers I observed during my research managed to connect with their students' social worlds. However, understanding youth culture did not mean backing down in the face of loud students; rather, students seemed to respond best to "tough love." Mr. Smith, a Scottish teacher in London, often addressed students with "precious" and "darling," as only an elderly male teacher could do, yet he was able to discipline an especially unruly Year 11 class. More than one student who often misbehaved told me that Mr. Smith was his or her favorite teacher, because he was strict but fair and he also joked with them. One day I observed Jamie, a weak student, reading silently in Mr. Smith's class; later in the day I observed her cause chaos in another classroom. In addition to using kind words and humor, when his class lost control, Mr. Smith could bellow and intimidate even me, an adult observer—although less than five feet tall, he could command silence.

In contrast, many of the same students in London expressed dislike for Mr. Jones, whom they perceived to be unfair. One day I observed Mr. Jones covering a class for another teacher. Most of the students seemed to know him from previous classes. Despite the class's reputation as a particularly well-behaved one, students were unusually disruptive, talking back when Mr. Jones yelled at students and laughing at his insistent admonishments. Indira, an Indian girl whose parents came to England from Kenya, sat at the front of the room by herself, quietly doing her work amidst the chaos. When I sat down next to her, she explained her classmates' behaviors to me, as if to apologize for their altered comportment compared to other days when I had come to their class: "Mr. Jones picks on certain people, and that's why everyone is rude to him. He singles out individuals." Fairness matters a great deal, and children are sensitive to teachers' biases.

Teachers who were fair and open but not tough could not teach effectively, either. In New York I encountered Ms. Davis, a very kind teacher who spoke lovingly of her students outside class and expressed great faith in and admiration for many of them. During class, however, Ms. Davis's lack of strictness often led students to take advantage of the lack of discipline in the classroom. Students often interrupted discussions with tangential comments that led the class astray; others carried on conversations with peers throughout the class period in spite of Ms. Davis's occasional requests to focus. On one occasion, I observed less than one-third of the class turn in a long-term project on the day it was due. Because Ms. Davis did not engage with the toughness element of her students' cultural dispositions, she could not teach them effectively, in spite of her positive relationship with most of her students (see also Chin and Phillips, 2004). Students expressed a preference for and seemed to thrive best with teachers who skillfully balanced toughness with support and who were consistently fair.

4. School structures should foster strong teacher-student relationships and peer relationships.

A significant contrast between the New York and London schools was their structures. Both were typical for their city. Traditional public high schools in New York range in size from 1,000 to 4,000 students (250 to more than 1,000 students per grade); in contrast, about 1,000 students (about 200 students per grade) attend the typical state secondary school in London. In New York City's public schools, students typically attend seven classes in one day with seven different groups of peers and seven teachers. Twice a year, these groups and teachers change, so that a student sees a peer and a teacher for just forty-three minutes every day for only four months, unless they happen to have another course together in the future. The most cohesive class I observed in New York was the rare special class that lasted for the full school year; the students were battling administrators to persuade them to approve another year together with the same teacher (they were unsuccessful). The anomie and lack of class cohesion the general structure created led students to cling to what was most familiar—ethnicity—rather than learning about other cultures, about peers of other backgrounds, and especially about those for whom they held negative stereotypes.

In contrast, London students typically attend classes with a Form Class, with whom most start in Year 7 (age eleven). The Form Classes I observed had strong bonds between the students, and generally classes stayed with the same form tutor from Year 7 to Year 11 (ages eleven to sixteen). The class tutor took attendance and kept track of students' bad (and good) behaviors in the classes of other teachers. He or she saw the class at least twice daily, for morning and afternoon registration times. This accountability system meant that it was difficult for students to slip by and go unnoticed by teachers. The longer-term relationships gave students and their form tutors a chance to understand each other and to move past stereotypes about style and race. Moreover, the smaller school size and continuity from ages eleven to sixteen (and eighteen for those who stayed for Sixth Form, ages sixteen to eighteen) fostered familiarity within the school building. After less than a month at Long Meadow, I began to recognize most students in the hallways; this was not my experience in New York. A familiar environment in which most staff and students know each other well and students from diverse backgrounds know each other well enables youth to dialogue across the usual ethnic and racial boundaries. Small schools have recently been promoted in many urban school districts, based on research showing that small schools improve academic achievement (Lawrence, 2004; Sizer, 1984); the research in this book shows that small schools can also improve race relations, a major goal of U.S. schools since the landmark *Brown v. Board of Education* decision in 1954. Happily, when I visited York High School one year after my research, a school administrator told me that the school was transitioning to four "Small Learning Communities," semi-autonomous "schools" within the building (interview with school administrator, June 2, 2005).

The reader may justifiably find these policy recommendations insufficient to close the achievement gap. My project deals with one small aspect of the lives of teenagers: youth culture. Other influences in their lives are at least equally important: socioeconomic inequality in their society; inadequate school funding; the ill effects of life in neighborhoods of concentrated poverty; parental resources; and many others. Also, although many studies suggest that changes in education can lead to many social changes, scholars should remember that schools can do only so much to change a society. In the most unequal society, excellent schools can only go so far to decrease inequality, because the resources and avenues for advancement may not exist. Hence, the policy implications I have listed here should be read with an understanding of the limitations as well as the potential positive effects.

Nevertheless, empowering second-generation teens to perform balancing acts between their peer status goals and academic achievement goals is surely one piece of the puzzle of how to improve academic achievement among children of immigrants. I begin this book by describing the trajectories my brother and I followed from working-class public schools in small-town America to professional careers that took us far away from our childhood peers. We integrated mainstream American culture, the youth cultures of our white working-class peers, and our parents' Indian culture. Later on, both of us became avid consumers of hip-hop. The research presented in this book suggests that children of immigrants, in both New York City and London, are pursuing the immigrant dreams of their parents, even if many attend school in environments where failure is more common than success. Empowering them to balance their youthful desires to be hip and cool among their peers while also achieving academically, through a better understanding of youth cultures, will surely improve their life trajectories.

Research Sites and Methods

The school-based research I describe in this book is based on fieldwork I con-ducted during the 2003–2004 academic year. My previous interest in the process of assimilation in multi-ethnic urban America led me back to New York City for my research, but with a twist. This time, I wanted to look beyond the American context to understand what was unique to the United States in terms of assimila-tion processes—more specifically, processes of cultural assimilation. New York and London have much in common: they both receive immigrants from diverse countries and regions of the world; they are both centers of cultural production; and they are both the financial centers of their respective countries. New York and London provide representative snapshots of the multiethnic global city. Thirty-five percent of New Yorkers are immigrants, and another 17 percent are second generation (March 2005 Current Population Survey in Kasinitz et al., 2008). Similarly, 22 percent of London's population was born outside the European Union (5 percent in the non-British EU), and 29 percent identify as racial minorities (Office for National Statistics 2001a, 2001c). Among their differences, what stands out most has historical roots: the presence in New York of a former slave population that is a native poor minority group, African Americans. To be sure, working-class whites have a distinct culture and identity in Britain. However, researchers have not explained negative school orientations among children of immigrants by fingering the influence of working-class whites (or any other group), as the culture of disadvantaged African Americans has been said to influence second-generation Americans.

To pursue my research questions about the cultural lives of children of immigrants and assimilation, I based my study in schools, where children spend one-third of their waking hours (Hofferth and Sandberg, 2001) and where they encounter a large concentration of peers on a daily basis. I chose to study high school students rather than younger children because teenagers consciously make many cultural choices, rather than simply participating in their parents' worlds as younger children do. At school, youth are confronted by peers as well as the authority of adults, beyond the eyes of their parents. For many teenagers, school is the site where most of their social activities take place and where their friendships are formed. The school environment provided a unique, bounded space in which to study cultural processes through observations of student interactions and behaviors in the classroom. The urban school contexts I chose bring youth of different ethnic and racial backgrounds together for extended periods of time, even if after school they return to neighborhoods dominated by their own ethnic or racial groups, especially in New York. These sites allowed me to study the dynamics of youth cultures across ethnic groups within the same context. In contrast, previous studies have either looked at multiple school sites, to compare ethnic groups, or else have studied just one ethnic group in one school. The school setting also facilitated conducting interviews and surveys across ethnic groups.

To choose schools, I first investigated neighborhoods in New York and London that were multiethnic, because I wanted to see what youth culture looks like in an environment in which no ethnic or racial group dominates and leads the way in defining the peer culture. I also wanted to interview students from a group thought to demonstrate positive youth culture (Indians) and from a group thought to demonstrate negative youth culture (Afro-Caribbeans). After narrowing down the choice of neighborhoods and visiting multiple areas in both cities, I identified an area in Queens, New York, and another in Brent, London. Finally, I identified, contacted, and sought permission to conduct research in schools in those areas.

In London I cold-called and then cold-visited a handful of schools before two sympathetic administrators allowed me to return to visit their schools for a day. Both were supportive of my research and eager to have a researcher come in and observe their schools. They both seemed confident about and proud of their schools, which I suspect made them comfortable with an outsider coming in for a detailed peek at their schools. I had contacts in London's East End (Tower Hamlets and Newham) as well and visited three schools there. In Tower Hamlets, schools were divided almost exclusively between white working-class and Bangladeshi students—an interesting setting but one that did not suit my research questions on downward assimilation and was not conducive to the comparison of London to New York and across different second-generation groups. The Newham school had few Indian students, which would have made for a difficult comparison with New York. I eventually chose Long Meadow Community School in Brent for its similarity to the Queens high schools I had in mind in terms of socioeconomic status of families sending their children to the school; the neighborhood's location on the edge of the city center; student achievement levels well below average, but not the worst in the city or country; and ethnic and racial diversity. The assistant headmaster quickly agreed to allow me to conduct my detailed research there and sought the headmistress's permission only on my insistence that she also be on board.

Although I tried, I had no luck with cold-calling or cold-visiting schools in New York. This problem was somewhat abated by my greater familiarity with New York Schools, having taught for four years in New York City public schools prior to starting work on my Ph.D. Friends of friends and former colleagues introduced me to teachers in their schools, and I made contact, as well, with other schools through my previous research in a New York high school and community. In contrast to the general openness of London schools, New York schools were difficult to penetrate, even when a sympathetic teacher was on my side. Most administrators were reluctant to agree to admit an outsider, and formal approval for research from the New York City Board of Education entailed a lengthy process. The Board of Education approval process was time-consuming and intensive, and I was barred from asking many kinds of questions. For example, I was not allowed to ask questions on students' religious backgrounds, because of the sensitive nature of the post 9/11 era (this research was done in New York almost three years after the 2001 tragedy). The threat of a lawsuit seemed to guide most responses to my requests to visit schools and to conduct research in New York. Through persistence, a bit of luck, and the help of sympathetic administrators, I eventually did manage to visit a handful of schools in Queens and Brooklyn. Finding the right mix of students proved more difficult than I expected, even in schools with more than three thousand pupils. A helpful representative of a South Asian youth organization introduced me to an administrator at York High School, and that assistant principal agreed to allow me to visit the school and, later, to conduct my research. During my first visit the school quickly struck me as the kind of place I was looking for: it was diverse, it hosted significant numbers of black and South Asian students, and student backgrounds were poor to lower-middle-class, like those at Long Meadow in London (see table 1).

THE SCHOOLS

York High School, New York

I spent four months at York High School in New York during the spring of 2004, attending school every day for at least the length of one student's school day. Like most public high schools in New York City, York High is vastly overcrowded. Home to more than three thousand students, the building operates at one-third more than its official capacity. Overcrowding affects most aspects of student life. Twenty-two trailers used as extra classrooms have become a permanent fixture on the school's former playground, eliminating play space. Including the trailers, York High has just over one hundred classrooms (including computer and special education rooms), which are not enough for the 3,100 students (interview with school administrator, May 31, 2005). Hence, a staggered schedule allows students to start and finish school at different times of day, so that fewer students are in the building during any given period. Students start school anywhere from before 7:30 A.M. to 10:30 A.M. and finish between 12:45 P.M. and 4 P.M.

Because of the school's staggered schedule, I could use different timings to observe different aspects of the school, and toward the end of my research I spent longer times at school to answer my research questions and complete interviews before the school year ended and classes and groups once again changed. I began my research at York by shadowing a teacher in the English

Department, Ms. McDuff, and her classes, which ranged from ninth to eleventh grade (ages fourteen to seventeen). These were the classes in which I also conducted the New York survey and recruited initial interview respondents. The overall combination of students taught by Ms. McDuff represented a good cross-section of York students who come to school regularly. After some time, Ms. McDuff introduced me to two other English teachers, whom I subsequently also shadowed. I also visited selected classes of other teachers I met, sometimes when I encountered an opportunity for different kinds of observations, such as when one student's drama class was putting on a performance for other classes in the school auditorium. I spent a lot of time in gym and computer classes as well, where the informal structure allowed me to observe different types of interactions and chat informally with students. The staggered lunch schedule at York High also meant that I could spend up to six periods a day in the cafeteria, a setting ripe for observation and discussions.

I kept my writing in front of students to a minimum, using a very small notebook during the day to jot down a few words here and there. When I felt my mind was saturated with observations and my notebook filled with shorthand, I would go to a corner of the teachers' cafeteria in the school's basement to add details to the scant notes while they were fresh in my memory. Every afternoon when I got home from school, I would transform these handwritten notes into even more detailed ones on my computer. The time rewriting my notes and filling in details helped me process my observations and thoughts, and often led to lengthy memos that sometimes hypothesized about processes that I was observing and other times fleshed out new questions and ideas that I wanted to think about as I continued my research. I also spent time in neighborhood religious organizations and with after-school clubs, and wandering the nearby streets and shops to better understand the neighborhood. My goal was to integrate as much as possible into the school community, while keeping in mind my questions about culture, peer status, and academic achievement.

Long Meadow Community School, London

In London I spent six months (three days per week) at Long Meadow Community School. During the 2003–2004 school year, twelve hundred students were enrolled at Long Meadow, including about two hundred students each in Years 7 to 11 (ages eleven to sixteen, the equivalent of grades 6–10 in the United States), and two hundred total in Sixth Form, the equivalent of eleventh and twelfth grades in the United States. I spent my days shadowing students in Years 10 and 11 (ages fourteen to sixteen) and in lower Sixth Form (ages sixteen to seventeen). When I started the research, I was first introduced to one student in each year group by an administrator, and I shadowed those students on different days. Later in the year, I shadowed two to three of their peers (eight total) through their school days. The students I shadowed represented a diversity of interests (elective classes), genders (gym classes were gender segregated), and most importantly, tracking level (high- and low-level science and math classes). During the school's breaks I wandered the halls, sometimes chatting with students in the schoolyard or in the hallways, at other times observing, and at still

TABLE 20   INTERVIEW RESPONDENTS

	New York		London
1.5- and 2nd-generation Indians	10 boys		10 boys
	10 girls		10 girls
1.5- and 2nd-generation Afro-Caribbeans	10 boys		10 boys
	10 girls		10 girls
1.5- and 2nd-generation Indo-Caribbeans	10 boys	Native whites	10 boys
	10 girls		10 girls
Total (New York)	30 boys	Total (London)	30 boys
	30 girls		30 girls

other times chatting with school staff. I spent time in the cafeteria as well, and sitting with students (and occasionally teachers) at the lunch tables outside. As in New York, I kept note-taking in front of students to a minimum. I had keys to an administrator's office in the school that I frequently used in the middle of the day, skipping a class or two, to jot down field notes. During those six months I also attended the few after-school functions that were held, including an MC (rapper) competition, parent-teacher conferences, a winter holiday celebration, and a staff Christmas dinner. I also got to know the surrounding area and the neighborhoods in which students lived, by attending religious services on Sundays and by visiting local markets and the local community gym that many boys frequented.

WHAT I DID

There were three components to this research in both schools: ethnographic observations, in-depth interviews, and a survey of a cross-section of students. Ethnographic observations allowed salient aspects of culture to emerge that I missed in my survey and interview questions, and enhanced my understanding of the cultural processes in both schools. Using ethnographic data also allowed me to compare what students *said* with what they *did*. This was one way of handling the "attitude-achievement paradox" (Mickelson, 1990) debate in the sociology of education, which highlights the difference between minority students' positive attitudes toward achievement and their negative behaviors in school and weak academic achievement.

The in-depth interviews were with twenty second-generation (and some 1.5-generation) Indians and twenty second-generation Afro-Caribbeans in each city. I also interviewed twenty native whites in London and twenty Indo-Caribbeans in New York, for a total of 120 in-depth interviews. Half of the students in each group were boys, half girls (see table 20).

Interviews lasted from forty to ninety minutes. I conducted most of the interviews in two parts (on occasion, three), to coincide with the short class periods at both sites that I had to accommodate. Interviews focused on various aspects of peer cultures: taste preferences in music and style, the meanings of those tastes, influences on style, ethnic and racial identities, extracurricular activities and interests, attitudes and beliefs about school and achievement, school experiences, handling conflict at school, fighting in school, school social groups, popularity at school, racial discrimination, peer and parental expectations and influences, police encounters, and friendships. I recruited students for interviews in the classes I initially observed and surveyed for the project and then in other classes I observed, interviewing almost all the students from particular classes who fit the interview criteria in order to have as much of a cross-section of the ethnic groups as possible. Because of York High School's greater diversity, I had some difficulty finding enough Indian and Afro-Caribbean students; hence, teachers helped me by introducing me to students they knew. Interview respondents in both cities ranged in age from fourteen to eighteen, with the exception of one twenty-year-old student in New York. The interviews were transcribed through an independent agency and then reviewed by me. I used ATLASti to code and analyze the interviews. The software allowed me to easily observe patterns in, for example, gender or ethnicity, in responses to questions. I spent much time creating extensive charts in the style of Miles and Huberman (1984) when I analyzed the data and disaggregated them by ethnicity, city, and gender into twelve subgroups. The use of qualitative data software allowed me to easily return to the data over and over again, whenever I had new ideas, hypotheses, and analyses that I wanted to test; when I needed to find a specific quote that I remembered but could not place; and when I needed to rethink and reevaluate claims I had made in earlier drafts of the dissertation in the process of writing this book.

Because I found that the majority of black students at York High were African American with U.S.-born parents, I approached a neighboring school in the same Board of Education Region to complete interviews with Afro-Caribbeans. Harrison High School lies less than two miles from York High School, and no other high schools are located between the two. A school administrator called Harrison York's "sister school." Many students at Harrison reported having friends at York, and vice versa. Although this was not an ideal choice, because the schools are demographically similar, I do not believe conducting interviews in two different schools affected my findings. Fifteen of the twenty interviews with Afro-Caribbeans in New York were with students at Harrison. Because I had conducted research at Harrison for a previous project, I was quite familiar with that school environment.

No prior survey data on either city had addressed the questions I wanted to answer in my research on youth culture among multiple ethnic groups, so I had to create my own. Hence, in addition to the ethnographies and 120 in-depth interviews, I surveyed 191 students at York High School and Long Meadow Community School. The surveys were conducted with diverse groups of students during four heterogeneous classes (by ethnicity/race, SES, gender, and skills) at each site; they gave a sense of overall attitudes, interests, tastes, beliefs, identities, and backgrounds in the schools. These were the same classes that I observed regularly and from which I recruited interview subjects, allowing me to triangulate my findings in many cases between ethnographic observations of school behaviors, survey responses, and interview responses. The survey was administered in four Personal, Social, and Health Education (PSHE) classes in London, and in four English classes in New York. PSHE is taught to Form Classes, which are, according to a school administrator, deliberately mixed in terms of gender, SES, ethnicity, and skill level. The English classes in New York included a "remedial" ninth-grade English class (fifteen of the nineteen ninth-grade English classes were remedial); a general tenth-grade English class; and two mixed tenth-and-eleventh-grade classes serving medium-achieving students. The highest achievers are not in the New York survey, because I did not include any honors classes. Students who were absent on the day of the survey were not included in the survey data, and those who had already dropped out of school or who did not attend school regularly are not part of this research; hence, my findings speak only to cultural life for *regular school attendees* and cannot speak to youth cultures among high school dropouts. Although the data are limited to the schools I visited, the robust data collection within the schools led to insights into youth culture at school that I believe are applicable in other settings in the two cities.

For topics addressed in both the survey and interviews, I compared my survey and interview findings for both cities in order to understand the degree to which my interview data mirrored data overall in the schools. Survey and interview data were generally in agreement. I wrote memos that summarized my survey, interview, and ethnographic findings on particular topics, such as tastes in music. Also, during the research process, in addition to field notes, I wrote analytical memos on overall thoughts and further questions I had, largely based on my ethnographic observations. I later used survey and interview data to confirm, refine, or add nuance to my ethnographic observations. During the research process I made it a point to transcribe interviews and begin coding them, so that my insights from interviews and the ethnography could lead to further observation and analysis in the schools and further probing in later interviews.

Using these data in this book I analyze the evidence for youth culture as a mechanism for behaviors not conducive to academic success. I employ the cross-national comparison to illuminate what is unique to the U.S. context and what is similar to multiethnic schools in the global metropolitan cities of New York and London. Having three sources of data enhanced my understanding. For example, after interviewing Olivia, an Afro-Caribbean girl in New York, and hearing about her strong focus on education and her high academic achievement, I routinely observed Olivia loitering in the hallways between classes, five to ten minutes after the late buzzer had rung. I then had to think through a situation that on the surface seemed contradictory. I later understood that because her schedule with no lunch break or homeroom period allowed no social time during the school day, Olivia took it when she could, so that she could maintain her popularity. Similarly, recall Carl in London, a white, working-class boy, who told me in an interview he was now straightening up his act after misbehaving a lot in school. After I interviewed Carl, I saw him misbehaving in class, so I cheekily asked him about his interview, which had taken place earlier that day, and he then sat in his seat, much to my surprise. It was as if my question reminded him of what he really wanted to do. This observation led me to understand that desire for success in school does not preclude misbehavior, nor vice versa. These moments of data triangulation strongly enhanced my understanding of the schools and their students, in ways that one type of data collection alone could not have done.

IDENTITY AND RESEARCH

My own identity as an Indian American and former New Yorker certainly impacted my research. Having lived in the United States all my life and in New York for more than four years prior to starting my research helped me to more quickly understand the sociocultural world of the teenagers in New York. As I explain in chapter 1, many of the questions and hypotheses I posed in this research grew out of my observations as a teacher in New York City's public schools for four years, as well as my own experiences growing up since birth in the United States with two immigrant parents from India.

Having parents from India meant that I understood more details of South Asian diasporic life, such as terminology and culture, perhaps making the South Asians I encountered in my research more comfortable with me than other groups may have been. I had many a discussion about Bollywood and bhangra music during the research process. When some South Asian girls heard that I was soon to be married (I got married the summer after completing my research), we had long discussions about what I would wear, where I should buy my jewelry, how long the ceremony would be, and whether my parents were upset that my fiancé was from a different part of South Asia from my family. South Asian students sometimes came to me looking for advice on how to handle dating with strict South Asian parents. Many Indo-Caribbeans in New York also saw me as a fellow Indian who shared their culture. In addition, having previously done research in their community, I was familiar with chutney, soca, and other aspects of the small community that signaled an understanding of their ethnic culture, which many students appreciated. Afro-Caribbeans, too, identified with my experiences with immigrant parents, with comments such as "You know how immigrant parents are"—they work hard, push their children to excel, and enforce very, very strict rules, especially with girls!

On the other hand, students in both sites, regardless of ethnicity, saw me as an outsider in some ways, and many of their perceptions of my identity focused on my being a Harvard student and a researcher, both of which many, if not most, had not encountered previously. In London, students thought of me first as an American, my accent setting me most apart from them, regardless of ethnicity. When I began my research four months after my initial visit to the London school, a South Asian boy recognized me in the hallway from my previous visit and shouted, "Hey! You're the American girl, aren't you?!" In fact, some students in both cities (Indians and non-Indians alike) did not recognize my Indian ethnicity until I told them my parents are from India or demonstrated ethnic knowledge, about which they sometimes seemed surprised. I attributed this to two factors. First, and probably more important, I bore many signals of cultural identity that went against their own understandings of Indian identity. For example, I wore thick, dark glasses during much of my research, a style more popular among the upper middle class and well educated. Also, I rarely wear ethnic markers such as gold jewelry, religious symbols, or ethnic clothing, as did many Indian students, especially girls. This was not a deliberate attempt at separation but simply a result of my upbringing in an almost exclusively white American environment, followed by attendance at elite universities and a stint in New York City (away from its Indian ethnic enclave). Second, my family's roots are not from Gujarat or Punjab, the most common origins of Indian emigrants in New York and London, and I do not speak Gujarati or Punjabi, the regional languages of most of my respondents' origins and the languages spoken in most of their homes (apart from English). This ethnic difference also means that I do not look like the typical Indian in Queens or Brent.

The things that marked me as an outsider were not always detrimental to my research. In New York, multiple students, upon hearing the name Harvard or simply that I had a lot of higher education, made it a point to get to know me and to seek my advice. Some asked me how I had made it to Harvard; others asked about how to study for the SAT; and one young woman asked for advice on how to obtain an athletic scholarship to college. I was more than happy to help when I could. Still, I also wished that students had someone who could address these questions on a more continuous basis at school after I left. This is a sad consequence of attending an overcrowded high school in which individual guidance counselors are responsible for tracking and guiding three hundred to four hundred students at a time.

In London, my outsider status provided other benefits. Students—and this is not an exaggeration—*marveled* at my American accent. After the initial excitement of having me say certain words, many in later conversations asked me to describe American high school proms, graduation parties, and cheerleading squads, all of which some wished for in their own high school. When they found out I had lived in Brooklyn, they were even more excited, mostly having heard about the place in hip-hop music. Some asked me about what the "ghetto" neighborhoods of New York are. Conveying a sad stereotype promoted around the world, one working-class white English student told me and his friends in a conversation that he wanted to visit the ghetto in New York and was curious about what it is like, and that he would do so someday in a bullet-proof car with tinted windows and with his head down low, so he wouldn't get shot. As I note in the text, for better or worse, American popular culture looms large in Britain, and British students saw me as its potential representative.

I tried to mitigate my image as an adult and hence an authority to kids in different ways. I had students address me as Natasha, rather than Miss or Ms. Warikoo, as they would a teacher in their schools. Second, I rarely intervened in misbehavior, except when I felt I could not keep silent as a responsible individual in the room. (For example, when I once observed two students on the brink of fighting, I intervened with a threatening look to remind them that an adult was in the room—which in that case seemed to do the trick.) Finally, I chose to wear more casual clothes than teachers and other staff. My relatively young age (I moved to London to start the research there on my thirtieth birthday) at least kept me out of the age category of students' parents, especially when they found out that I was neither married nor a mother at the time. I am under no illusion that students behaved in front of me exactly as they would have had there been no adult in the room; still, I did my best to put them at ease with me as quickly as possible, and in both cities they soon began treating me as a nonthreatening, regular—but curious—presence.

Notes

CHAPTER 1. UNDERSTANDING CULTURAL INCORPORATION

1. For an overview of cultural explanations for racial and ethnic stratification in academic achievement, see Warikoo and Carter, 2009.

2. Barth (1969) introduced the concept of ethnic boundaries, suggesting that "ethnicity is a matter of social organization above and beyond questions of empirical cultural differences: it is about 'the social organization of culture difference'" (6).

3. Indo-Caribbeans come mostly from Guyana and Trinidad. Their ancestors came from India to the West Indies during the nineteenth and early twentieth centuries as indentured laborers.

4. British public discourse regarding assimilation and socioeconomic inequality often focuses on Muslims, especially Pakistani and Bangladeshi Muslims (see, for example, Office for National Statistics, 2004b). Still, I chose to focus on Afro-Caribbeans for downward assimilation because they are the ethnic minority group most often cited as "resisting" the dominant culture and maintaining an oppositional stance (Majors, Gillborn, and Sewell, 2001; Modood 2004; Sewell, 1997).

5. In both countries, Indians are also stereotyped as working-class, especially as convenience store owners. However, overall they are seen as "successful" minorities (Khandelwal, 2002; Prashad, 2000).

6. Most British Indian students had some ties to East Africa (Uganda, Kenya, or Tanzania)—just two interviewees out of twenty did not. (The two exceptions were both Punjabi Sikhs.) Some British Indians had a parent who was actually born in East Africa, and in two cases, both parents were born in East Africa; these students' grandparents were all from India. East African Indians in Britain have done exceptionally well in terms of education and labor market outcomes (Modood, 1997).

7. Mary Waters (1999) describes second-generation Afro-Caribbeans in the United States as either employing ethnic identity to distance themselves from African American identity and its negative associations, or identifying as African American and experiencing similar stereotypes and discrimination as do African Americans. She links *ethnic* identity to those living in middle-class areas, and *African American* identity to those living in more disadvantaged areas.

8. New York City's public schools are significantly more racially segregated than London's (Burgess and Wilson, 2004). Hence, no high school with significant numbers of Afro-Caribbeans and Indians had significant (native) white populations, so I could not include U.S.-born whites in the New York segment of my study. Because of the lack of a comparison group, I did not focus on Latinos in New York.

9. I have changed the names of the schools, my respondents, and teachers in the interest of confidentiality.

10. A school administrator explained to me that because many students do not have a lunch period at school, many do not bring in their free/reduced-price lunch form. In the 2005–2006 school year, in fact, the school pushed students to bring in their forms, and as a result, 92 percent qualified for free or reduced-price lunch.

11. I chose to report mother's rather than father's education because one-third of the students in New York and over half of the students in London reported that they did not know their father's education level. A significant though lower number of students also did not know their mother's education level. The percentages are based on students who reported their mother's education level.

12. The school where I conducted additional interviews with Afro-Caribbeans in New York, Harrison High School, had demographics similar to those of York. Harrison's student body was 9 percent non-Hispanic white, 26 percent non-Hispanic black, 37 percent Hispanic, and 33 percent Asian and other (New York City Department of Education, 2004–5). Forty-nine percent of Harrison's 3,500-plus students were eligible for free school lunches.

13. In Britain, *mixed race* most commonly refers to someone with one black parent and one white parent. It sometimes also refers to children of other partnerings as well, such as Asian-white.

14. The GCSE exams are the exit exams for schooling in Britain, taken at age sixteen. Five C-or-above GCSE grades (one grade is awarded for each subject) are the minimum requirement for entering most British universities.

15. British secondary education ends at age sixteen, Year 11, when mandatory schooling ends; this is equivalent to tenth grade in the United States. After secondary school, students can enroll in a college (ages sixteen to eighteen), enroll in a Sixth Form (ages sixteen to eighteen), or work. College and Sixth Form education are highly specialized, including vocational tracks and specific academic subjects.

16. Half of U.K. mothers with higher-education degrees were born in Britain, and one-third were white.

17. The population of Brixton, known as London's Afro-Caribbean neighborhood, is less than 25 percent Afro-Caribbean. Tower Hamlets, known as London's Bangladeshi enclave, is just one-third Bangladeshi (Office for National Statistics, 2001c).

18. Bhangra is traditional Punjabi folk music. It has become popular among South Asians worldwide, especially in remixed music.

CHAPTER 2. MUSIC AND STYLE

1. Hip-hop includes rap music, DJing (someone spinning melodies and remixed music, often overlaid with rapping), certain styles of dancing, dress styles, and graffiti art (Chang, 2005). I use the phrase *hip-hop music* to mean rap, remixed music with rap, rhythm and blues, and U.K. garage (a British form of rap music, with faster beats and rapping than American rap).

2. Shell Toes are a style of Adidas sneakers popular among hip-hop artists.

3. Students at Oxford University and at Stanford University have reported this to me in personal conversations.

4. Missy Elliott, a popular rapper, often raps lyrics similar to those of her male counterparts, reversing the traditional roles of male rappers expressing aggressive, sexual lyrics about women and about their fame and fortunes; Elliott raps similarly about men and about her successes, skills, and wealth.

5. Just one student I interviewed—a New Yorker—admitted to being in a gang at the time of the interview. Others described past involvement with gangs, and friends who are in gangs.

6. *Ghetto* as an adjective used among youth has two meanings. First, it means something cheap or of low quality—of the ghetto. Second, it means ostentatious or over-the-top. This meaning derives from the phrase "ghetto fabulous," which describes those from ghetto neighborhoods who ostentatiously wear heavy jewelry and name-brand clothing—the look's appeal is in its extreme display of conspicuous consumption.

7. MTV Base is a U.K. MTV station that exclusively plays hip-hop and R&B music videos.

8. The gender difference was not significant among other groups.

9. The finding that London students preferred American music and styles to British music and styles is not exclusive to the second generation or to teenagers in Britain: Bennett (2009) found that young adults in Britain tend to prefer American to British-made television and movies.

CHAPTER 3. RACIAL AUTHENTICITY, "ACTING BLACK," AND CULTURAL CONSUMPTION

1. Recall that most Indian students at York High were Punjabi Sikhs, so that in this case, religion and ethnicity coincided.

2. For a general discussion of Indian authenticity among Indian American New Yorkers, see Maira, 1999, 2002.

3. *Coolie* is used in the Caribbean to describe Indo-Caribbeans. This is sometimes pejorative, but it is used self-referentially as well.

4. "Asian" in Britain commonly means South Asian–origin: having forefathers from India, Pakistan, Bangladesh, Sri Lanka, or Nepal.

5. Terry is referring to the film *Don't Be a Menace to South Central While Drinking Your Juice in the Hood,* a parody of movies featuring African American characters and settings, such as *Menace II Society* and *Boyz in the Hood.*

6. Ragga is a modern style of reggae music that incorporates electronic sounds.

7. In the contemporary U.S. and U.K. contexts, "bhangra" implies bhangra–hip-hop remixed music. Although all but two of the Indian youth I met at Long Meadow Community School are Gujarati, they listen to bhangra. It has become the popular music of all South Asian youth, in both Great Britain and the United States (Maira, 2002).

8. Indians came to Britain in large numbers well before 1965, when significant numbers of Indians started coming to the United States. A small wave of Indian men did come to the United States around the turn of the twentieth century; however, the population did not sustain itself, because no Indian women came (Leonard, 1992). Today, approximately 4 percent of Britain's population is South Asian, compared to less than 1 percent of the U.S. population (Office for National Statistics, 2001c; U.S. Census Bureau, 2000a).

9. Because Richie looked South Asian, he identified religiously as Hindu, and his parents were from Guyana, I categorized him as Indo-Caribbean, in spite of his self-identification as black. Because students called their ethnic and racial identities a variety of different names, I chose to stay with the categories I established at the beginning of the study, even if students called themselves differently when asked about their racial and ethnic identities.

10. A *salwar kameez* is a common South Asian outfit consisting of a long tunic worn over loose-fitting pants. Both women and men wear *salwar kameezes,* although women's tend to be more ornate and colorful, and men's are generally white and quite loose.

11. This includes Indian women and men ages sixteen to thirty-four, including both first- and second-generation.

12. Note that consuming black-identified taste culture does not necessarily signify identifying with or even liking blacks as individuals. Sunaina Maira (2002) has shown that young South Asians in New York enjoy hip-hop music and dance while simultaneously expressing disdain for African Americans (see also Kasinitz, Mollenkopf, Waters, and Holdaway, 2008, chapter 10). This suggests the critical importance of paying attention to cultural meanings and the reception of culture.

13. I define white English students as those who are racially white and whose parents were both born in England (third and subsequent generations). A few students with Irish ancestry fell into this category. However, I found that students with Irish heritage exhibited symbolic ethnicity (Gans, 1979; Waters, 1990; for a critique of this perspective, see Hickman, 1998), so I chose to include them.

14. Richard Peterson and his colleagues (R. Peterson and Kern, 1996; R. Peterson and Simkus, 1992) have suggested that American elites have increasingly omnivorous, rather than exclusive, tastes.

15. A taste for punk and rock music did not generally signal the same social or political views in New York. I met many students of color (especially Hispanics) in New York who listened to rock or punk music, or both, and others whose primary interest was hip-hop yet who also appreciated rock, a phenomenon less common in London.

CHAPTER 4. TWO TYPES OF RACIAL DISCRIMINATION

1. A few Indians reported post-9/11 racial harassment outside school directed at their older male relatives, as well.

2. British sociologist of immigration Tariq Modood (2005) has suggested that in Britain, South Asians face a qualitatively different kind of racism—cultural racism—than do Afro-Caribbeans, who experience color racism. Modood argues that racism toward South Asians in Britain emphasizes their cultural distinctiveness and foreignness, in contrast to biological and color racism aimed at blacks in that country.

3. A patka is a hair covering worn by Sikh boys that is simpler than the turban worn by adult Sikh men.

4. Some students from Asia, including East and South Asia, had a faint smell of spices on their bodies, due perhaps to living in close. poorly ventilated quarters where spicy food was cooked. In addition, some recently arrived Indian immigrants wore sweet-smelling hair oil, a common practice in India. These influences were not the kind of Indian cultural practices that peers took up or appreciated, such as henna tattoos. Cultural practices needed popular icons to make them acceptable and even hip—for example, Madonna's use of henna tattoos (Warikoo, 2005).

5. Recall that in London Indians did not report experiencing racial discrimination; hence, I do not include London Indians in this analysis.

6. The difference between Afro-Caribbean interview and survey responses regarding experiences with racial discrimination suggests perhaps that in interviews Afro-Caribbean students tried to think of particular incidents of racial discrimination, and experiences outside school came to mind first as the most egregious cases, while experiences with teacher racial discrimination were less obvious. The survey question measures teachers' "fairness" with respect to race—perhaps a softer test than the actual accounts of racial discrimination probed in interviews.

CHAPTER 5. POSITIVE ATTITUDES AND (SOME) NEGATIVE BEHAVIORS

1. As mentioned in chapter 4, the greater perception of teacher bias in survey responses than that found in interviews may be due to the questions asked.

The survey asked about teacher fairness, while interviews asked about experiences with racial *discrimination,* perhaps a stronger test. Furthermore, "racial discrimination" may have been interpreted as a question about explicit, overt discrimination, such as that found in more anonymous settings. Responses to the survey question on teacher fairness with regard to race were similar across ethnic groups, with 17 percent of Afro-Caribbean students disagreeing compared to 19 percent of Indian students disagreeing. Still, it is unclear whether students reported bias toward their own group or toward a commonly mistreated group, such as African Americans.

2. In Britain, *college* means the two years after secondary school, which are the equivalent of grades 11 and 12 in the United States. Hence, the London survey said "university" while the New York survey said "college."

3. The difference between New York and London in terms of beliefs about college likely stems from the higher rates of participation in the United States versus Britain. According to the 2000 U.S. Census, 24 percent of Americans over age twenty-five have a bachelor's degree (U.S. Census Bureau, 2000b), in contrast to just 20 percent of English adults (aged sixteen to seventy-four) holding *any* form of higher-education degree (post age eighteen), including vocational degrees (Office for National Statistics, 2001b). Unfortunately, these universally high aspirations are not likely to translate into universally high outcomes. In the York High School neighborhood, just 20 percent of adults age twenty-five or more have completed college. Similarly, Feliciano and Rumbaut (2005) find that among second-generation youth who expected to attend college, six years later only 54 percent of boys and 46 percent of girls were enrolled in college. Still, educational aspirations are good predictors of relative future educational attainment and occupational prestige among the second generation (Feliciano and Rumbaut, 2005).

4. Morrill and his colleagues (2000) similarly describe the "rational tales" youth tell about conflicts as "tales in which the author represents him- or herself as a rational decision maker navigating through the events of [a] story" (534). They contrast rational tales with tales that focus on morality, emotion, or instinct.

5. Similarly, Zukin and Maguire (2004) find that working-class mothers feel conflicted between "shopping by necessity"—similar to Pradeep's fighting to prevent physical violence—and "shopping for status"—similar to Pradeep's later gang membership (193).

CHAPTER 6. BALANCING ACTS

1. Remarkably, 53 percent of white students admitted to sometimes skipping school. This finding resonates with Kasinitz and his colleagues' finding (2008) that white males in New York had rates of contact with the criminal justice system similar to those of second-generation Dominican, Afro-Caribbean, and South American men, though the consequences of these criminal justice encounters seemed to be more severe for racial minorities than for whites.

CHAPTER 7. ETHNIC AND RACIAL BOUNDARIES

1. In addition, tracked classes had about one-third of the pupils from three different Form Classes, and a gym class has all the same-gender members of two Form Classes.

2. Others have used "likeability" to measure peer status—that is, how likely peers are to name an individual as someone they would like to hang out with (Eder and Kinney, 1995; Merten, 1997). This is certainly a measure distinct from popularity, but for the reasons listed I chose instead to operationalize status as popularity.

3. Answers like Nikki's were coded as "Misbehavior or bullying" rather than "Race" because she talked about race only in response to a probe.

4. The same is true of suburban schools, at least in the popular imagination. A 2004 film, *Mean Girls,* takes place in a suburban Chicago school and portrays the mean ways of the school's most popular girls. Rather than being black, the popular girls in the film embody a different image of popularity and status—white and mostly blonde. The 2003 film *Thirteen* portrays the most popular girl at school as manipulative and deeply troubled.

5. From the context of each case in which the respondent said "Indian," I gathered that he or she meant Punjabi Indians, not Indo-Caribbeans. Most Indians at the school were in fact Punjabi Sikhs, so for many there, Indian, Punjabi, and Sikh were synonymous. Three of the twenty Indians I interviewed in New York were *not* Punjabi Sikhs, and five of the eight Sikh boys I interviewed wore a turban over uncut hair, as prescribed by their Sikh religion.

6. Because students in New York identified Indo-Caribbeans and Indians as separate social groups but African Americans and Afro-Caribbeans as one, for this analysis Afro-Caribbean–African American friendships were seen as an in-group friendship, while Indian–Indo-Caribbean friendships were counted as out-group friendships. The results are similar if Afro-Caribbeans are separated from African Americans, and if Indo-Caribbeans are grouped with Indians.

7. Singer Alicia Keys, from New York, has a white mother and an African American father.

8. In contrast to blacks, Asian Indians are slightly more integrated in the United States than their counterparts in Britain with respect to intermarriage: 6.5 percent of married Asian Indians in the United States have non-Asian spouses, compared to 6 percent of married Indians in Britain (C.N. Lee, 2007; Office for National Statistics, 2005). However, the difference is much smaller than the difference between Afro-Caribbean rates in the U.S. and Britain.

9. The index of dissimilarity measures the percentage of a group that would need to move to create an even distribution of two groups, given their relative proportions of the population. In New York City, the index of dissimilarity (census tract level) between blacks and whites was 0.75 (75 percent) in 2000; in London, the index of dissimilarity between whites and Afro-Caribbeans (ward level, a smaller unit of analysis than the census tracts) in 1991 was 0.49 (49 percent) (Beveridge, 2008; Peach, 1996).

10. Other research has shown that freshman college students with room-mates of a different race tend to have more interracial friends by the end of the first year (Stearns, Buchmann, and Bonneau, 2009).

CHAPTER 8. EXPLAINING YOUTH CULTURES, IMPROVING ACADEMIC ACHIEVEMENT

1. Nevertheless, West founded the Kanye West Foundation, whose mission is to "help combat the severe dropout problem in schools across the United States" (www.kanyewestfoundation.org/about/).

2. Some suggest that industry leaders in fact determine what to market by taking cues from poor black youth, and thus construct the meaning of hip to be countercultural (Klein, 2000; Frank, 1997). Klein (2002) cites a designer quoted in *Vogue* magazine: "It's terrible to say, [but] very often the most exciting outfits are from the poorest people" (73).

Works Cited

Adler, Patricia A., and Peter Adler. 1998. *Peer power: Preadolescent culture and identity.* New Brunswick, NJ: Rutgers University Press.

Ainsworth-Darnell, James W., and Douglas B. Downey. 1998. Assessing the oppositional culture explanation for racial/ethnic differences in school performance. *American Sociological Review* 63 (4):536–554.

Alba, Richard D. 2005. Bright vs. blurred boundaries: Second-generation assimilation and exclusion in France, Germany, and the United States. *Ethnic and Racial Studies* 28 (1):20–49.

Alba, Richard D., and Victor Nee. 2003. *Remaking the American mainstream: Assimilation and contemporary immigration.* Cambridge, MA: Harvard University Press.

Alexander, Claire. 2000. *The Asian gang: Ethnicity, identity, masculinity.* Oxford: Berg.

Allport, Gordon W. 1954. *The nature of prejudice.* Cambridge, MA: Addison-Wesley.

Anderson, Elijah. 1999. *Code of the street: Decency, violence, and the moral life of the inner city.* New York: W. W Norton.

Appiah, Kwame Anthony. 1996. Race, culture, identity: Misunderstood connections. In *Color conscious: The political morality of race,* edited by K. A. Appiah and A. Gutmann. Princeton, NJ: Princeton University Press.

Arlidge, John. 2004. The new melting pot. *Observer,* January 4, p. 19.

Barboza, Craigh. 2001. Friend or foe? *USA Weekend,* January 28.

Barth, Fredrik. 1969. Introduction. In *Ethnic groups and boundaries: The social organization of culture difference,* edited by F. Barth. Bergen, Germany: Universitetsforlaget; Prospect Heights, IL: Waveland Press.

Bendix, Regina. 1997. *In search of authenticity: The formation of folklore studies.* Madison: University of Wisconsin Press.

Bennett, Andy. 2000. *Popular music and youth culture: Music, identity, and place*. Basingstoke, UK: Macmillan; New York: St. Martin's Press.

———. 2001. *Cultures of popular music: Issues in cultural and media studies*. Buckingham, UK, and Philadelphia: Open University Press.

Bennett, Tony, et al. 2009. *Culture, Class Distinction*. New York: Routledge.

Beveridge, Andrew A. 2008. A century of Harlem in New York City: Some notes on migration, consolidation, segregation, and recent developments. *City and Community* 7 (4):358–365.

Binder, Amy. 1993. Constructing racial rhetoric: Media depictions of harm in heavy metal and rap music. *American Sociological Review* 58 (6):753–767.

Bleich, Erik. 2003. *Race politics in Britain and France: Ideas and policymaking since the 1960s*. Cambridge: Cambridge University Press.

Bourdieu, Pierre. 1984. *Distinction: A social critique of the Judgment of taste*. Cambridge, MA: Harvard University Press.

———. 1986. The forms of capital. In *Handbook of theory and research for the sociology of education,* edited by J.G. Richardson. New York: Greenwood Press.

Bourdieu, Pierre, and Jean-Claude Passeron. 1977. *Reproduction in education, society and culture*. Translated by R. Nice. *SAGE Studies in Social and Educational Change*, Vol. 5. London: SAGE Publications.

Bowles, Samuel, and Herbert Gintis. 1976. *Schooling in capitalist America: Educational reform and the contradictions of economic life*. New York: Basic Books.

Brown, B. Bradford. 1990. Peer groups and peer cultures. In *At the threshold: The developing adolescent,* edited by S.S. Feldman and G.R. Elliot. Cambridge, MA: Harvard University Press.

Bryson, Bethany. 1996. "Anything but heavy metal": Symbolic exclusion and musical dislikes. *American Sociological Review* 61 (5):884–899.

Burgess, Simon, and Deborah Wilson. 2004. Ethnic segregation in England's schools. CASE paper, Centre for the Analysis of Social Exclusion, London School of Economics.

Carter, Prudence. 2003. "Black" cultural capital, status positioning, and schooling conflicts. *Social Problems* 50 (1):136–155.

———. 2005. *Keepin' it real: School success beyond black and white*. New York: Oxford University Press.

Chang, Jeff. 2005. *Can't stop, won't stop: A history of the hip-hop generation*. New York: St. Martin's Press.

Chin, Tiffani, and Meredith Phillips. 2004. "Oppositional to what? Achievement ideologies, resistance, and ethnic authenticity among urban youth." Paper presented at the American Sociological Association Annual Meeting, San Francisco, August 14, 2004.

———. 2005. "The ubiquity of oppositional culture." Unpublished paper in author's possession.

Cohen, Albert Kircidel. 1955. *Delinquent boys: The culture of the gang*. Glencoe, IL: Free Press.

Cohen, Cathy J. 2007. *The attitudes and behavior of young black Americans: Research summary*. Chicago: University of Chicago.

Cohen, Phil. 1997 [1972]. Subcultural conflict and working-class community. In *The Subcultures Reader*, edited by K. Gelder and S. Thornton. London: Routledge.

Coleman, James Samuel. 1961. *The adolescent society: The social life of the teenager and its impact on education*. Glencoe, NY: Free Press.

Coley, Richard J. 2001. Differences in the gender gap: Comparisons across racial/ethnic groups in education and work. Educational Testing Service, Policy Information Center Report.

Conchas, Gilberto Q. 2001. Structuring failure and success: Understanding the variability in Latino school engagement. *Harvard Educational Review* 71 (4):475–504.

Connell, R. W. 2002. *Gender*. Short Introductions. Cambridge: Polity Press; Malden, MA: Blackwell.

Cook, Philip J., and Jens Ludwig. 1998. The burden of "acting white": Do black adolescents disparage academic achievement? In *The black-white test score gap*, edited by C. Jencks and M. Phillips. Washington, DC: Brookings Institution Press.

Cornell, Stephen E., and Douglas Hartmann. 1998. *Ethnicity and race: Making identities in a changing world*. 1st ed. Sociology for a New Century. Thousand Oaks, CA: Pine Forge Press.

Crain, Robert L., and Rita E. Mahard. 1978. School racial composition and black college attendance and achievement test performance. *Sociology of Education* 51 (2):81–101.

Davies, Scott. 1995. Reproduction and resistance in Canadian high schools: An empirical examination of the Willis thesis. *British Journal of Sociology* 46 (4):662–687.

Davis, Fred. 1992. *Fashion, culture, and identity*. Chicago: University of Chicago Press.

Dawkins, Marvin P., and Jomills Henry Braddock II. 1994. The continuing significance of desegregation: School racial composition and African American inclusion in American society. *Journal of Negro Education* 63 (3):394.

Delpit, Lisa D. 1995. *Other people's children: Cultural conflict in the classroom*. New York: New Press; distributed by W. W. Norton.

Dench, Geoff, Kate Gavron, and Michael Dunlop Young. 2006. *The new East End: Kinship, race and conflict*. London: Profile Books.

Department for Communities and Local Government. 2004. *Indices of Deprivation 2004: Local Authority Summaries*.

Diamond, John, Amanda Lewis, and Lamont Gordon. 2007. Race, culture, and achievement disparities in a desegregated suburb: Reconsidering the oppositional culture explanation. *International Journal of Qualitative Studies in Education* 20 (6):655–680.

DiMaggio, Paul. 1987. Classification in art. *American Sociological Review* 52 (4):440–455.

Dixson, Adrienne D., and Celia K. Rousseau. 2005. Editorial. *Race, Ethnicity, and Education* 8 (1):1–5.

Dolby, Nadine. 2001. *Constructing race: Youth, identity, and popular culture in South Africa*. Albany: State University of New York Press.

Donahue, Patricia L., Kristin E. Voelkl, Jay R. Campbell, and John Mazzeo. 1999. NAEP 1998 reading report card for the nation and the states. National Center for Education Statistics, Office of Educational Research and Improvement, U.S. Department of Education.

D'Souza, Dinesh. 1991. *Illiberal education: The politics of race and sex on campus.* New York: Free Press; Toronto: Collier Macmillan Canada.

Durham, Meenakshi Gigi. 1999. Girls, media, and the negotiation of sexuality: A study of race, class, and gender in adolescent peer groups. *Journalism and Mass Communication Quarterly* 76 (2):193–216.

Eder, Donna, and David A. Kinney. 1995. The effect of middle school extracurricular activities on adolescents' popularity and peer status. *Youth and Society* 26 (3):298–324.

Edin, Kathryn, and Maria Kefalas. 2005. *Promises I can keep: Why poor women put motherhood before marriage.* Berkeley: University of California Press.

Erickson, Bonnie. 1996. Culture, class, and connections. *American Journal of Sociology* 102 (1):217–251.

Erickson, Rebecca J. 1995. The importance of authenticity for self and society. *Symbolic Interaction* 18 (2):121.

Ewick, Patricia, and Susan S. Silbey. 1995. Subversive stories and hegemonic tales: Toward a sociology of narrative. *Law and Society Review* 29 (2):197–226.

Favell, Adrian. 1998. *Philosophies of integration: Immigration and the idea of citizenship in France and Britain.* Migration, Minorities, and Citizenship. New York: St. Martin's Press, in association with the Centre for Research in Ethnic Relations, University of Warwick.

Feliciano, Cynthia, and Rubén G. Rumbaut. 2005. Gendered paths: Educational and occupational expectations and outcomes among adult children of immigrants. *Ethnic and Racial Studies* 28 (6):1087–1118.

Ferguson, Ann Arnett. 2000. *Bad boys: Public schools in the making of black masculinity, law, meaning, and violence.* Ann Arbor: University of Michigan Press.

Fine, Gary Alan. 2003. Crafting authenticity: The validation of identity in self-taught art. *Theory and Society* 32 (2):153.

Flores-González, Nilda. 2002. *School kids/street kids: Identity development in Latino students.* Sociology of Education. New York: Teachers College Press.

Foner, Nancy. 2005. *In a new land: A comparative view of immigration.* New York: New York University Press.

Fordham, Signithia. 1988. Racelessness as a factor in black students' school success: Pragmatic strategy or Pyrrhic victory? *Harvard Educational Review* 58 (1):54–84.

Foster, Peter. 1993. Some problems in establishing equality of treatment in multi-ethnic schools. *British Journal of Sociology* 44 (3):519–535.

Frank, Thomas. 1997. *The conquest of cool: Business culture, counterculture, and the rise of hip consumerism.* Chicago: University of Chicago Press.

———. 2004. *What's the matter with Kansas? How conservatives won the heart of America.* New York: Metropolitan Books.

Frey, William H., and Dowell Myers. 2005. *Racial segregation in U.S. metropolitan areas and cities, 1990–2000: Patterns, trends, and explanations.* Ann Arbor: Population Studies Center, University of Michigan Institute for Social Research (report 05–573).

Frosh, Stephen, Ann Phoenix, and Rob Pattman. 2002. *Young masculinities: Understanding boys in contemporary society.* Basingstoke, UK: Palgrave.

Fry, Richard. 2005. *The high schools Hispanics attend: Size and other key characteristics.* Washington, DC: Pew Hispanic Center. http://pewhispanic. org/files/reports/54.pdf.

Gans, Herbert J. 1979. Symbolic ethnicity: The future of ethnic groups and cultures in America. *Ethnic & Racial Studies* 2:1–20.

———. 1992. Second-generation decline: Scenarios for the economic and ethnic futures of the post–1965 American immigrants. *Ethnic and Racial Studies* 15 (2):173.

———. 1999. *Popular culture and high culture: An analysis and evaluation of taste.* Rev. ed. New York: Basic Books.

Gates, Henry Louis. 1997. Black London. *New Yorker,* April 28 and May 5, 194–205.

Gibson, Margaret A. 1988. *Accommodation without assimilation: Sikh immigrants in an American high school.* Ithaca, NY: Cornell University Press.

Giddens, Anthony. 2006. Misunderstanding multiculturalism. *The Guardian,* October 14. www.guardian.co.uk/commentisfree/2006/oct/14/tonygiddens.

Gillborn, David. 2005. Education policy as an act of white supremacy: Whiteness, critical race theory, and education reform. *Journal of Education Policy* 20 (4):485.

———. 2006. Rethinking white supremacy. *Ethnicities* 6 (3):318.

Gillborn, David, and Caroline Gipps. 1996. Recent research on the achievements of ethnic minority pupils. London: Office for Standards in Education.

Gillborn, David, and Heidi Safia Mirza. 2000. Educational inequality: Mapping race, class, and gender. London: Office for Standards in Education.

Gillborn, David, and Deborah Youdell. 2005. "*Whose* children left behind? The impact of institutional arrangements and practices on pathways through education." Paper presented at the Educating Immigrant Youth: Mobility and Citizenship in International Perspective conference, sponsored by the Social Science Research Council and the Nuffield Foundation, London, February 11–12.

Gillespie, Marie. 1995. *Television, ethnicity, and cultural change.* London: Routledge.

Gilroy, Paul. 1987. *"There ain't no black in the Union Jack": The cultural politics of race and nation.* London: Hutchinson.

———. 1993. *The black Atlantic: Modernity and double consciousness.* Cambridge, MA: Harvard University Press.

Giroux, Henry A. 1983. *Theory and resistance in education: A pedagogy for the opposition.* Critical Perspectives in Social Theory series, edited by S. Aronowitz and R. Bologh. London: Heinemann Education Books.

Glaser, Barney G., and Strauss, Anselm L. 1967. *The discovery of grounded theory: strategies for qualitative research.* Chicago: Aldine.

Goodhart, David. 2004. Too diverse? *Prospect,* January 22, 2004. www .prospectmagazine.co.uk/2004/02/toodiverse.

Grazian, David. 2003. *Blue Chicago: The search for authenticity in urban blues clubs.* Chicago: University of Chicago Press.

Hacker, Andrew. 1992. *Two nations: Black and white, separate, hostile, unequal.* New York: Scribner's.

Hall, Kathleen. 2002. *Lives in translation: Sikh youth as British citizens.* Philadelphia: University of Pennsylvania Press.

Hall, Stuart. 1996. Politics of identity. In *Culture, identity, and politics,* edited by T. Ranger, U. Samad, and O. Stuart. Aldershot, UK: Avebury.

———. 1997. The Local and the global: Globalization and ethnicity. In *Culture, globalization and the world-system: Contemporary conditions for the representation of identity,* edited by A. D. King. Minneapolis: University of Minnesota Press.

Hall, Stuart, and Tony Jefferson. 1976. *Resistance through rituals: Youth subcultures in post-war Britain.* London: Hutchinson.

Hallinan, Maureen T., and Richard A. Williams. 1990. Students' characteristics and the peer-influence process. *Sociology of Education* 63 (2):122–132.

Haywood, Chris, and Mairtin Mac an Ghaill. 2003. *Men and masculinities: Theory, research, and social practice.* Philadelphia: Open University Press, McGraw-Hill Education.

Hebdige, Dick. 1979. *Subculture: The meaning of style.* London: Routledge.

Held, David. 1999. *Global transformations: Politics, economics and culture.* Cambridge: Polity Press.

Hewitt, Roger. 1986. *White talk, black talk: Inter-racial friendship and communication amongst adolescents.* Comparative Ethnic and Race Relations. Cambridge: Cambridge University Press.

Hewstone, Miles, and Rupert Brown. 1986. Contact is not enough: An intergroup perspective on the "contact hypothesis." In *Contact and conflict in intergroup encounters,* edited by M. Hewstone and R. Brown. Oxford: Blackwell.

Hickman, Mary J. 1998. Reconstructing deconstructing "race": British political discourses about the Irish in Britain. *Ethnic and Racial Studies* 21 (2):288.

Hochschild, Jennifer L. 1996. *Facing up to the American dream: Race, class, and the soul of the nation.* Princeton, NJ: Princeton University Press.

Hofferth, Sandra L., and John E. Sandberg. 2001. How American children spend their time. *Journal of Marriage and Family* 63 (2):295.

Hollinger, David A. 1995. *Postethnic America: Beyond multiculturalism.* New York: Basic Books.

Horkheimer, Max, and Theodor W. Adorno. 1972. *Dialectic of enlightenment.* New York: Herder and Herder.

Jackson, John L. 2001. *Harlemworld: Doing race and class in contemporary Black America.* Chicago: University of Chicago Press.

———. 2005. *Real Black: Adventures in racial sincerity.* Chicago: University of Chicago Press.

Jacobson, Matthew Frye. 1998. *Whiteness of a different color: European immigrants and the alchemy of race.* Cambridge, MA: Harvard University Press.

Jay, Michelle. 2003. Critical race theory, multicultural education, and the hidden curriculum of hegemony. *Multicultural Perspectives* 5 (4):3–9.

Kasinitz, Philip, John H. Mollenkopf, and Mary C. Waters. 2004. *Becoming New Yorkers: Ethnographies of the new second generation.* New York: Russell Sage Foundation.

Kasinitz, Philip, John H. Mollenkopf, Mary C. Waters, and Jennifer Holdaway. 2008. *Inheriting the city: The children of immigrants come of age.* Cambridge, MA: Harvard University Press.

Katznelson, Ira. 1973. *Black men, white cities: Race, politics, and migration in the United States, 1900–30, and Britain, 1948–68.* London: Published for the Institute of Race Relations by Oxford University Press.

Kessler, Ronald C., Kristin D. Mickelson, and David R. Williams. 1999. The prevalence, distribution, and mental health correlates of perceived discrimination in the United States. *Journal of Health and Social Behavior* 40 (3):208.

Khandelwal, Madhulika S. 2002. *Becoming American, being Indian: An immigrant community in New York City.* The Anthropology of Contemporary Issues. Ithaca, NY: Cornell University Press.

Kimmel, Michael S. 2002. Toward a pedagogy of the oppressor. *Tikkun* 17 (6):42–45.

Kimmel, Michael S., and Matthew Mahler. 2003. Adolescent masculinity, homophobia, and violence: Random school shootings, 1982–2001. *American Behavioral Scientist* 46 (10):1439–1458.

Klein, Naomi. 2002. *No logo: No space, no choice, no lobs.* New York: Picador; distributed by Holtzbrinck.

Knapp, Laura G. 2005. Postsecondary institutions in the United States: Fall 2003 and degrees and other awards conferred, 2002–2003. Institute of Education Sciences, U.S. Department of Education, NCES 2005-154.

Koppel, Niko. 2007. Are your jeans sagging? Go directly to jail. *New York Times,* August 30.

Kozol, Jonathan. 1991. *Savage inequalities: Children in America's schools.* New York: Crown.

La Ferla, Ruth. 2003. Generation E.A.: Ethnically ambiguous. *New York Times,* December 28, ST1.

Lamont, Michèle. 1992. *Money, morals, and manners: The culture of the French and American upper-middle class, morality and society.* Chicago: University of Chicago Press.

———. 2000. *The dignity of working men: Morality and the boundaries of race, class, and immigration.* New York: Russell Sage Foundation; Cambridge, MA: Harvard University Press.

Lamont, Michèle, and Marcel Fournier. 1992. *Cultivating differences: Symbolic boundaries and the making of inequality.* Chicago: University of Chicago Press.

Lamont, Michèle, Jason Kaufman, and Michael Moody. 2000. The best of the brightest: Definitions of the ideal self among prize-winning students. *Sociological Forum* 15 (2):187–224.

Lamont, Michèle, and Virág Molnár. 2002. The Study of boundaries in the social sciences. *Annual Review of Sociology* 28:167–95.

Lamont, Michèle, and Mario Luis Small. 2008. How culture matters for poverty: Enriching our understanding. In *The colors of poverty: Why racial and ethnic disparities persist,* edited by Ann Lin and David Harris. New York: Russell Sage Foundation.

Lareau, Annette. 2003. *Unequal childhoods: Class, race, and family life.* Berkeley: University of California Press.

Lawrence, Barbara Kent. 2004. For authentic accountability, think small. *Journal of Education* 185 (3):41.

Lee, C.N. 2007. "Interracial dating and marriage." *Asian-Nation: The landscape of Asian America.* www.asian-nation.org/interracial.shtml (accessed June 9, 2010).

Lee, Valerie E. 2000. School size and the organization of secondary schools. In *Handbook of the sociology of education,* edited by M.T. Hallinan. New York: Kluwer Academic/Plenum.

Leonard, Karen Isaksen. 1992. *Making ethnic choices: California's Punjabi Mexican Americans.* Philadelphia: Temple University Press.

Lieberson, Stanley. 1992. Small N's and big conclusions: An examination of the reasoning in comparative studies based on a small number of cases. In *What is a case? Exploring the foundations of social inquiry,* edited by C.C. Ragin and H.S. Becker. Cambridge: Cambridge University Press.

Liebes, Tamar, and Elihu Katz. 1990. *The export of meaning: Cross-cultural readings of Dallas.* New York: Oxford University Press.

López, Nancy. 2002. *Hopeful girls, troubled boys: Race and gender disparity in urban education.* New York: Routledge.

Louie, Vivian S. 2004. *Compelled to excel: Immigration, education, and opportunity among Chinese Americans.* Stanford, CA: Stanford University Press.

Loury, Glenn C. 2002. *The anatomy of racial inequality: W.E.B. Du Bois lectures.* Cambridge, MA: Harvard University Press.

Lundy, Garvey F., and Glenn Firebaugh. 2005. Peer relations and school resistance: Does oppositional culture apply to race or to gender? *Journal of Negro Education* 74 (3):233–245.

Mahon, Maureen. 2004. *Right to rock: The Black Rock Coalition and the cultural politics of race.* Durham, NC: Duke University Press.

Maira, Sunaina. 1999. Ideologies of authenticity: Youth, politics, and diaspora. *Amerasia Journal* 25 (3):138.

———. 2002. *Desis in the house: Indian American youth culture in New York City.* Philadelphia: Temple University Press.

Majors, Richard, ed. 2001a. *Educating our black children: New directions and radical approaches.* London: Routledge.

Majors, Richard. 2001b. Introduction. In *Educating our black children: New directions and radical approaches,* edited by Richard Majors. London: Routledge.

Majors, Richard, and Janet Mancini Billson. 1992. *Cool pose: The dilemmas of black manhood in America.* New York: Simon and Schuster.

Majors, Richard, David Gillborn, and Tony Sewell. 2001. The exclusion of black children: Implications for a racialised perspective. In *Educating our black children: New directions and radical approaches,* edited by R. Majors. London: Routledge.

Marriott, David. 1996. Reading black masculinities. In *Understanding masculinities: Social relations and cultural arenas,* edited by M. Mac an Ghaill. Philadelphia: Open University Press, McGraw-Hill Education.

Martin, Karin A. 1996. *Puberty, sexuality, and the self: Boys and girls at adolescence.* New York: Routledge.

———. 1998. Becoming a gendered body: Practices of preschools. *American Sociological Review* 63 (4):494–511.

Massey, Douglas S., and Mary J. Fischer. 2006. The effect of childhood segregation on minority academic performance at selective colleges. *Ethnic and Racial Studies* 29 (1):1–26.

Massey, Douglas S., Margarita Mooney, Camille Z. Charles, and Kimberly C. Torres. 2007. Black immigrants and black natives attending selective colleges and universities in the United States. *American Journal of Education* 113 (2):243.

Massey, Douglas S., and Nancy A. Denton. 1993. *American apartheid: Segregation and the making of the underclass.* Cambridge, MA: Harvard University Press.

Mehan, Hugh, Lea Hubbard, and Irene Villanueva. 1994. Forming academic identities: Accommodation without assimilation among involuntary minorities. *Anthropology and Education Quarterly* 25 (2):91–117.

Menjívar, Cecilia. 2006. Liminal legality: Salvadoran and Guatemalan immigrants' lives in the United States. *American Journal of Sociology* 111 (4):999–1037.

Merten, Don E. 1997. The meaning of meanness: Popularity, competition, and conflict among junior high school girls. *Sociology of Education* 70:175–191.

Mickelson, Roslyn Arlin. 1990. The attitude-achievement paradox among black adolescents. *Sociology of Education* 63 (1):44–62.

Miles, Matthew B., and A.M. Huberman. 1984. *Qualitative data analysis: A sourcebook of new methods.* Beverly Hills: Sage Publications.

Milner, Murray. 2004. *Freaks, geeks, and cool kids: American teenagers, schools, and the culture of consumption.* New York: Routledge.

Mirza, Heidi Safia. 1992. *Young, female, and black.* New York: Routledge.

———. 1999. Black masculinities and schooling: A black feminist response. , *British Journal of Sociology of Education* 20 (1):137–147.

Mirza, Munira, Abi Senthilkumaran, and Zein Ja'far. 2006. *Living apart together: British Muslims and the paradox of multiculturalism.* London: Populus and Policy Exchange.

Model, Suzanne, and Gene Fisher. 2002. Unions between blacks and whites: England and the US compared. *Ethnic and Racial Studies* 25 (5):728–754.

Modood, Tariq. 1996. "The limits of America: Rethinking equality in the changing context of British race relations." In *The making of Martin Luther King and the Civil Rights Movement,* edited by B. Ward and T. Badger. New York: New York University Press.

———. 1997. *Ethnic minorities in Britain: Diversity and disadvantage.* PSI Research Report 843. London: Policy Studies Institute.

———. 2004. Capitals, ethnic identity, and educational qualifications. *Cultural Trends* 13 (2):87–105.

———. 2005. *Multicultural politics: Racism, ethnicity, and Muslims in Britain.* Minneapolis: University of Minnesota Press.

Morrill, Calvin, Christine Yalda, Madelaine Adelman, Michael Musheno, and Cindy Bejarano. 2000. Telling tales in school: Youth culture and conflict narratives. *Law and Society Review* 34 (3):521–565.

National Center for Education Statistics. 2007. *Indicators of School Crime and Safety.* Washington, DC.

Neckerman, Kathryn M. (ed.). 2004. *Social inequality.* New York: Russell Sage Foundation.

Newman, Katherine S. 2004. *Rampage: The social roots of school shootings.* New York: Basic Books.

New York City Department of Education. 2004–5. *School Report Cards.* New York.

New York State Education Department. 2005–6. *New York State School Report Card: Accountability and Overview Report.*

Nightingale, Carl Husemoller. 1993. *On the edge: A history of poor black children and their American dreams.* New York: Basic Books.

Oakes, Jeannie. 1985. *Keeping track: How schools structure inequality.* New Haven: Yale University Press.

Office for National Statistics. 2001a. Census 2001: Country of Birth, Table UV08.

Office for National Statistics. 2001b. Census 2001: Education, Skills and Training: Qualifications, Table UV24.

Office for National Statistics. 2001c. Census 2001: Key Statistics. People and Society: Population and Migration, Table KS06.

Office for National Statistics. 2001d. Census 2001: National Report for England and Wales. Table T13.

Office for National Statistics. 2004a. Census 2001: Focus on Ethnicity and Identity, Population Size.

Office for National Statistics. 2004b. Census 2001: Focus on Religion Report.

Office for National Statistics. 2005. Census 2001: Focus on Ethnicity and Identity, Inter-ethnic Marriage Report.

Ofsted (Office for Standards in Education, Children's Services, and Skills). 2004. *School Inspection Report.*

Ogbu, John. 1990. Minority education in comparative perspective. *Journal of Negro Education* 59 (1):45–57.

———. 1991. Immigrant and involuntary minorities in comparative perspective. In *A comparative study of immigrant and involuntary minorities,* edited by J. Ogbu and M. Gibson. New York: Garland.

———. 1995. Cultural problems in minority education: Their interpretations and consequences—Part two: Case studies. *Urban Review* 27 (4):271–297.

———. 2004. Collective identity and the burden of "acting white" in black history, community, and education. *Urban Review* 36 (1):1–35.

Pager, Devah, and Hana Shepherd. 2008. The sociology of discrimination: Racial discrimination in employment, housing, credit, and consumer markets. *Annual Review of Sociology* 34 (1):181–209.

Parker, Laurence, Donna Deyhle, and Sofia A. Villenas, eds. 1999. *Race is—race isn't: Critical race theory and qualitative studies in education.* Boulder, CO: Westview Press.

Pattillo-McCoy, Mary. 1999. *Black picket fences: Privilege and peril among the Black middle class.* Chicago: University of Chicago Press.

Peach, Ceri. 1996. Does Britain have ghettos? *Transactions of the Institute of British Geographers* 21 (1):216–235.

———. 2005. Social integration and social mobility: Spatial segregation and intermarriage of the Caribbean population in Britain. In *Ethnicity, social mobility, and public policy: Comparing the US and UK,* edited by G. C. Loury, T. Modood, and S. M. Teles. New York: Cambridge University Press.

Perry, Pamela. 2002. *Shades of white: White kids and racial identities in high school.* Durham, NC: Duke University Press.

Peterson, Richard, and Roger Kern. 1996. Changing highbrow taste: From snob to omnivore. *American Sociological Review* 61 (5):900–917.

Peterson, Richard, and Albert Simkus. 1992. How musical tastes mark occupational status groups. In *Cultivating differences: Symbolic boundaries and the making of inequality,* edited by M. Lamont and M. Fournier. Chicago: University of Chicago.

Peterson, Richard A. 1997. *Creating country music: Fabricating authenticity.* Chicago: University of Chicago Press.

Phinney, Jean S. 1991. Ethnic identity and self-esteem: A review and integration. *Hispanic Journal of Behavioral Sciences* 13 (2):193–208.

Pollock, Mica. 2004. *Colormute: Race talk dilemmas in an American school.* Princeton, NJ: Princeton University Press.

Portes, Alejandro, Patricia Fernández-Kelly, and William Haller. 2005. Segmented assimilation on the ground: The new second generation in early adulthood. *Ethnic and Racial Studies* 28 (6):1000–1040.

Portes, Alejandro, and Rubén G. Rumbaut. 2001. *Legacies: The story of the immigrant second generation.* Berkeley: University of California Press; New York: Russell Sage Foundation.

Portes, Alejandro, and Min Zhou. 1993. The new second generation: Segmented assimilation and its variants. *Annals of the American Academy* 530:74–96.

Prashad, Vijay. 2000. *The karma of Brown folk.* Minneapolis: University of Minnesota Press.

Quillian, Lincoln. 2006. New approaches to understanding racial prejudice and discrimination. *Annual Review of Sociology* 32 (1):299–328.

Radway, Janice A. 1991. *Reading the romance: Women, patriarchy, and popular literature.* Chapel Hill: University of North Carolina Press.

Ramos-Zayas, Ana Y. 2003. *National performances: The politics of class, race, and space in Puerto Rican Chicago.* Chicago: University of Chicago Press.

Rigsby, Leo C., and Edward L. McDill. 1975. Value orientations of high school students. In *The Sociology of Education: A Sourcebook*, edited by H.R. Stub. Homewood, IL: Dorsey Press.

Roscigno, Vincent J. 1998. Race and the reproduction of educational disadvantage. *Social Forces* 76 (3):1033.

Rose, Tricia. 1994. *Black noise: Rap music and black culture in contemporary America*. Hanover, NH: Wesleyan University Press/University Press of New England.

Rumbaut, Rubén G. 2004. Ages, life stages, and generational cohorts: Decomposing the immigrant first and second generations in the United States. *International Migration Review* 38 (3):1160–1205.

Rumbaut, Rubén G., Douglas S. Massey, and Frank D. Bean. 2006. Linguistic life expectancies: Immigrant language retention in Southern California. *Population and Development Review* 32 (3):447–460.

Sandhu, Sabeen. 2004. Instant karma: The commercialization of Asian Indian culture. In *Asian American youth: Culture, identity, and ethnicity*, edited by J. Lee and M. Zhou. New York: Routledge.

Schudson, Michael. 1989. How culture works. *Theory and Society* 18 (2):153–180.

Sewell, Tony. 1997. *Black masculinities and schooling: How Black boys survive modern schooling*. Stoke on Trent, UK: Trentham Books.

Sewell, Tony, and Richard Majors. 2001. Black Boys and Schooling: An intervention Framework for Understanding the Dilemmas of masculinity, Identity and Underachievement. In *Educating our Black Children: New Directions and Radical Approaches*. Edited by R. Majors. London: Routledge.

The Sikh Coalition. 2008. *Making our voices heard: A civil rights agenda for New York City's Sikhs*. New York.

Sizer, Theodore R. 1984. *Horace's compromise: The dilemma of the American high school*. Boston: Houghton Mifflin.

Skiba, Russell J., Robert S. Michael, Abra Carroll Nardo, and Reece L. Peterson. 2002. The color of discipline: Sources of racial and gender disproportionality in school punishment. *Urban Review* 34 (4):317.

Skrentny, John D. 2008. Culture and race/ethnicity: Bolder, deeper, and broader. *Annals of the American Academy of Political and Social Science* 619:59–77.

Smith, Caspar Llewellyn. 2005. Hey, music lovers. *The Observer*, July 2005, 18–43.

Solomos, John. 1988. *Black youth, racism and the state: The politics of ideology and policy*. Comparative Ethnic and Race Relations. Cambridge: Cambridge University Press.

Solorzano, Daniel G., and Armida Ornelas. 2004. A critical race analysis of Latina/o and African American Advanced Placement enrollment in public high schools. *High School Journal* 87 (3):15–26.

Stapinski, Helene. 2004. Preppy Punks. *New York Times*, City Weekly Desk, February 22, p. 1.

Stearns, Elizabeth, Claudia Buchmann, and Kara Bonneau. 2009. Interracial friendships in the transition to college: Do birds of a feather flock together once they leave the nest? *Sociology of Education* 82 (2):173–195.

Steele, Claude M., and Joshua Aronson. 1995. Stereotype threat and the intellectual test performance of African Americans. *Journal of Personality and Social Psychology* 69 (5):797–811.

Stepick, Alex. 1998. *Pride against prejudice: Haitians in the United States.* New Immigrants series. Boston: Allyn and Bacon.

Stevens, Mitchell. 2008. Culture and education. *Annals of the American Academy of Political and Social Science* 619:97–113.

Suárez-Orozco, Carola, and Marcelo M. Suárez-Orozco. 1995. *Trans-formations: Immigration, family life, and achievement motivation among Latino adolescents.* Stanford, CA: Stanford University Press.

Swidler, Ann. 1986. Culture in action: Symbols and strategies. *American Sociological Review* 51 (2):273–286.

Tajalli, Hassan, and Cynthia Opheim. 2005. Strategies for closing the gap: Predicting student performance in economically disadvantaged schools. *Educational Research Quarterly* 28 (4):44.

Taylor, Charles. 1992. *The ethics of authenticity.* Cambridge, MA: Harvard University Press.

Thernstrom, Stephan, and Abigail M. Thernstrom. 1997. *America in black and white: One nation, indivisible.* New York: Simon and Schuster.

Thorne, Barrie. 1993. *Gender play: Girls and boys in school.* New Brunswick, NJ: Rutgers University Press.

Trent, William T. 1997. Outcomes of school desegregation: Findings from longitudinal research. *Journal of Negro Education* 66 (3):255.

Trilling, Lionel. 1972. *Sincerity and authenticity.* Cambridge, MA: Harvard University Press.

Tuan, Mia. 1998. *Forever foreigners or honorary whites?: The Asian ethnic experience today.* New Brunswick, NJ: Rutgers University Press.

———. 1999. Neither real Americans nor real Asians? Multigeneration Asian ethnics navigating the terrain of authenticity. *Qualitative Sociology* 22 (2):105.

Tyack, David B. 1974. *The one best system: A history of American urban education.* Cambridge, MA: Harvard University Press.

Tyson, Karolyn, William Darity Jr., and Domini Castellino. 2005. It's not "a black thing": Understanding the burden of acting white and other dilemmas of high achievement. *American Sociological Review* 70 (4):582–605.

U.K. Department for Education and Skills. 2004. Statistics First Release, SFR23/2004.

U.S. Census Bureau. 2000a. 2000 Census of Population and Housing, Summary File 2.

U.S. Census Bureau. 2000b. 2000 Census of Population and Housing, Summary File 3.

U.S. Census Bureau. 2000c. 2000 Census of Population and Housing, Summary File 4.

Valenzuela, Angela. 1999. *Subtractive schooling: Issues of caring in education of U.S.-Mexican youth.* Social Context of Education. Albany: State University of New York Press.

Varshney, Ashutosh. 2001. Ethnic conflict and civil society. *World Politics* 53 (3):362.

Vertovec, Steven. 2006. Super-diversity and its implications. *Ethnic and Racial Studies* 30 (6):1024–1054.

Vickerman, Milton. 1999. *Crosscurrents: West Indian immigrants and race.* New York: Oxford University Press.

Waldinger, Roger. 1996. *Still the promised city? African-Americans and new immigrants in postindustrial New York.* Cambridge, MA: Harvard University Press.

Waldinger, Roger, and Cynthia Feliciano. 2004. Will the new second generation experience "downward assimilation"? Segmented assimilation re-assessed. *Ethnic and Racial Studies* 27 (3):376–403.

Warde, Alan, David Wright, and Modesto Gayo-Cal. 2007. Understanding cultural omnivorousness: Or the myth of the cultural omnivore. *Cultural Sociology* 1 (2):143–164.

Warikoo, Natasha. 2004a. Cosmopolitan ethnicity: Second generation Indo-Caribbean identities. In *Becoming New Yorkers: Ethnographies of a new second generation,* edited by P. Kasinitz, J. H. Mollenkopf, and M. C. Waters. New York: Russell Sage Foundation.

———. 2004b. Race and the teacher-student relationship: interpersonal connections between West Indian students and their teachers in a New York City high school. *Race, Ethnicity, and Education* 7 (2):135–147.

———. 2005a. Gender and ethnic identity among second generation Indo-Caribbeans. *Ethnic and Racial Studies* 28 (5):803–832.

———. 2005b. In a teenage waistland, fitting in. *Washington Post,* July 31, 2005, B01.

Warikoo, Natasha, and Prudence Carter. 2009. Cultural explanations for racial and ethnic stratification in academic achievement: A call for a new and improved theory. *Review of Educational Research* 79 (1):366–394.

Waters, Mary C. 1990. *Ethnic options: Choosing identities in America.* Berkeley: University of California Press.

———. 1999. *Black identities: West Indian immigrant dreams and American realities.* New York: Russell Sage Foundation; Cambridge, MA: Harvard University Press.

Watson, James L. 1997. *Golden Arches East: McDonald's in East Asia.* Stanford, CA: Stanford University Press.

Weber, Max. 1968. Ethnic groups. In *Economy and society,* edited by G. Roth and C. Wittich. Berkeley: University of California Press.

Willis, Paul E. 1977. *Learning to labour: How working class kids get working class jobs.* Farnborough, UK: Saxon House.

———. 1990. *Common culture: Symbolic work at play in the everyday cultures of the young.* Boulder, CO: Westview Press.

Wilson, William J. 1996. *When work disappears: The world of the new urban poor.* New York: Knopf.

Wimmer, Andreas. 2007. How (not) to think about ethnicity in immigrant societies: A boundary making perspective. Oxford: ESRC Centre on Migration, Policy and Society, University of Oxford.

———. 2008a. Elementary strategies of ethnic boundary making. *Ethnic and Racial Studies* 31 (6):1025–1055.

———. 2008b. The making and unmaking of ethnic boundaries: A multilevel process theory. *American Journal of Sociology* 113 (4):970–1022.

Yun, John T., and Michal Kurlaender. 2004. School racial composition and student educational aspirations: A question of equity in a multicultural society. *Journal of Education for Students Placed at Risk* 9 (2):143–168.

Zerubavel, Eviatar. 1991. *The fine line: Making distinctions in everyday life.* New York: Free Press.

Zhou, Min. 1997. Segmented Assimilation: Issues, Controversies, and Recent Research on the New Second Generation. *International Migration Review* 31 (4):975–1008.

Zhou, Min, and Carl L. Bankston. 1998. *Growing up American: How Vietnamese children adapt to life in the United States.* New York: Russell Sage Foundation.

Zolberg, Aristide R., and Litt Woon Long. 1999. Why Islam is like Spanish: Cultural incorporation in Europe and the United States. *Politics and Society* 27 (1):5–38.

Zukin, Sharon, and Jennifer Smith Maguire. 2004. Consumers and consumption. *Annual Review of Sociology* 30 (1):173–198.

Index

academic achievement: among grungies, 66–67; among Indian students, ix, 121–22; attitudinal predictors of, 96; bragging about, 94; conflict with peer status, 8, 9, 86, 108, 114; conflict with teachers and, 104–5; daily choices in, 172; downward assimilation and, 92; effect of racial integration on, 126; effect of school size on, 152; effect of school structure on, 22, 157, 169–70; effect of symbolic status on, 161; and fighting in school, 106; good choices for, 171–78; impediments to, 96–106; influence of culture on, 4; low, xiii, xiv, 20, 107, 163; negative factors for, xiv, 90, 94–95, 171; oppositional attitudes and, 90–94; and perception of discrimination, 95, 107; popularity and, 141; pride in, 89; privileging of youth culture over, 119–20; reactive ethnicity in, 74; role of cultural assimilation in, 4; role of cultural capital in, 110; role of peer culture in, 20, 91, 92, 93–94, 95, 106, 107, 115, 124, 161, 173; within school, 123; school policies affecting, 171–78; self-pride and, 104; students' view of, 92, 94–96, 120, 171; and style, 111; and success in life, 94, 115; youth cultures' view of, 91, 160, 185. *See also* behaviors, achievement related; education

acting black, 8; among British white students, 55, 65; chastisement for, 19; in enjoyment of hip-hop, 50; failure in, 46; peer status through, 53, 54, 110; racial inauthenticity in, 52–54; South Asian students on, 53
Adidas sneakers, 65, 191n2
Adorno, Theodor W., 6
adult culture, 71; conflict with peer status, 115–16; students' privileging of, 121–23; versus youth culture, 114–17
adults: advice on code-switching, 159; assumptions of delinquency, 35, 79, 116, 174; consumption of hip-hop music, 27; cultural capital of, 71; ethnic identity scripts of, 50–51; experience of discrimination, 92; misunderstanding of youth styles, 35–40, 158, 174, 178; perception of coolness, 162; racial stereotyping by, 84; respect for, 104
African American culture: Afro-Caribbean identification with, 13, 21, 58–59, 61, 153, 156; effect on downward assimilation, 12; influence on children of immigrants, 91; oppositional elements of, xi, 9–10, 12, 24, 95, 107, 159–60; role in disadvantage, x
African Americans: dissimilarity index with whites, 195n9; job discrimination against, 76; South Asians' view of, 192n12; workplace successes of, xi

TEXT
10/13 Sabon

DISPLAY
Sabon

INDEXER
Roberta Engleman

COMPOSITOR
Toppan Best-set Premedia Limited

PRINTER AND BINDER
Maple-Vail